OUT OF THE BOX

OUT OF THE BOX

ROBERT HOEKMAN, JR.

O'REILLY®

BEIJING • CAMBRIDGE • FARNHAM • KÖLN • PARIS • SEBASTOPOL • TAIPEI • TOKYO

Flash Out of the Box

by Robert Hoekman, Jr.

Published by O'Reilly Media, Inc., 1005 Gravenstein Highway North, Sebastopol, CA 95472.

O'Reilly books may be purchased for educational, business, or sales promotional use. Online editions are also available for most titles (*safari.oreilly.com*). For more information, contact our corporate/institutional sales department: 800-998-9938 or *corporate@oreilly.com*.

Print History:	**Editor:**	Bruce Epstein
November 2004: First Edition.	**Production Editor:**	Emily Quill
	Art Direction:	Michele Wetherbee
	Cover Designer:	Ellie Volckhausen
	Interior Designer:	David Futato
	Cover Illustration:	Dan Masi/Mayzee Illustration

 This book uses RepKover™, a durable and flexible lay-flat binding.

0-596-00691-8
[C]

CONTENTS

PREFACE

Flash Out of the Box is a user-centric introduction to Flash MX 2004. This book is designed for people who want to get up to speed in Flash with minimal effort and without being shortchanged. The Preface provides a quick orientation to get you off on the right foot. All the software you need is included on the CD-ROM that comes with this book.

Welcome to *Flash Out of the Box*, a user-centric introduction to Flash MX 2004. This book includes everything you need to get started in Flash, including trial versions of the software and all the example files from the exercises on the enclosed CD-ROM.

WHO THIS BOOK IS FOR

A funny thing happened on the way to publication. I originally intended this book as purely for beginners. But during the review process, beta readers of diverse experience levels told me they found it tremendously useful. Having incorporated the suggestions of numerous readers, I feel this book serves a number of potential audiences.

This book is primarily geared toward beginning Flash users who want to bring their project ideas to life. Even if you're a beginner, I assume you're relatively intelligent and motivated, that you have a general familiarity with typical graphics programs and web browsers, and perhaps some HTML experience. I don't assume any programming experience, but familiarity with JavaScript will make it easier to follow the programming examples (which I introduce gently). If you don't understand all the code examples, don't worry. You can use the code examples verbatim without fully understanding them, but I felt it was important to at least introduce readers to ActionScript, which is used to implement some important functionality. Most of the ActionScript is presented in the later chapters, and beginners will be well prepared by that time to take Flash to the next level.

This book is also an excellent choice for readers who may have a superficial familiarity with Flash MX 2004 (or previous versions) and want to learn more about the latest version's capabilities. This group includes developers with previous ActionScript experience who may never have mastered Flash's drawing tools and other animation and media-related features.

This book should also suit experienced programmers with no prior Flash experience who need to learn the Flash development environment. If you want to learn more advanced ActionScript, refer to the resources in Chapter 13. Regardless, the book is designed for people who want to get up to speed in Flash with minimal effort and without being shortchanged.

Because this book is designed for a range of users, it covers considerable ground. For beginners, it covers the basics in a way that you'll appreciate and absorb quickly. We were all beginners in Flash once, but most authors seem to have forgotten what it was like to be brand new to Flash. I haven't forgotten. Flash can have a steep learning curve, but with the right guide, you can be comfortable in no time. Even if you're not a Flash beginner, the coverage of Flash features acts as both a refresher and a stepping-stone to greater expertise.

The first time I cracked open Flash (more specifically, Flash 3), I went through the Help documentation to find some hands-on exercises and found one of the most useful tutorials I've ever read. In those days, Flash was best known as an animation tool, and the mission of this particular tutorial was to animate a bouncing ball. I quickly learned to draw in Flash, use gradients, reuse graphics in an efficient way, animate the bouncing ball, set the tempo for a movie, and finally, publish the movie for use on the Web. All that in one tutorial! I felt like a genius, and I was immediately hooked on Flash.

The tutorial was effective because it revealed information on a need-to-know basis. I didn't have to read a dry chapter on drawing tools outside the context of a real project. Instead, I learned to draw a circle and turn it into a bouncing ball with realistic motion. I started at point A and followed a story to point C. (The rest of the alphabet came later on.)

When I asked members of my user group (the Flash and Multimedia Users Group of Arizona) to divulge their first experiences with Flash, the stories were very similar. The ironic part is that when you look through the Help documentation in Flash MX 2004, the bouncing ball tutorial is nowhere to be found. The focus has changed from animation and basic design to Rich Internet Applications (RIAs), a term coined by Macromedia to represent web applications with a rich media interface. And while Flash's evolution is good for developers at all levels, it also means that new users have a lot more to learn than they once did. While Flash development used to mean simple interactivity and motion graphics, modern Flash development can involve data connectivity, web services, and multiplatform deployment.

But even the latest version of Flash shares the same underpinnings as older versions, and new users still need a foundation to use as a stepping-stone to reach their goals. Somewhere in the evolutionary process, tutorials on the fundamentals got lost, so I'm bringing them back in style. Much like the bouncing ball tutorial, this book docs not teach Flash, per se—it *reveals* Flash through tasks that every Flash designer performs during the course of a typical project.

However, this book isn't merely a wading pool in which to get your feet wet. With this book's lessons and guidance, you'll be treading water, doing some laps, and swimming in the deep end in no time. You might even be brave enough to jump off the diving board, but regardless, I won't just throw you overboard and wait for you to sink.

WHAT'S IN A NAME?

Flash Out of the Box offers a unique approach to learning Flash.

You'll learn how to use the tools that come in the box with Macromedia Flash to accomplish your goals—goals that ultimately exist outside of Flash. You'll learn how to animate, make efficient Flash movies, implement basic interactivity and logic, stream and play video, publish Flash content, and more. But the goal isn't to teach you Flash, per se. Rather, the goal is to enable you to implement your vision with Flash as the tool of choice. So rather than constrain your ideas with Flash's authoring metaphor, I'll get you thinking outside the proverbial box in ways that other introductory books often fail to do.

Another reason for the book's name is that you're going to learn a lot about Flash while using a box as a unifying theme throughout.

Why a box?

Boxes are representative of all aspects of design and development. A box represents form and structure (as in building blocks), transition (as in the boxes that hold your memories on moving day), and adventure (like the boxes you unwrap on your birthday). A box encompasses everything you include in its confines and excludes everything you bar from its interior. A box is a metaphor for your own preconceptions and the ability to understand and overcome them. A box is an atomic unit that can be transformed in endless ways. Every piece of paper, computer screen, and web browser window starts as an empty box, and it is up to you to fill it.

You're going to use, abuse, and transform the box as you step through exercises that will reveal the basics of Flash in an intuitive way. Instead of running through chapter after chapter of information about the major facets of Flash, you'll learn organically as we complete interesting exercises that present and reinforce the important concepts you'll need to maximize your creativity. You play the starring role and Flash is the supporting cast.

In this book, we'll use a box as the basis for graphic layouts, buttons, animations, interactive widgets, cartoon characters, containers for externally loaded assets, advertisements, and even as a television set for displaying video. The exercises show you how Flash can help you accomplish your goals, and the "Get Out of the Box" section at the end of each chapter inspires you to go beyond what you've learned to that point.

A box is never just a box. It's a window. It's a door. It's the artwork on an album cover. It's the canvas waiting to become an oil painting. It's the jack-in-the-box longing for you to turn the crank. Millions of possibilities exist inside the constraints of a box, and I'll show you how to implement, build upon, and transcend them.

You'll learn to think and operate outside the box if you take this opportunity to explore Flash and ultimately bend its capabilities to your will.

What makes Flash Out of the Box better?

If you're standing in a bookstore right now, reading this Preface to determine how *Flash Out of the Box* compares to other books on Flash basics, set this one down for a moment. Find two other introductory Flash books and peruse the table of contents in each one.

The chapter list probably looks something like this:

Chapter 1: Interface
Chapter 2: Drawing

These topics are things I would expect to see in a book on Flash basics, because I already know how to use Flash. But they are not things *you* are likely to expect, because you do not already know about the various features of Flash or how they can help you create the projects in your head that brought you to this bookstore in the first place. Instead of a mental model of Flash, you have only a design goal, and you have no way to know if the preceding list will help you accomplish your goals. These books cover Flash in an order that is nonintuitive for the beginner because they are Flash-centric. They often cover Flash concepts without regard to when or why (or even *if*) you should use a particular feature or technique.

Now look through the table of contents for *Flash Out of the Box*:

While you see some of the same topics in this book's table of contents, the topics are presented in a very different way. For one thing, my book is considerably shorter than

many because I assume you're smart and experienced with other programs even if you're inexperienced with Flash. Furthermore, I focus on the material you really need, and do so efficiently. So you won't spend half your time learning features you'll likely never use. Rather than teaching concepts in the abstract, I introduce them in a context in which they're meaningful to the exercise at hand. I explain things to help you get where you want to go. After all, you're not just shopping for a book on Flash. You're shopping for a book that will help you achieve your goals of creating something spectacular using Flash. The difference is paramount.

THE PROMISE OF THIS BOOK

Several techniques are used in this book to help you better understand and retain the information you are given. This approach is what makes *Flash Out of the Box* a more effective learning tool than other books on the shelf. Here's a breakdown of the approach:

Learning by doing

People learn by repetition, so you should perform all the exercises. Techniques presented in one chapter are used again in later chapters, offering practice while you learn new techniques. After you've initially learned an operation, such as drawing a box, I gradually offer less hand-holding until you can perform the task as second nature. This means that you won't have to absorb too much information at once.

Shortcuts

Shortcuts and alternative techniques are introduced after you have performed an operation at least once. Becoming more familiar with each operation from multiple perspectives reinforces the material, helping you to transfer it from short-term to long-term memory.

Chunking

Information in this book is grouped together in small pieces, revealing larger concepts through collections of digestible parts. This process is known as *chunking*. To see how this works, try to remember the following nine-letter sequence: *pnggifjpg*. Not too easy. Now try to remember the following chunks: PNG,

GIF, and JPG. The difference is in the presentation. In the first case, you are expected to remember nine unrelated and abstract items (most people's limit is three to five items). In the second example, you are asked to remember only three items, and the items are familiar and related to one another (they are all graphic file types). For example, instead of repeating four steps for drawing a box, I might just say "draw a box." This gives you practice at flying solo and lets me take advantage of the chunks of information you've already learned.

Keeping it concrete

It is always easier to remember things that have meaning for you. So I'll make abstract concepts concrete before expecting you to absorb too much more. Everything is presented in context, so you'll understand when and why to use each feature, not just how.

Need-to-know basis

Some books try to teach you everything about a given topic before you're ready. This book features "progressive disclosure" in which a topic is revisited in more depth as your knowledge and needs grow. This is the way we learn most things in life. We learn to tell time before we worry about time zones and daylight savings and leap years. Learning Flash should be no different. This book teaches what you need to know, when you need to know it, without getting bogged down in minutiae that isn't relevant at the time. In other words, don't go through this book expecting to learn everything there is to know about a topic in one chapter. Instead, expect to be introduced to a topic or tool and revisit it later to learn more.

Narration

The exercises are presented in a narrative style. New information is given as you go along, so the book follows a typical, iterative learning process. Sometimes steps are undone and restarted to simulate working alongside a teacher or a colleague. This gives the exercises a flow that's more realistic than other books. It also helps you learn. If you see the mistakes now, you'll be able to catch your own mistakes later on. I'll show how to do it right and, on occasion, what happens when you do it wrong.

Sidebars

Sidebars are used to expand upon topics introduced in text sections. The topic is explained in the text enough to perform the exercise and explained in more detail in the sidebar. I cover important concepts in sidebars to avoid bogging down the main text with too many tangents for readers with more Flash experience. Beginners who want a deeper understanding of underlying Flash concepts are well advised to read all the sidebars.

Tips

In addition to the formatted notes and warnings, many tips are offered within the body text, without any special formatting. This may not sound like much of a selling point, but it is. This way, tips are woven seamlessly into your learning experience without being intrusive. You'll learn deceptively more than you think you are learning.

Terminology

Flash terminology and operations are offered throughout the book in a way that makes it easy to remember the names of things and the purposes of the various panels. After I mention how to perform various operations in the Properties panel, for example, you'll understand that panel intimately without our ever having discussed it in isolation. You will become familiar with standard Flash terminology, so that you can understand discussion groups and support lists and can ask questions in an intelligent manner.

"Get Out of the Box" sections

Each chapter ends with a section called "Get Out of the Box," which offers suggestions about what can be accomplished with the skills you gained in the preceding exercises. Suggestions like these are also spread throughout the chapters, so you always have a reason for completing an exercise and always know how you can apply your new knowledge later on.

Accomplish instead of learn

Flash Out of the Box focuses on Flash as a tool, not as an end in itself. The book offers you a path to follow, a reason to follow it, and somewhere to go. All information is presented in a reader-centric, task-oriented fashion, and reasons are offered for completing each exercise. This book presents goals and helps you reach them, and I hope your own interest in the topic provides additional motivation apart from the reasons the book offers.

Make a mess

Flash design and development is rarely a linear process. More often than not, you end up with extraneous code, graphics that don't get used, multiple versions of the same file, and a whole arsenal of ideas that may or may not work for a particular project. In other words, it's fun. Design is about the process, and learning should occur the same way. Making a mess is not only acceptable, it's desirable. And we'll make plenty of messes...er, "serendipitous excursions" in this book. (Of course, it is always wise to clean up your files before handing them off to clients or other developers.)

The basics and beyond

You will learn what you hope to learn by using this book: the basics of using Flash so you can accomplish your design goals. But I also cover lots of more-advanced features that really add interest to the topic and to your project. The book is not an exhaustive Flash reference, so it won't leave you exhausted. You'll get up to speed quickly and be equipped to learn more in the future. Aside from information on the basics, I also offer lots of best-practice advice on everything from design to optimization to usability.

WHY USE FLASH?

I assume, since you are reading this Preface, that you have some idea of what Flash can do, and you have some things you'd like to do with it. If you don't, here is some background information.

Flash started as an animation tool with a very basic programming language (ActionScript). From the heyday of the dot-com boom, Flash offered lightweight animations that could be incorporated into any web site, providing a compelling way to bring designs to life. However, instead of using Flash for practical reasons that users would appreciate, such as the animation of a diagram, designers everywhere were using it for convoluted, animated introductions that repelled users in droves. As a poor remedy, Skip Intro buttons became prevalent, and Flash quickly got a bad rap from usability experts such as Jakob Nielsen, who claimed Flash was "99% Bad." (Since then, Macromedia has made great efforts to improve the usability of Flash content for users, and Nielsen and others have changed their tune.)

Soon enough, Flash made its appearance on our television sets, with Flash animators producing several full-length, broadcast cartoons. Next, the Flash Player made its way into handheld devices, starting with the Pocket PC platform and eventually PDAs and cell phones. Flash even showed up in kiosks in shopping malls. My personal favorite was an animated billboard on top of a taxicab in Las Vegas, the last place I ever expected to see Flash in use.

Over the past several years, with the advent of robust web applications, new usability concerns arose over the number of online transactions that failed. Upon recognizing this, Macromedia began morphing Flash into a serious application development environment, capable of loading dynamic information and exposing web services on the Web, CD-ROM, handhelds, and now, Macromedia Central (*http://www.macromedia.com/software/central*). The purpose is to use the ubiquitous Flash Player as a front end for web applications, helping to consolidate multiple screens into a single dynamic interface, creating a more engaging and effective application.

Flash is the ultimate tool for creating rich media experiences that engage, entertain, and even facilitate business processes. Of course, plenty of people still use it to make cartoons, and I, for one, think that's pretty cool.

What you do with Flash is up to you, so I hope you've got some projects in mind. Soon, you'll see just how easy it is to implement your designs in Flash, and by the end of this book you'll be ready to transcend Flash's limits and, in doing so, push your own.

HOW TO USE THIS BOOK

If you read the book from cover to cover, you'll find many tidbits in unlikely places that you'd miss if you skip around. You're strongly encouraged to perform all the exercises so you get some practice and gain familiarity with Flash. Most of the exercises build on concepts and operations learned earlier, so unless you're already familiar with Flash, you should definitely start at the beginning. The exercises are refreshingly brief, so give them a shot and pick up the finer points hidden along the way.

Getting the examples working

Nothing is more frustrating than a tutorial book in which you can't get the examples to work. In anticipation of that, I offer the following guidance. This explanation will make much more sense once you get further into the book, learn to use Flash, and experience difficulties first-hand. You may want to just skim this advice now and revisit this section if you are having trouble getting something to work.

This book assumes you are using either the Flash MX 2004 or Flash MX Professional 2004 (Flash Pro) authoring environment. See *http://www.macromedia.com/software/ flash/productinfo/features/comparison* for a comparison between the two. Flash development is largely identical on both Windows and Macintosh, although some of the keyboard shortcuts or locations of menu commands vary slightly across platforms. I point out differences where necessary.

The example files for the exercises and installers for both Flash MX 2004 and Flash MX Professional 2004 are included on the enclosed CD-ROM. I recommend you install Flash Pro if you don't already have Flash MX 2004 installed.

If you have lost the CD-ROM and have a high-speed connection, you can download the trial software from Macromedia's site (*http://www.macromedia.com*). I generally don't use features that are exclusive to Flash Pro, and I warn you when I do. Almost everything works identically in Flash MX 2004 and Flash Pro.

The most common reason for being unable to get an example to work (assuming you haven't made any typos) is a failure to set up the Flash file according to the instructions. Reread the surrounding text and follow the steps carefully. Be sure to place the code where it belongs (usually in the first frame of the *actions* layer).

> **NOTE**
>
> Refer to Appendix A for important tips on how to configure your workspace for maximum ease-of-use. The enclosed CD-ROM includes a sample panel layout, as described in the appendix.

Any code example that accesses movie clips, buttons, or text fields via ActionScript won't work unless you set the item's instance name properly. To set the instance name for a movie clip, button, or text field, select it on stage and enter the instance name on the left side of the Properties panel (accessible via the Window → Properties menu command) where you see the placeholder "<Instance Name>".

> **NOTE**
>
> In case of errors, updated examples and sample files can be downloaded from the book's support web site at *http://flashoutofthebox.com*.

If you still can't get it working, be sure to check the example files on the CD-ROM, contact O'Reilly book support, or check the book's errata page.

To ensure the examples compile, set the ActionScript Version to ActionScript 2.0 under File → Publish Settings → Flash. All examples have been tested in Flash Player 7 (the latest version of the plugin corresponding to the release of Flash MX 2004 and Flash Pro), but many will work in Flash Player 6 or even Flash Player 5. Most examples can also be exported in Flash Player 6 format from Flash MX 2004 or Flash Pro by setting the export format (i.e., the Version option) to Flash Player 6. If you have trouble getting an example to work, especially an example that uses ActionScript, be sure to export it in Flash Player 7 format.

Flash MX—the previous version of the Flash authoring tool—does not support ActionScript 2.0. However, most of the exercises and example code work in Flash MX (some of the menu options and panel items may be slightly different, but you shouldn't have any trouble adapting the exercises to Flash MX). If using Flash MX, set the Actions panel to Expert Mode (using the Options menu in the upper-right corner of the panel). In Expert Mode, you can enter ActionScript directly in the Script pane of the Actions panel rather than using Normal Mode's menu-driven approach. Flash MX 2004 and Flash Pro no longer support a menu-driven mode for entering ActionScript, and all code is either entered directly in the Script pane of the Actions panel or created via the Behaviors panel.

CONVENTIONS

The following typographical conventions are used in this book:

Keyboard shortcuts

Keyboard shortcuts for Windows and Macintosh are often listed for a command. If only one keyboard shortcut is specified, it is the same on both platforms. If different, the platform is mentioned. For example, "Ctrl-G (Windows)" means to press the Ctrl key and the G key at the same time on the Windows operating system. "Cmd-G (Mac)" means to press the Command key and the G key at the same time on the Macintosh operating system. Shorthand notation such as "Ctrl/Cmd-G" means to use Ctrl-G on Windows and Cmd-G on Mac.

Menu commands

Menu commands are indicated using the arrow symbol (→). For example, Edit → Copy indicates that you should select the Copy command from the Edit menu. Similarly, Modify → Arrange → Send Backward indicates choosing a menu item several levels

deep. The same convention is used to indicate that you should choose a tab or suboption in a dialog box, such as File → Publish Settings → Flash → Action-Script Version.

Plain text

Indicates menu titles, menu options, menu buttons, and keyboard accelerators (such as Alt, Ctrl, and Cmd).

Italic

Indicates new terms, function names, method names, class names, layer names, URLs, email addresses, filenames, file extensions, pathnames, and directories. In addition to being italicized in the body text, method and function names are also followed by parentheses, such as *stop( )*.

Constant width

Indicates code samples, clip instance names, symbol names, symbol linkage identifiers, frame labels, variables, attributes, properties, parameters, values, objects, XML tags, HTML tags, the contents of files, or the output from commands.

Constant width bold

Shows commands or other text that should be entered literally by the reader.

Constant width italic

Shows text that should be replaced with user-supplied values.

> **NOTE**
>
> This icon signifies a tip, suggestion, or general note, although many tips are integrated throughout the text.

> **WARNING**
>
> This icon indicates a warning or caution. Ignore at your own peril.

COMMENTS AND QUESTIONS

Please address comments and questions concerning this book to the publisher:

> O'Reilly Media, Inc.
> 1005 Gravenstein Highway North
> Sebastopol, CA 95472
> (800) 998-9938 (in the United States or Canada)
> (707) 829-0515 (international or local)
> (707) 829-0104 (fax)

We have a web page for this book, where we list errata, examples, and any additional information. You can access this page at:

> *http://www.oreilly.com/catalog/flashbox*

To comment or ask technical questions about this book, send email to:

> *bookquestions@oreilly.com*

For more information about our books, conferences, Resource Centers, and the O'Reilly Network, see our web site at:

> *http://www.oreilly.com*

ACKNOWLEDGMENTS

I offer my sincerest gratitude to the following people:

Bruce "I correct everything" Epstein
> You took my fledgling of an idea for *Flash Out of the Box* to the O'Reilly editorial board and convinced them to let me write this book. Then you helped me shape the book's vision, taught me to be the writer I thought I already was, offered sage advice at all the best (and worst) times, and suffered through quite a few nights of serious sleep deprivation to get this book ready for production. All of this makes you either brilliant or crazy. In either case, Bruce, you rock.

O'Reilly Media, Inc.
> You have all been wonderful throughout this process. Even Tim O'Reilly himself kept close tabs on the book's progress to make sure it lives up to the O'Reilly name. And believe me, I *really* hope it does. Thanks also to the O'Reilly staff, including Emily Quill, Rob Romano, Claire Cloutier, Glenn Bisignani, Bill Takacs, and Robert Luhn, and to my conscientious copyeditor, Norma Emory.

Robert Eckstein
> You were kind enough to answer questions, offer advice, and even shoot video of your dog for this book. Thanks, Robert. May Scrappy and you both live long and healthy lives.

Ron Haberle
> You put together the custom timeline effect featured in Chapter 6, and then offered yourself up as a reference when the opportunity came along for me to join the KnowledgeNet team. Why you did any of this, I'll never know, but you're a swell cat in my book (and this is, in fact, my book, so I get final say). Thanks, Ron.

Liatt Bailey
> You used to be the guy who asked way too many questions about how to do the simplest things you could possibly do on a computer (I'm so glad that's over). You're also the guy who makes me laugh more than anyone else. Ironically, you're terrible at telling jokes. For that, I'm appreciative. And a bit confused.

The beta readers and tech reviewers
> I thank you for keeping me accurate and honest. Sham Bhangal, Paul Catanese, Lisa Coen, Marc Garrett, Mark Jonkman, Andy Rayne, Darron Schall, Drew Shefman, Dana Stokes, Karen Vagts, and Edoardo Zubler.

The Macromedia Flash Engineering team
> Words cannot possibly describe how great you have been. In particular, I'd like to thank Mike Downey (Flash Project Manager), Mike Chambers (guru of everything Macromedia), and Ed Sullivan and Amy Brooks (Macromedia User Group Coordinators). All of you have been a tremendous help and have contributed to the Flash community in ways I can't begin to explain.

FMUG.az (Flash and Multimedia Users Group of Arizona)

John C. Bland II, Shane "can't design" Anderson, Bob Wohl, Ron Haberle, Muharem Lubovac, Shaun Jacob, Jeff "cross-homogenization" Garza, and everyone else in the group (all 180 of you) make this whole experience worth everything I have put into it. Without you, I'd still be wondering if there were other Flash geeks in Phoenix.

Above all else, I thank my wife, Christine Rose Pearson, without whom none of the possibilities in my life would have become reality. You are my eternal inspiration. You are my best friend. You are, quite simply, the place I call home. See you in Dreamland.

—*Robert Hoekman, Jr.*
Phoenix, Arizona
October 2004

The best way to get started with Macromedia Flash is to jump right in, so let's start with something you can show off immediately. We'll get your brain moving by doing some drawing, creating some funky designs, and learning to reuse graphics. The concepts behind the fun stuff will be discussed at the end of each chapter, but right now, let's get our hands dirty.

As explained in the Preface, the object of this book is to teach you to use Macromedia Flash to help you accomplish your goals, whatever they may be, and to give you a lot of good information on the basics without drowning you in details. *Flash Out of the Box* is much shorter than many other introductory books on Flash because it focuses on the information you need to know to accomplish your goals. It isn't intended as an exhaustive reference of every feature, but rather concentrates on the features you're likely to use and presents them in an engaging and digestible format. You'll learn to do what you want to do with Flash, and by the end of this book, you'll have the skills you need to explore further study or experiment more on your own.

Furthermore, you'll learn through progressive disclosure, which means the book provides information in the context of an exercise, when and where it's relevant. For example, this chapter doesn't cover everything there is to know about Flash's drawing tools. Instead, I'll show you how to use a few drawing techniques to create your first design in Flash, add color, and make an image reusable. In later chapters, I'll show you other ways to draw in Flash and expand on the skills gained here. Throughout the book, I'll also offer suggestions about how to apply your new skills in other projects and a reason to learn each technique.

This approach avoids inundating you, the reader, with more information than you can assimilate. Instead, we'll tackle Flash in small chunks so that you'll be able to absorb each concept and the required actions, allowing you to build confidence and a larger skill set over time. Most people can remember only four or five new things at once, but by chunking them into larger operations, you have to remember fewer things. For example, instead of having to remember every twist and turn of a road, you might simply follow directions that tell you to drive to the next light. Of course, this assumes you have the fundamental abilities to see the road, depress the gas pedal or brake pedal, and steer the car. If so, you can pursue the overall goal by remembering just one instruction: drive to the next light. This book revisits certain techniques and provides reminders to help reinforce the operations learned earlier to help you transfer them to your long-term memory. Over time, you'll master the mechanics of using Flash, allowing you to comfortably focus on your overall goal, such as creating a compelling application or animation.

I know you're just dying to get started, so let's do it. In this chapter, we'll draw a box, fill it with color, and then push the box further by turning it into a psychedelic image of Jimi Hendrix. Later on, we'll make a box graphic reusable to eliminate the need to re-create it.

The techniques used in this chapter are the first steps in learning to animate with Flash and are used in almost every Flash project you'll take on. Even if you're not into Jimi Hendrix, this chapter is a building block for the animations we'll create in Chapter 3. To begin your journey of becoming a Flash "master of the universe," let's get started with some of Flash's built-in tools.

EXERCISES AND SOFTWARE

All of the exercise files in the book are available on the accompanying CD-ROM or from *http://www.flashoutofthebox.com*. Copy or download the examples, and put them somewhere on your hard drive where you can find them easily. The content (such as images) you need for the exercises in each chapter are in numbered folders, such as folder *01* for Chapter 1. The folders also contain the completed exercises in some cases, but you'll benefit most by going through the exercises step-by-step.

If you don't already have it installed, a 30-day trial version of Macromedia Flash MX 2004 (version 7.2) is included on the accompanying CD-ROM. Trial software can also be downloaded from *http://www.macromedia.com/go/software/flash*. The enclosed CD-ROM also includes Fireworks and other trial software you may need for some of the exercises.

NOTE

Refer to Appendix A for important tips on how to configure your workspace for maximum ease-of-use. The enclosed CD-ROM includes a sample panel layout, as described in the appendix.

DRAWING YOUR FIRST BOX

Many of Flash's drawing tools are similar to those in other graphics programs, which means you can apply information here to other programs, but some of Flash's tools behave in unique ways. Be aware that Flash's drawing tools are vector based. Mastering Flash's tools allows for precision drawing, so you'll quickly be creating visual masterpieces worthy of international design awards (right?).

We'll start with a method for drawing a box, which is one of the most commonly used shapes in design. If you are new to Flash, you'll feel comfortable in no time. And if you've already cracked it open a few times, you'll expand your horizons quickly.

Setting up the file

Before we can start a design, we need to create a new Flash file:

1. Make sure you have copied the sample files (from the CD-ROM or web site) into a folder named *FOTB* (for *Flash Out of the Box*) on your hard drive, and make sure you have another folder, named *01,* inside it.

2. Launch either Flash MX 2004 or Flash MX Professional 2004 (Flash Pro). The exercises in this book work the same in either version, as both share basic features.

3. When you launch Flash, the Start screen appears, as shown in Figure 1-1. Start screens are used in all Studio MX 2004 products, including Flash and Flash Pro. One cool reason to use the Start screen is that it keeps track of the last 10 opened documents,

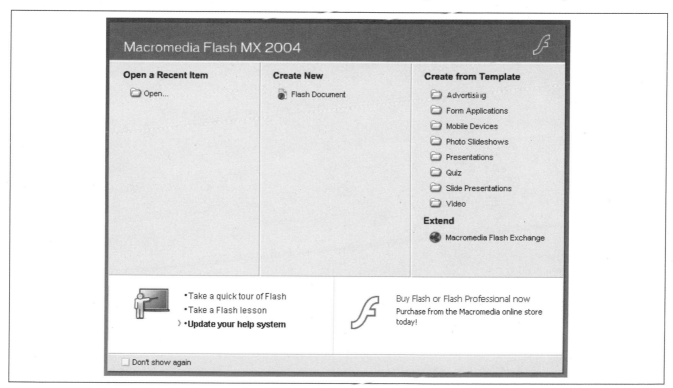

Figure 1-1. The Start screen knows what you've been doing.

so those files are handy when you come back from lunch. Figure 1-1 shows the Start screen from Flash MX 2004. If you're using Flash Pro, the Start screen contains some additional templates and file types, which we'll ignore for now. Regardless, your Start screen will show your recently used files and may reflect automatic online updates provided by Macromedia, so each user's screen will vary slightly.

4. Under the Create New heading of the Start screen, click on Flash Document to create a new, blank Flash

NOTE

Flash documents are often called *movies*, but some developers prefer to use that term only for distributable *.swf* files (pronounced "swiff") published from the *.fla*, which we'll learn about later.

document (a *.fla* file, pronounced "flah"). Of course, you can use File → New → Flash Document to create a new document at any time.

5. Save your new document as *box.fla* in the *01* folder (inside the *FOTB* folder you created earlier) using the File → Save As menu option.

Now take a moment to look around the world of Flash. Notice the Tools panel, shown in Figure 1-2. (If your Tools panel isn't visible, you can open it using Window → Tools.) Many of the tools will look familiar if you've worked with other graphics programs. As you roll your cursor over each icon in the Tools panel, a tool tip indicates the tool's name and shows the shortcut key in parentheses. For example, you can select the Pencil tool by pressing Y. The Options portion at the bottom of the Tools panel reflects the options for the currently selected

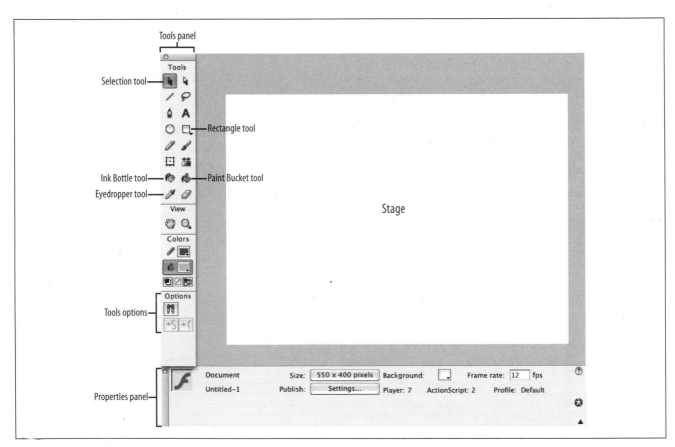

Figure 1-2. The Flash interface, showing the Tools panel, Stage, and Properties panel.

tool (i.e., this section changes depending on what tool is selected).

Creating a rectangle

Let's draw a rectangle shape as a starting point for a design. To draw a rectangle:

1. In the Tools panel, select the Rectangle tool, indicated in Figure 1-2.

2. With the Rectangle tool active, roll your cursor over to the Stage (the large white area in the Document window). Your cursor should look like a crosshair (a big + sign).

3. Click and drag somewhere on the Stage to create a rectangle, then pat yourself on the back for doing such a great job.

Creating a square

Before you get too excited, try to draw a square box instead of a rectangular one:

1. Use the Edit → Undo menu command to get rid of the previous rectangle. Alternatively, you can press Ctrl-Z (Windows) or Cmd-Z (Mac) to undo the previous step. Now we're back to square one! (You saw that joke coming a mile away, didn't you?)

2. With the Rectangle tool active, click and drag on the Stage again to draw another box, but this time, try to make it perfectly square.

3. When you're done, choose the Selection tool (shown in Figure 1-2) from the Tools panel.

4. Double-click inside the box you just drew to select both the box and its border.

5. With the box selected, locate the Properties panel (shown in Figure 1-3), which appears below the Stage by default. (If it's not visible, choose Window → Properties to open it. It is also sometimes called the Property inspector or PI.) The Properties panel looks different in Figure 1-3 than it does in Figure 1-2 because its appearance and contents change depending on what item is selected (that is, it's context-sensitive). At the bottom of Figure 1-2, the Properties panel displays the Stage's properties. In Figure 1-3, it displays the selected rectangle's properties.

6. The W and H fields in the Properties panel represent the width and height of the rectangle. If the width and height match, you've drawn a perfect square and deserve a snack (but you'll have to get it yourself). More likely, the two numbers will be slightly different. You can make the rectangle a perfect square by entering the same value in the W and H fields.

Drawing a perfect square

There is a way to draw a perfect square without eyeballing it or setting the dimensions manually, so give this a shot instead:

1. Undo the previous steps to get rid of the box. (Remember, to undo, use Ctrl-Z or Cmd-Z. You can undo up to 1000 steps by default.)

2. Choose the Rectangle tool from the Tools panel again (or use the R keyboard shortcut).

3. This time, press and hold down the Shift key, then click on the Stage and drag the crosshair cursor to draw a box. Don't release the Shift key until after you've released the mouse button (or lifted your stylus, if you are using a graphics tablet). The Shift

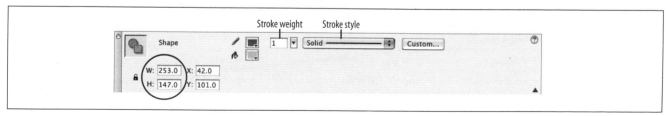

Figure 1-3. The Properties panel, as it appears when a shape is selected.

key constrains the shape's proportions to a perfect square as it is drawn.

4. Double-click inside the box to select both the box and its border, then consult the Properties panel again. The box's width and height values are now identical.

5. Save your work using File → Save (Ctrl-S or Cmd-S). Leave the file open.

Constraining the shape of the box as it's drawn is a great way to ensure your squares are actually square. The same rule applies to the Oval tool for drawing circles, and both of these shapes can be used as the basis for countless designs. There are several other ways to draw in Flash, but we'll save those for other chapters. For now, let's learn to manipulate the shape we've got.

FILLING SHAPES WITH COLOR

If you went through the exercises in the preceding section and didn't change the default colors, you should now have a blue box with a black border sitting on the Stage. Flash draws new shapes using whatever colors are already chosen in the Tools panel or Properties panel, which represent the shape's *fill* and *stroke* colors. See the "Fills and Strokes" sidebar for details.

Figure 1-4 shows the strokes and fills of a simple rectangle and how the stroke appears when selected partially or in its entirety.

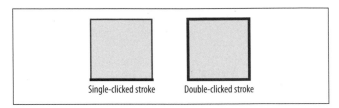

Single-clicked stroke   Double-clicked stroke

Figure 1-4. Strokes and fills (a single-clicked stroke on a box versus a double-clicked stroke on a box).

Solid fills and gradients

Next we'll use new colors to create a gradient pattern. *Gradients*, which are a type of fill, are useful because they produce a smaller file size than bitmap images, while still creating interesting effects.

Let's start by creating a solid fill:

1. Choose the Selection tool from the Tools panel, and click once inside the box on the Stage. The fill area inside the box should appear as a large collection of dots, indicating that it is selected.

2. In the Properties panel (which you can open with Ctrl-F3 on Windows or Cmd-F3 on Mac), notice the Pencil and Paint Bucket icons shown in Figure 1-5. The Stroke Color swatch (next to the Pencil icon) represents the current stroke color, and the Fill Color swatch (next to the Paint Bucket icon) represents the current fill color. A white box with a red line through it indicates "no color."

FILLS AND STROKES

Unlike many other drawing programs, Flash elements are drawn using *fills* and *strokes*, which are easier to understand if you experiment a bit with the various drawing tools. A *fill* is the area of color that fills up or constitutes a shape.

For example, if you draw a free-form blob on the Stage, the colored area inside its border is its fill (even if the fill color matches the movie's background color, making the fill unnoticeable). The colored area is called a fill even if no border surrounds it.

Fills can be split into multiple fills, and separate fills can be joined to create new shapes. They can also be grouped together (Ctrl-G or Cmd-G) or broken apart (Ctrl-B or Cmd-B) for editing purposes.

A *stroke* is simply the name for the border. The stroke can be a solid, dotted, or dashed line, as controlled via the Properties panel.

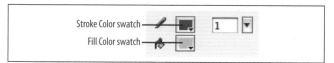

Figure 1-5. The stroke and fill color choosers.

3. Click on the Fill Color swatch to open the color chooser. This reveals the Web 216 color palette, the default color palette for Flash.

4. Choose any color from the Web 216 color palette. Choosing a new color automatically changes the color for the selected fill. Your world is in full, living color, so go for something orange, just for fun.

5. Click once somewhere outside of the box to deselect it.

6. Select the box's stroke. Since the stroke in this case consists of four lines, clicking once selects only one side of the box. Double-click any side to select the entire stroke (the box's perimeter).

7. Click on the Stroke Color swatch in the Properties panel to change the color of the stroke. Choose something that will clash with orange, such as a nice shade of olive green. Knowing what colors look bad together is an important part of designing good color schemes, and this color choice is perfectly awful. Deselect the stroke when you're done to see how it looks.

8. Save your work using Ctrl-S or Cmd-S.

Creating a multicolor gradient fill

Gradient fills are more versatile than solid fills. Gradients can help you design a sunrise or sunset, lighting effects, and the illusion of depth in otherwise two-dimensional drawings (as shown in Figure 1-6), so don't be afraid to experiment. Gradients can be applied only to fills, not to strokes.

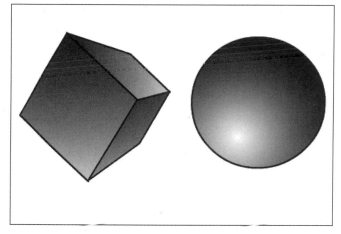

Figure 1-6. 3D shading effects created with gradients.

We're all done with bad colors, so let's fix the color scheme from the previous exercise. This time, let's use a multicolor gradient fill to create a psychedelic look for a 1960s-style poster for a Jimi Hendrix concert:

1. Select the fill again (by clicking once in the center of the box you've drawn on the Stage).

Clicking once inside a shape selects only the fill. Double-clicking a shape selects both its fill and stroke (if a stroke is present).

If the stroke is a continuous line, such as the stroke for a circle, you need to click it only once to select the entire stroke. However, if the stroke consists of multiple lines, such as the four sides of a rectangle, a single-click selects only one line. To select all parts of the stroke, double-click any part

of it. See Figure 1-4 for a comparison of single-clicking and double-clicking strokes.

As discussed, double-clicking selects both the fill and the stroke. If you don't double-click fast enough, the unselected part (usually the stroke) gets left behind if you drag the shape. If this happens, undo your last step to move the fill back to its original position inside the stroke. Then double-click again to select them both before attempting to drag them.

2. Choose Window → Design Panels → Color Mixer to open the Color Mixer panel, shown in Figure 1-7.

3. In the Color Mixer panel, change the Fill Type to Linear using the drop-down list. On the Stage, the solid fill automatically changes to a linear gradient, blending from black to white. A colored bar, which shows how the gradient looks, also appears in the Color Mixer.

Take a look at the Color Proxy sliders in the Color Mixer, shown in Figure 1-7. Notice that the Color Proxy slider on the left is black and the one on the right is white. Notice also that the Color Proxy swatch at the top of the panel is set to black.

You can change the gradient color as follows:

1. Click on the leftmost Color Proxy slider, as seen in Figure 1-7. Then click on the Color Proxy swatch to pick a color from the color palette. Changing this swatch changes the beginning color of the gradient. To keep going with the psychedelic look, choose bright green from the pop-up.

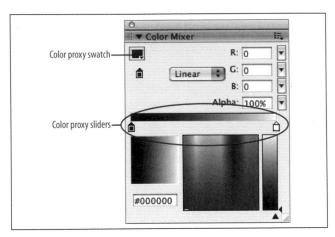

Figure 1-7. Color Proxy sliders in the Color Mixer panel control the blending of gradients.

2. Click on the white (rightmost) Color Proxy slider to change the end color for the gradient. Again, use the color palette pop-up to choose pink as the ending gradient color.

Now, that's one ugly gradient. Some additional steps are necessary to achieve the psychedelic effect we want.

THE COLOR MIXER

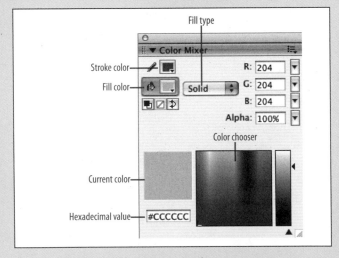

Figure 1-8. The Color Mixer panel.

The Color Mixer panel, shown in Figure 1-8, gives us some great options for changing strokes and fills, and even enables us to change the fill completely by converting it to a gradient.

Here is a breakdown of the options for the Color Mixer:

Stroke color
Changes the color of the stroke. The stroke color option appears only when the Fill Type is set to None or Solid.

Fill color
Changes the color of the fill.

Fill type (menu)
Changes the fill style. Options include None (which deletes the fill), Solid (for a solid, one-color fill), Linear (for a gradient that blends on a linear path), Radial (for a gradient that blends outward, in a circular path, from a

Gradients on LSD

To turn the gradient into a more psychedelic frenzy of color, try this:

1. With the gradient on the Stage selected, click once halfway between the two Color Proxy sliders below the gradient bar in the Color Mixer panel. This adds a third slider to the gradient. With the new slider selected, change its new color to aqua by using the pop-up palette accessible via the Color Proxy color chooser.

2. Move the aqua Color Proxy slider to the right a little bit by clicking and dragging (hence the name "Color Proxy *slider*").

3. Click halfway between the leftmost and middle sliders in the gradient bar to add another new Color Proxy slider. (You can remove Color Proxy sliders, except for the beginning and ending ones, by dragging them off the slider area.) Make it red by choosing the red swatch in the lefthand column of the Color Proxy color chooser. Now green blends to red, red blends to aqua, and aqua blends to pink. Beautiful, and very strange. Jimi would be proud.

4. To create a background more like the psychedelic posters from the 1960s, change the Fill Type drop-down list choice in the Color Mixer panel to Radial. This changes the gradient so it blends outward from a central point, creating a "tripped-out" backlighting effect, as though the sun is shooting out acidic rays of light.

5. Save your work and leave this file open.

Strokes (and other medical emergencies)

The stroke for this image could be improved to further induce flashbacks of Woodstock, so let's change it from a solid line to something funkier:

1. Deselect the fill for the box, and select the entire stroke.

2. In the Properties panel, click on the Stroke Style drop-down list, shown back in Figure 1-3. Choose the fourth style down from Solid (Solid is the default stroke style). The styles aren't named in the menu, so you'll have to count down to the right one. (It looks a bit like splattered paint, and is known as Stipple.)

focal point), and Bitmap (for a fill made of tiled bitmap images).

RGB (three separate slider bars)
Changes the density of the red, green, and blue (RGB) colors in a fill.

Alpha
Sets the percentage of opacity for a solid fill (or the currently selected Color Proxy slider for a gradient fill). Zero percent alpha makes it invisible, while 100% alpha makes it opaque.

Current color
Displays the currently selected color.

Color chooser
Provides a quick, visual way to choose any color. Simply click on the color chooser and drag the cursor around to locate the color you want. You can open a platform-specific color selector using the icon in the upper right of the pop-up palette (not shown). This allows you to specify colors other than RGB, such as hue, saturation, and brightness (HSB).

Hexadecimal value
Displays the current color's hexadecimal (a.k.a. hex) value, which you can manually override by entering a new one. Commonly used in HTML, hex values are six-digit number and/or letter (A–F) combinations that represent a color, such as #000000, which represents black, or #FFFFFF, which represents white.

3. Use the Stroke Color swatch to change the stroke color. Choose the blue swatch in the lefthand column of the chooser.

4. Using the stroke weight text field or slider in the Properties panel, set the stroke weight to 10 to fatten it up.

5. Deselect the stroke to see what it looks like. You should now have a 10-pixel-wide stroke that appears as an array of spots that resemble paint splatters, as seen in Figure 1-9.

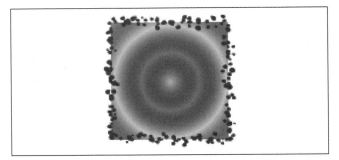

Figure 1-9. The new stroke.

Things are looking good now, but the stroke doesn't seal off the border as well as it could, so let's modify the stroke to fix that:

1. Select the entire stroke again. In the Properties panel, click the Custom button to open the Stroke Style dialog box. The Type drop-down list is already set to Stipple (unless you chose a different type of stroke earlier).

2. Set Dot Size to Medium, Dot Variation to Varied Sizes, and Density to Dense. This tightens up the stroke to seal up the edges of the fill it surrounds.

3. Click OK and deselect the stroke to see your work by clicking somewhere outside of the box. Nice, huh?

4. Save the file, but leave it open.

Using the Pencil tool to resurrect Hendrix

Adding a silhouette of Jimi Hendrix in the foreground of this gradient would finish this thing off nicely, so let's do it. If your drawing skills aren't that good, don't sweat it. The silhouette of Jimi, just like the rest of this image, can be as psychedelic as you want. The objective is to see how the Pencil tool can be used to draw shapes freehand:

1. Choose the Pencil tool from the Tools panel (which changes the cursor to a pencil) and set the Pencil tool options to Smooth (instead of the default Straighten). In the Properties panel, set the stroke weight to 5, set the stroke color to black, and change the stroke style back to a solid line.

2. Click and drag inside the box to draw a silhouette of Jimi, like the one in Figure 1-10.

Figure 1-10. A silhouette of Jimi Hendrix drawn with the Pencil tool.

You can stop and start as much as you want using the Pencil tool, so feel free to use as many lines or curves as you need. If you make a mistake, either undo it or remember that mistakes can be just as cool as the lines you draw intentionally. (The trick is to know when to let go. The brilliance of artists like Picasso and Matisse is in their subjective interpretations, not in painting straight lines or rendering reality with fidelity.)

> **NOTE**
>
> If you prefer not to draw the silhouette yourself, open *hendrix_silhouette.fla*, located in the *01* folder (inside the *FOTB* folder on your hard drive, from the CD-ROM, or from the book's web site). It contains the drawing shown in Figure 1-10. Select the stroke, choose Edit → Copy to copy it, return to *box.fla*, and choose Edit → Paste to paste it into *box.fla*. Close *hendrix_silhouette.fla* by choosing File → Close when you're done.

If your drawing skills are no better than your dog's, then do what you can and tell your friends you took some "artistic liberties."

If you're not satisfied with your drawing, try smoothing the stroke with the Pencil tool options in the Tools panel:

1. Select the stroke you drew (Jimi's silhouette) with the Selection tool. If the lines are all connected, double-clicking selects them all. If they are not all connected, press Shift and select each line individually until you have selected all of them.

2. Click once on the Smooth option at the bottom of the Tools panel. This makes the stroke smoother. If you're happy with the new look, leave it alone. If not, click Smooth one or two more times until you are satisfied. The trick is remembering when to stop smoothing it. Making it too smooth will diminish the hand-drawn quality. Deselect the stroke when you're done.

3. Choose the Paint Bucket tool, and change the fill color to solid black using the Properties panel.

4. With the Paint Bucket tool active, click once inside the outline to fill in the silhouette of Jimi.

Gotcha. The entire image turned black, huh? When you drew the silhouette, you didn't draw a line at the bottom to complete the stroke, and the gap is large enough that it prevents the fill from knowing where to go, so it fills up the entire image. Let's fix it by sealing off the fill area by closing the stroke:

1. Undo the last step to remove the black fill from the image.

2. Using the Pencil tool, draw a line from the lower-left corner of the Hendrix silhouette to the lower-right corner, connecting the stroke. When you're done, the pencil stroke may disappear behind the stroke for the box.

3. Activate the Paint Bucket tool again, select the Gap Size icon from the Options section of the Tools panel, and choose Close Small Gaps from the menu. Then, click inside the shape to see if the fill is applied. If not, choose Close Medium Gaps and try again. If that doesn't work, choose Close Large Gaps.

The Gap Size option dictates how large a gap can be bridged when applying a fill with the Paint Bucket tool.

Next, let's try grouping shapes together so their fills can't be accidentally deleted:

1. Activate the Selection tool and select the black fill you just applied to the silhouette, then delete it. Everything inside the fill area is removed, including the gradient that was once behind the silhouette's fill!

2. Undo the last step. We'll need the silhouette fill for something else in a minute.

3. Select the gradient fill and the box's stroke (by double-clicking in the box but outside Jimi, or by holding down the Shift key while making multiple selections). Press Ctrl-G or Cmd-G. This creates a *group* of the fill and stroke so that they can be easily moved together (i.e., they cannot be edited separately). Everything is now grouped except for the black fill inside the silhouette. A line appears around the box, indicating it is a grouped image.

> **NOTE**
>
> Groups are typically used to make a semipermanent selection when animating or creating content. For example, you might group together a gaggle of geese for an animation in which they fly in a V pattern, then ungroup them at a later time so you can animate each bird separately. To create a permanent grouping, you can group the items inside a symbol instead (see the "Symbols" sidebar on the next page).

4. Drag the group to the right. You see that the inside of the box where the silhouette overlapped is empty.

5. In the Color Mixer panel, change the Fill Type from Solid to Radial. The gradient that appears in the gradient bar is the same as the one we last used.

6. Use the Paint Bucket tool to apply the gradient to the black silhouette fill on the left side of the Stage. Notice that the radial gradient's center point is determined by the position of your click. Click several times

inside the silhouette area to change the center point for the gradient until you are happy with the look.

7. Activate the Lock Fill option at the bottom of the Tools panel and try to apply the fill again. The Lock Fill option prevents the fill from being changed. When you're done, disable the Lock Fill option by clicking it again.

8. Save your work.

To compare your work to the preceding exercises, open *box_2.fla*, located in the *01* folder. It contains a version of the image as it should appear at this point of the chapter.

Scaling images

You often can't tell when starting a drawing how big or small it needs to be. In this case, the gradient image should fill up the Stage, so let's resize it. We'll experiment a bit to get you familiar with Flash drawing tools. The Stage is rectangular, but the image is square, so we'll need to make some changes to the image as well:

1. Select the silhouette image on the left side of the Stage (using the Selection tool), and activate the Ink Bottle tool from the Tools panel, shown in Figure 1-2.

2. Click inside of the fill. The Ink Bottle tool adds a stroke to the silhouette fill. Use the Selection tool (which you can activate by simply pressing V) to select the stroke, and change the stroke weight to 5.

3. Double-click to select both the silhouette's fill and its stroke, and group them (using Ctrl-G or Cmd-G). Then move the group offstage to get it out of the way for a moment.

4. Select every part of the box except for the stroke (by holding down the Shift key and making multiple selections) and delete it (using the Delete or Backspace key). You may need to break apart the box first by choosing Ctrl/Cmd-B.

5. Select the box's stroke and, using the Properties panel, set the width (W) to 550 and the height (H) to 400. The stroke now matches the dimensions of the Stage (550 × 400 is the default Stage size for new Flash documents). You may need to unlock the padlock icon to change the box's width and height independently.

SYMBOLS

A *symbol* is a reusable asset, or *object*, that resides in the Library of a Flash document. A symbol in Flash is like a set of instructions for an asset that has been wrapped up like a birthday present and named. Each symbol can contain graphics data and/or ActionScript that is used to tell Flash how *instances* of the symbol behave. When you drag a symbol from the Library to the Stage, you're not moving the symbol itself. Instead, you're creating an instance of that symbol in the movie, based on the symbol's intrinsic instructions. In a typical Flash project, your Library will be full of these symbols, and your Stage will be full of symbol instances that were created from them.

Symbols can be reused as many times as you want, and multiple instances of a symbol will add almost no file size to your movie (which is important for optimizing download time). For example, Flash can use a single box symbol to create one or more box instances. Flash stores unique attributes (*properties*) for each instance, such as its name, color, width, height, and position. This allows Flash to draw (*render*) hundreds of boxes separately even though they are all derived from a single symbol.

6. Also in the Properties panel, change the X (horizontal) and Y (vertical) positions to 0. The registration point for objects is in the center by default. So change the registration point of the box to the upper-left corner using the Info palette (Window → Design Panels → Info). This aligns the stroke to the upper-left corner of the Stage, which is its origin. We'll discuss more about Flash's coordinate system in Chapter 2.

7. In the Color Mixer panel, set the Fill Type to Radial (if it's not already). The gradient that appears is the same one we used earlier.

8. Activate the Paint Bucket tool and apply the gradient fill to the area inside the box stroke. This time, click near the upper-left corner of the area to start the radial gradient from that point, giving the illusion of sunlight made of multicolored rays.

9. Select both the fill and stroke of the Stage-sized box and group them by pressing Ctrl-G or Cmd-G.

10. Break apart the silhouette image off stage by selecting it (with the Selection tool) and pressing Ctrl-B or Cmd-B, then delete the stroke. It's not necessary to keep it as part of the silhouette.

11. Select the fill for the silhouette and change its fill color to black. When you're done, group the image again (you can use Modify → Group instead of Ctrl-G or Cmd-G).

12. Move the silhouette onto the Stage and place it on the right side of the gradient-filled box.

To compare your work to the figures shown in this chapter, open *box_3.fla*, located in the *01* folder. It contains the final version of the Hendrix image.

Stacking graphics

The image's composition is good, but the silhouette appears in front of the stroke for the box. Let's fix that, so that the stroke appears as a frame for the image:

1. Drag the silhouette back off stage, and break apart the box. We need these two elements split apart so we can put the background in the back, the silhouette in front of that, and the stroke in front of both.

2. Select the stroke and choose Edit → Cut to remove it temporarily.

3. Drag the silhouette back into place on the Stage.

4. Right-click in Windows (Cmd-click on Mac) off stage somewhere and choose Paste in Place from the contextual menu. This command pastes the stroke back into its original position and leaves it selected.

5. Group the stroke (this doesn't group the stroke with another element; it simply makes the stroke noneditable).

The stroke appears in front of the silhouette, so it looks like a frame for the image. This occurs because Flash creates a visual *stacking order* when new graphics are added or drawn within a single *layer* (we'll discuss layers in Chapter 3). If you draw a box, then draw a second box, the second box will appear in front of the first. If you then group the first box, it appears in front of the second box. Grouped objects appear in front of ungrouped objects, in the order that they were grouped.

6. Undo (Ctrl-Z or Cmd-Z) to place the silhouette image in front of the frame. There is another way to organize the stacking order that you may prefer:

   Choose the Modify → Arrange → Send Backward menu option. This sends the silhouette image back one step in the stacking order, so it appears behind the frame (you may need to do this more than once). The four options in this menu (Bring to Front, Bring Forward, Send Backward, and Send to Back) enable us to stack objects in any order we want.

7. Save your work, and close the *box.fla* file.

> **NOTE**
>
> If you are having trouble achieving the desired results with the Modify → Arrange menu options, remember that grouped objects are always drawn in front of ungrouped objects. If necessary, ungroup the box and stroke before using Modify → Arrange → Bring to Front to place the silhouette in front.

Perfect! It's hard to believe now that this image started as a simple box, but it did. Making use of a few drawing tools, fill and stroke options, and some ingenuity turned this simple shape into a background for a 1960s poster for a rock concert.

CREATING REUSABLE GRAPHICS

You may often need to use a graphic several times in one movie, whether it's a box, logo, or character. To avoid adding substantial file size to the finished project as a result, we use *symbols*. See the earlier "Symbols" sidebar for the scoop on symbols and their benefits.

Creating symbols

Let's create a reusable box symbol that we can use in our designs. To create the symbol:

1. Create a new, blank document using File → New. Activate the Rectangle tool in the Tools panel and, using the Properties panel, set the stroke weight to 1, the stroke color to dark gray, and the fill color to light gray.

2. Before drawing anything, double-click on the Rectangle tool icon in the Tools panel. This opens the Rectangle Settings dialog box. (If you click and hold on the Rectangle icon, it lets you choose between the Rectangle and PolyStar tools, so be sure to double-click.)

3. Set the Corner Radius to 10 and click OK. The Corner Radius option sets the roundness of the corners drawn with the Rectangle tool. Setting the Corner Radius to 0 gives our box sharp corners, while setting it to 10 gives our box a more rounded look.

4. Draw a square box (remember to hold down the Shift key to constrain the shape). You now have a nice, light gray box on the Stage with a dark gray stroke and rounded corners. Very stylish.

5. Select both the fill and stroke for the box (using the Selection tool).

6. Choose Modify → Convert to Symbol (F8). This opens the Convert to Symbol dialog box, shown in Figure 1-11.

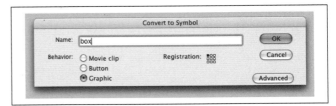

Figure 1-11. *The Convert to Symbol dialog box.*

7. In the Name field, type the word **box**.

8. For the Behavior type, choose Graphic, then click OK to close the dialog box. You should see a blue line around the box you just drew. This indicates that it is now a symbol and is currently selected.

THE LIBRARY

Every Flash movie (*.fla* document) you create has its own Library, which acts as a repository for all your movie's assets. You can open the Library panel using Window → Library, Ctrl-L (Windows), or Cmd-L (Mac). When you import an asset, such as a PNG file, it is accessible from the Library. The same is true for sounds, video clips, and anything else you can import into Flash. The Library is convenient and efficient because it makes assets easy to find and reuse. The Library also holds all symbols (whether button, graphic, or movie clip symbols). Don't confuse the Library panel with, say, collections of ActionScript files that are sometimes referred to colloquially as libraries.

It's important to understand that a grouped image is not the same as a symbol. A grouped image is raw graphic data on the Stage, whereas a symbol is the defined blueprint for one or more instances of the same graphic.

Reusing symbols

Now that we have a symbol, we can reuse it as many times as we want without re-creating the drawing or adding significant file size to a project. To create an instance of a symbol:

1. Open the Library (Window → Library or Ctrl-L or Cmd-L). The *box* symbol, created in the previous exercise, is stored there so you can find it easily.

2. Choose the Control → Test Movie menu option to open the Preview window (sometimes called Test Movie mode), which shows you how your movie will look when it's published. Right now, you just have a box sitting there doing nothing.

> **NOTE**
>
> You should try to memorize the shortcut key for Test Movie mode (Ctrl-Enter on Windows or Cmd-Enter on Mac), as you'll use it frequently.

3. With the Preview window open, choose View → Bandwidth Profiler. The third line down in the Bandwidth Profiler (shown in Figure 1-12) displays the file size of your movie. It says 0 KB (85 B), but this may vary depending on your computer's operating system. This means your movie is very small, and that's great, because the smaller a file is, the faster it downloads (some developers refer to a file's size as its "weight," so lightweight files are a good thing).

4. Close the Preview window.

5. Click on the *box* symbol in the Library and drag it out to the Stage. This adds an instance of the *box* symbol to the movie. Position it wherever you want.

6. Test the movie again (using Control → Test Movie). The movie size should say something similar to 0 KB (92 B). Adding a second box increased the file by only 7 bytes, which is a trivial amount.

7. Close the Preview window and drag 10 more instances of the *box* symbol out of the Library, placing them randomly around the Stage. If dragging instances to the Stage is too monotonous for you, press the Alt key (on Windows) or the Option key (on Macintosh), then click and drag an instance that is already on the Stage. Alt-clicking (or Option-clicking) duplicates the instance (remember to release your mouse button before letting go of the Alt or Option key).

8. Test the movie again. The size is still only 0 KB (193 B). You have 12 instances of the *box* symbol on the Stage, and your movie still fits into less than 1 KB!

9. Close this file, but don't bother saving it. We won't need it again.

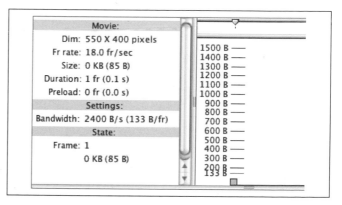

Figure 1-12. The Bandwidth Profiler.

We've only just begun, but we've already covered many fun and useful techniques. So far, you've learned about:

- Basic Flash terminology such as *Stage* and *movie*

- The Tools panel and its drawing tools, including the Rectangle tool, Pencil tool, and Selection tool

- Gradients, strokes, and fills

- The Properties panel

- Symbols and how to reuse them

You may notice that many Flash terms and concepts, such as the Stage and movie, sound as if they came from a movie studio. Flash often uses a filmmaking metaphor. Much like a film, anything that appears on the Stage appears in the finished movie. A graphic appearing off stage is not seen in the published movie unless it moves onto the Stage at some point.

You also learned that the Properties panel (which is common to all Studio MX 2004 products) is useful for checking and changing the properties of objects and options for tools. The Properties panel is context-sensitive, so its options change depending on which tool or object you have selected. For example, if you select the Text tool, the Properties panel displays options for text, such as font size, bold, text field type, and so forth. If you activate the Rectangle tool, the Properties panel shows options for the fill color, stroke color, type of stroke, and stroke weight. The Properties panel can also be used to change the properties of the movie itself if the Stage is selected, and to set component parameters when a particular component is selected (you'll work with components in Chapter 10).

If you want to experiment for a while, try using some of the other drawing tools. Which operations can be constrained by holding down the Shift key? Try finishing off the Hendrix poster image, perhaps by adding some text (using the Text tool) or brightly colored flowers. Use the Oval tool to create a circle for the center of a flower, and use the Pencil tool to draw the petals. Fill them in with funky gradients and spread them all over the image to see how crazy it can get. If you want a more realistic-looking flower, see Hack #12, "Borrow Color Schemes from Nature," in *Flash Hacks* (O'Reilly).

With your new knowledge of the drawing tools in Flash, you can start drawing everything from cartoon characters and backgrounds to logos and layouts, so get to it. This book is all about playing around, so have some fun. Chapter 2 will be waiting for you when you're done.

TWO

CREATING LAYOUTS QUICKLY

The techniques used in this chapter enable you to create and modify layouts efficiently, leaving you more time to daydream about the next project and prepare your speech for the awards ceremony that will inevitably follow.

Having to manually repeat common tasks, such as drawing a box, can slow you down. To speed up development, Flash can automate almost any set of steps. In this chapter, we'll explore some cool ways to streamline your workflow by automating the creation of a symbol, editing multiple instances of it at once, and getting things aligned with precision using almost no energy.

KNOW YOUR HISTORY PANEL

If you created all of those boxes in Chapter 1, you may be looking for a faster way to get the job done. Fortunately, there is a way! Understanding how Flash tracks the tasks we perform helps us automate the process. Soon, you'll be able to create a box with a mere flick of the wrist, so nothing will get in the way of your creative process.

Tracking history

The History panel is new to Flash MX 2004 and Flash Pro. The History panel begins as a blank slate and tracks actions as they occur so that tasks can be undone and redone step-by-step, recorded, and replayed, saving you time and energy. To take advantage of this feature, let's make some history:

1. Create a new, blank document and save it as *history. fla* in the *02* folder (in the *FOTB* folder on your hard drive).

2. Choose Window → Other Panels → History to open the History panel.

3. Activate the Rectangle tool (R), choose any fill and stroke colors you like in the Properties panel, and draw a square box (remember to hold down the Shift key to constrain the shape).

4. Use the Selection tool (V) to select the fill, then change the fill color to light gray.

5. Select the stroke by double-clicking on any edge, and change the stroke color to dark gray. Then deselect the stroke.

6. Double-click in the fill area of the square to select both its fill and stroke. Then move it off stage.

Have you noticed the History panel filling up with information? It tracks each task we perform in order, resulting in something like the history list shown in Figure 2-1.

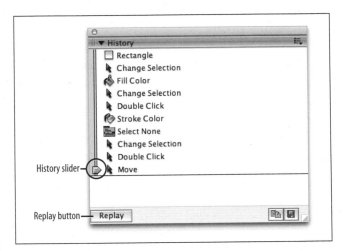

Figure 2-1. The History panel.

We've already seen how the Undo command can help us travel back in time, but the History panel allows us to retrace as many steps as we please by stepping through a written list of the tasks we have performed. At any point, we can step backward in the History panel and start again from a previous step, or simply repeat a sequence by choosing the steps to replay.

Let's see how it works:

1. Drag the history slider, indicated in Figure 2-1, up two steps to the step marked Double Click. The box on the Stage becomes selected again and moves back to its original position. Essentially, you're going back in time (so congratulations on figuring out the whole space-time continuum issue).

2. Drag the history slider up to the first step in the history list, marked Rectangle. The box on the Stage returns to its original state.

3. Drag the history slider back down to the last step to send the box off stage once again. The box is deselected, as you've come full circle.

4. Click once on the first step (Rectangle) in the history list, then hold down the Shift key and click on the second-to-last step (Move). Shift-clicking highlights the entire sequence, selecting the steps in between.

5. Click on the Replay button at the bottom of the History panel, as indicated in Figure 2-1, to replay the sequence.

Instantly, the steps selected in the History panel are replayed, creating a box in the same position as the first one you drew (you can't see the first box because the new one is obscuring it).

Let's move the new box to reveal the old one:

1. Drag the selected box to the left of the Stage. This reveals the original box so you can see both. If moving the second box doesn't reveal the original, the second fill overwrote the first one as described in the sidebar below. To create separate boxes, you can move the first box away from its original position, then replay the appropriate steps from the History panel to create a new box in the vacated space.

2. Save your work and leave this file open.

You now know how to perform a sequence of steps and replay them, but the process of drawing the box needs to be simplified so Flash can replay the sequence faster. In this case, we drew a box and immediately changed its

colors. It is easier for Flash to replay the sequence if we choose the colors we want before drawing the box, so let's simplify.

Economizing a sequence

A long list of actions in the History panel, like the one we have now, can be difficult to read, and we need to be able to identify which steps to save as part of the sequence. So before starting over to simplify the creation of our box, let's clean up the History panel.

To clear the history for the document:

1. Delete the two boxes from the Stage.

2. Open the History panel's Options menu and choose Clear History, as shown in Figure 2-2. Flash warns us that the action cannot be undone. Disregard the warning and click Yes to continue. (Be aware that

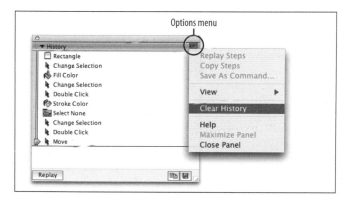

Figure 2-2. Using the Options menu to clear the history.

OVERLAPPING FILLS/STROKES

When Flash draws a fill, it combines the new fill with any existing fill with which it overlaps. To prevent two fills from being combined, put them on separate layers or avoid overlapping them.

A single fill can be separated into multiple fills by a stroke. For example, a straight line stroke drawn through a fill splits that fill into two separate fills. Likewise, intersecting strokes

split each other into separate strokes. For example, drawing two intersecting lines in the shape of an X creates four separate strokes (each line splits the other line into two strokes). Play around with Flash drawing tools until you are comfortable with the ways that strokes and fills behave and interact.

clearing the history deletes the entire contents of the History panel and not just the selected steps. But clearing the history does not undo any steps.)

3. Save your work.

Now let's cut the drawing process down to four steps, so we have an economical sequence that can be saved and quickly replayed by Flash. While we're at it, let's add a step that converts the graphic to a symbol, so Flash will also do that when we replay the sequence.

Perform the following steps exactly as they are listed, without any extra clicks or other actions:

1. Activate the Rectangle tool, then choose light gray and dark gray for the fill and stroke colors, respectively.

2. Draw a square box on the Stage.

3. Using the Selection tool, double-click the box to select both its fill and stroke.

4. Convert the box to a graphic symbol (using Modify → Convert to Symbol or F8), and name it **box**, being sure to set the Behavior radio button to Graphic and the registration point to the upper-left corner. The list in your History panel should match Figure 2-3.

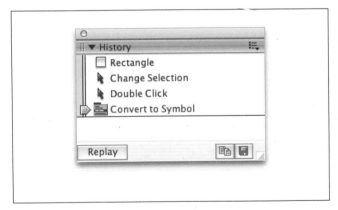

Figure 2-3. The history of a box.

Our new, more efficient sequence is easier for us to read and faster for Flash to execute. Next, we'll save and reuse the sequence.

Commands: next-generation macros

To make a sequence of steps reusable (like the macros common to many other applications), we need to save it as a *command*, as follows:

1. Select the first step (Rectangle) in the History panel, then press the Shift key and select the last step (Convert to Symbol) to highlight all four steps. (You can also click and drag from the top of the list to the bottom to select all the steps simultaneously.)

2. Click the Save Selected Steps as a Command button in the History panel, as indicated in Figure 2-4. This opens the Save As Command dialog box.

3. In the Command Name field, type **Make a Box**, and click OK to close the dialog box.

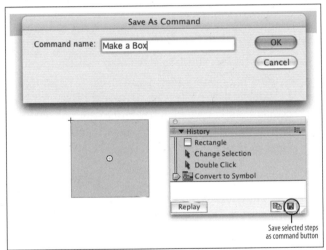

Figure 2-4. Saving selected steps as a command.

Now we have a command that creates a gray box any time we need it. To use it, just follow these steps:

1. Move the *box* symbol offstage somewhere to get it out of the way. You'll see why in just a moment.

2. Open the Commands menu at the top of the Document window, as shown in Figure 2-5. The Commands menu shows our brand-new Make a Box command. Congratulations—you've added a new command to the Flash interface (you can rename or delete it using Commands → Manage Saved Commands).

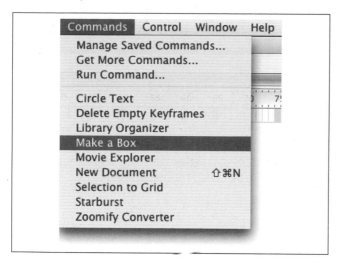

Figure 2-5. The Commands menu showing the custom Make a Box command (and a few others I've picked up along the way).

3. Choose the Make a Box command from the Commands menu.

4. Open the Library (Ctrl-L or Cmd-L). Aside from seeing the *box* symbol, you should see another graphic named *Symbol 1*, which was created via the Make a Box command. Flash names new symbols using the default naming convention *Symbol 1*, *Symbol 2*, and so on, unless we enter custom names.

Each time we execute the command, Flash creates a brand-new box and places it in the same position as the box we drew originally. Why? Because the History panel, in addition to tracking steps, tracks the position of the box as you draw it. Also, each time we run the Make a Box command, Flash converts the box to a symbol for us, eliminating the need to repeat the process manually. This is a great time-saver.

So why doesn't Flash use the name *box* every time we run the Make a Box command? If Flash named every new symbol *box*, there would be no way to distinguish among them without renaming each symbol. The default naming convention used by Flash (*Symbol 1*, *Symbol 2*, etc.) keeps each symbol identifiable in the meantime.

You may notice that the two symbols now in the Library (*box* and *Symbol 1*) are identical. And you may think, "Hey! You said I could use one symbol as many times

as I want." And you would be right. For faster download times, it is better to create multiple instances from only one symbol, because it helps minimize file size. So let's delete the extra symbol:

1. Delete the *Symbol 1* instance from the Stage. Even after you delete the instance from the Stage, the original symbol remains in the Library.

2. In the Library, select *Symbol 1* and click the trash can icon (or press the Delete key). A dialog box requests confirmation that you want to delete the symbol. Choose Yes to delete the symbol.

3. Save your work, and close the *history.fla* file.

Congratulations! You've automated the task of creating a box symbol, setting yourself up to save time in the future. We're all done with the History panel for now, but let's use the Make a Box command in a new file and learn to design a layout using only one symbol. By doing this, we'll see how to use one symbol multiple times and alter instances of it.

ALIGNMENT FOR UNLICENSED CHIROPRACTORS

Layout is vital when designing any project. The organization of elements on a page can make or break a good idea. A good layout can improve the user experience and ensure that you're communicating effectively, but planning and organizing a complex layout can quickly become difficult. One way to get started is to create a box symbol and use instances of it as placeholders before replacing them with real content. This way, you can design a layout without having to deal with text, images, animations, or other assets. I use this technique to get design ideas onto the screen and the creative juices flowing. Let's create a box symbol, design a layout, and employ some of Flash's alignment tools to speed up the process.

Use the guides, Luke

Let's create and position the first box in our layout using *rulers* and *guides*.

1. Create a new Flash Document (File → New → Flash Document) and save it as *layout.fla* in the *02* folder.

2. Run the Make a Box command (Commands → Make a Box). This adds *Symbol 1* to the Library and an instance of the symbol to the Stage.

3. In the Library, change the name of *Symbol 1* to *box*. To do this, double-click on the name of the symbol in the Library, type the new name, and press Enter or Return to commit the change. (Be sure to double-click the symbol's name; if you double-click the symbol icon in the Library instead, you enter Symbol Editing mode as described in the later sidebar "Symbol Editing Mode.")

4. Go get a ruler, preferably 12 inches or longer. You'll hold it up to your monitor to measure the distance between objects on the Stage. (I'm just kidding. Really. Put the ruler down.)

5. Choose the View → Rulers menu option. Rulers appear, using pixels for measurement, along the top and left sides of the Stage, as shown in Figure 2-6. Notice that the upper-left corner of the Stage is aligned to (0, 0).

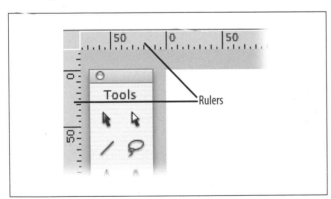

Figure 2-6. Rulers help align elements on the Stage.

6. Click on the horizontal ruler, which is parallel to the top edge of the Stage, and drag downward. This creates a *guide* (a green line). Drag the guide down, past the top edge of the Stage, and watch the vertical ruler (which runs parallel to the left edge of the Stage) as you do it. Release the guide when it is aligned to 10 pixels below the top edge of the Stage (when the vertical ruler's measurement mark for 10 turns white).

7. Now drag a guide from the vertical ruler past the left edge of the Stage and align it to the 10-pixel mark in the horizontal ruler (i.e., 10 pixels from the left edge of the Stage).

8. Drag the *box* instance so that its upper-left corner is aligned at the intersection of the guides (10, 10). When the bounding box for the *box* instance is directly over a guide, the bounding box line changes colors. If you have a hard time positioning it perfectly, use the arrow keys on your keyboard to nudge the object one pixel at a time.

We have used guides to align the first box for our layout to (10, 10) on the Stage. Guides are also helpful when you have a background image or other graphic covering up the edges of the Stage. Use guides so you always have a reference to which to align each edge.

If you can't stand seeing green lines all over your workspace, or if they're hard to see against your Stage's background color, you'll be happy to know you can change the color used for guides. Choose View → Guides → Edit Guides and change the color using the color chooser in the Guides dialog box.

Precision alignment

Using guides isn't always an accurate method for aligning objects, and the Properties panel can position objects without the use of your mouse or stylus. Let's try it:

1. Undo (Ctrl-Z or Cmd-Z) the last step of the preceding procedure so the *box* instance is no longer aligned at (10, 10).

2. With the *box* instance selected, use the Properties panel to set the X and Y values for the *box* instance to **10**. This aligns the instance perfectly to (10, 10), as shown in Figure 2-7. Using the Properties panel to align the *box* instance eliminates the guesswork.

3. With the *box* instance still selected, use the Properties panel to resize the *box* instance to 120 × 120. Before doing this, make sure the padlock icon in the Properties panel is locked (clicking the padlock toggles between locked and unlocked), and enter **120** into the W field. Locking the padlock ensures that when you alter either the width (W) or height (H)

value, the other value is changed proportionately. In this case, changing the box's width to 120 automatically changes the height to 120, maintaining a perfect square.

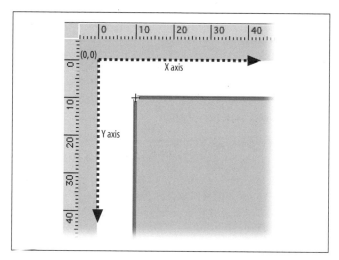

Figure 2-7. The X and Y axes, relative to the Stage.

The X and Y values represent the horizontal and vertical positions of an object, relative to the upper-left corner of the Stage. The upper-left corner of the Stage represents 0 for both the X and Y axes, as shown in Figure 2-7, so the *box* instance is aligned relative to its upper-left corner. A higher X value positions an object to the right, and a higher Y value positions the object lower down on the screen (that is, Flash's Y axis points down, in the opposite direction from the Y axis of the familiar Cartesian coordinate system).

Snap it in place

We need to align several more boxes to create a complete layout. However, dragging guides onto the Stage is time-consuming, and since we don't know the exact X and Y positions for the new objects, using the Properties panel won't be very effective (unless you're really good at guessing).

So let's get Flash to help us align graphic elements using one of its automatic alignment features to speed things up:

1. Alt-click (Windows) or Option-click (Mac) on the *box* instance and drag it to the right to create a second instance of the *box* symbol.

2. Unlock the padlock icon in the Properties panel and change the dimensions of the new *box* instance to 400 × 30 (using the W and H fields in the Properties panel).

3. Drag the new instance to the right of the first box and align its top edge to the horizontal guide (the green line) created earlier. Then hold down the Shift key and drag the new box toward (or away from) the first box until you see vertical and horizontal dashed lines appear on the Stage. These are *snap align guides*. When you release the mouse button (or lift your stylus), the new *box* instance has X and Y positions of 140 and 10. Consult the X and Y fields in the Properties panel to verify the position.

The snap align guides tell Flash to "snap" objects along invisible, intersecting gridlines. Positioning an object creates a virtual grid based on that object's position, and every object you arrange in close proximity to it reveals snap align guides. Snap align guides appear when the second object is within 10 pixels of the first object, as shown in Figure 2-8. The Snap Align feature is enabled by default, but you can toggle it by choosing View → Snapping → Snap Align. See Appendix A for more tips on customizing your workspace.

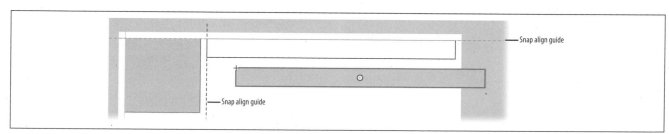

Figure 2-8. Snap align guides in action.

Now, let's create and align a third instance of our box:

1. Alt-click (Windows) or Option-click (Mac) the second *box* instance and drag it down to create a third instance of the *box* symbol. Position it below the second *box* instance. Keep the third instance vertically in line with the second instance (use the vertical snap align guide as a visual aid).

2. Resize the third *box* instance to 400 × 80 using the Properties panel.

And finally, let's create and align a fourth instance of our box to complete the layout:

1. Create a fourth instance of the *box* symbol (Alt-click or Option-click and drag from an instance on the Stage) and set its dimensions to 530 × 250.

2. Align the fourth *box* instance 10 pixels below the first *box* instance, in a straight, vertical line. Use the snap align guides to aid your positioning.

3. Save your work and leave this file open.

Using only the *box* symbol, we've designed an entire layout. Notice, though, that the stroke for each box instance gets larger when we resize it. This doesn't look too good, so let's consider how to fix it.

Behind every good symbol is a good editor

An important factor in feeling good about your design choices is knowing that you can experiment now and always change things later. You may be wondering how to change an existing symbol. In this case, we need to get rid of the stroke in our *box* symbol to refine the look of the layout and eliminate the distraction of the distorted lines.

To edit the symbol:

1. Select any instance of the *box* symbol on the Stage.

2. Choose Edit → Edit Symbols.

You've just entered the fourth dimension, where there are no physical boundaries, and space exists endlessly. Actually, you've entered *Symbol Editing mode*, but some strange things have happened nonetheless. For starters, the other content on the Stage fades into the background. Also, the Edit bar, as shown in Figure 2-9, now says

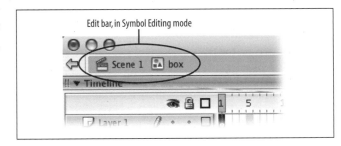

Figure 2-9. The Edit bar, while in Symbol Editing mode for the box symbol.

SYMBOL EDITING MODE

As discussed in Chapter 1, a symbol is an *object*, or a set of instructions used to define how all the instances of the symbol appear and function in a movie, and Symbol Editing mode is the editing environment for the instructions. Anything you do in Symbol Editing mode affects each and every instance of that symbol in your movie—instantly. If you change the color of the *box* symbol, and there are 10 instances of the symbol in your movie, every instance will reflect the change instantly.

Although all instances of a symbol share a common instruction set, each instance can have its own characteristics or *properties*. For example, instances of the *box* symbol can have different colors, dimensions, and levels of opacity while still being derived from a single symbol. Altering the properties of symbol instances allows us to use the same symbol in many different ways. For example, in Chapter 3, we change the color of several instances of the *box* symbol to create a color fade effect.

Scene 1, box. Finally, there is a small + (crosshair) symbol in the upper-left corner of your box. Before you go Jerry Maguire (and just *freak out*), take a deep breath and see the "Symbol Editing Mode" sidebar for more information.

Many properties of instances can be changed (as we'll see in later chapters) without creating multiple symbols or editing existing ones, but the stroke weight is an intrinsic attribute of a symbol, so it must be changed in Symbol Editing mode.

To change the stroke attribute of the symbol:

1. Delete the stroke from the *box* symbol. Every instance of the *box* symbol on the Stage, as we'll see in a minute, is instantly updated to reflect the change.

2. Use the Edit bar to return to Scene 1 (by clicking on *Scene 1*). The layout on the Stage is unaffected, but those ugly strokes are gone for good.

The *layout_1_complete.fla* file (in the *02* folder) shows a completed version of the layout. Notice that each box is aligned 10 pixels from an edge of the Stage and the boxes are 10 pixels apart from one another.

The layout is well organized, and now you have a starting point from which to continue designing or adding content. There are many ways you can use this layout. I often make a list of the elements I need to add to a page, create one *box* instance for each of the necessary elements, and then place them in different arrangements to see which one best achieves the look I want. If a box isn't enough,

I'll add ovals and other shapes until I have a folder full of possible designs saved on my hard drive. After choosing the final layout, I'll replace each shape on the Stage with a piece of real content, such as navigation, text, images, or animations. The result is limited only by your imagination.

Save your work and close the *layout.fla* file. If you have *layout_1.fla* open as well, choose File → Close All to close everything at once.

Distributing objects

Often, a layout of repeating patterns is helpful for displaying a series of images, such as a photo gallery, and many Flash developers are faced with this task at some point. Let's see how to do this efficiently by designing a layout for a Flash photo album. By the time you're done with this book, you'll know how to load images into these boxes on the fly (while the movie is running), but for now, we'll just focus on efficient positioning.

To create our photo album:

1. Create a new Flash document and save it in the *02* folder as *photo_album_layout.fla*.

2. Run our custom Make a Box command to add a box to the Stage. Change the name of the new symbol in the Library from *Symbol 1* to *box*.

3. Edit the *box* symbol to change its dimensions to 90 × 90. (You can either edit it in place or double-click on the symbol icon in the Library to enter Edit mode.

The Edit bar at the top of the Document window, as indicated in Figure 2-9, is the key to keeping track of our location. If you can't see the Edit bar, activate it using Windows → Toolbars → Edit bar. When in Symbol Editing mode (or simply "Edit mode"), the Edit bar tells us that instead of editing Scene 1, we are now editing a symbol that is used in Scene 1. The distinction is important to remember, because if you

accidentally enter Edit mode by double-clicking a symbol (which has the same result as choosing Edit → Edit in Place), you'll have to undo any inadvertent changes made to the symbol. Not that *I've* ever made this mistake (yeah, right). To return to editing the scene instead of the *box* symbol, click on Scene 1 in the Edit bar.

Double-clicking the symbol's name simply allows you to rename the symbol, not edit it.) Return to Scene 1 when you're done.

4. Choose Window → Design Panels → Align to open the Align panel, shown in Figure 2-10.

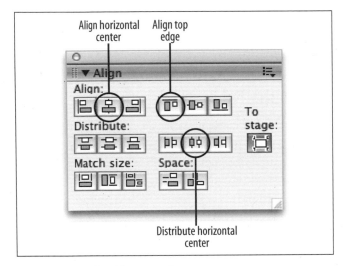

Figure 2-10. The Align panel.

5. In the Align panel, enable the Align/Distribute to Stage option. Clicking the To Stage button toggles the feature on and off.

6. With the *box* instance selected, click the Align Horizontal Center button in the Align panel to position the *box* instance in the horizontal center of the Stage.

The Properties panel's X and Y coordinates refer to the position of the upper-left corner of an object's bounding box. To align an object by the left, right, top, bottom, or center of its bounding box, you can use the Align panel (or the Modify → Align menu).

Let's finish our layout by creating multiple rows of boxes:

1. Click the Align Top Edge button in the Align panel to align the *box* instance to the top edge of the Stage.

2. Add four more instances of the *box* symbol to the Stage. To do this, click on the symbol in the Library and drag it to the Stage (this is another way to add symbol instances to your movie).

3. To position the boxes in a horizontal row, shift-select all five *box* instances and click the Distribute Horizontal Center button in the Align panel. This distributes all the boxes at equal intervals.

4. Shift-select all five *box* instances and click the Align Top Edge button in the Align panel. This aligns every instance to the top edge of the Stage so they are in a perfectly straight row.

5. Shift-select the five instances and Alt-drag in Windows (or Option-drag on Mac) to make another full row.

6. Repeat the last step until you've filled up the Stage with horizontal rows of boxes.

Now we've got a complete layout of boxes, ready to be replaced with photographs or other artwork. In a later chapter, we'll discuss how to load images into Flash while the movie is running.

In this chapter, you've learned how to:

- Work with the History panel to track tasks you perform

- Create a command to automate a sequence of tasks

- Align objects on the Stage using the Properties panel, guides, snap align guides, and the Align panel

- Edit symbols in Edit mode (a.k.a. Symbol Editing mode)

The layout we created in this chapter can serve as a great launching point from which to design the interface for a Flash-based web site.

To build on your work so far, replace each box instance on the Stage with content, such as navigation (we'll discuss how to create buttons in a later chapter), text, a logo, and perhaps an animation piece to bring some content to life. If you don't feel confident enough yet to take on a project like this, keep reading—you'll learn everything you need to know.

If you're interested in finding more commands to use while working with Flash, visit the Macromedia Flash Exchange at *http://www.macromedia.com/exchange/flash*. The Flash Exchange is filled with *components* (premade widgets, such as UI elements) and other *extensions* (add-on utilities) that enable you to do things like add a preloader to your movie, make text searchable, provide tool tips in applications, create dynamic navigation menus, and many other things, saving you lots of time and energy.

3

YOUR FIRST ANIMATION

Now that you have some
drawing skills under your
belt, you're ready to start
making graphics fly around
the screen—but please
don't. Animation can
be an effective method
of communication, or it
can seriously damage
the user experience. So
animate responsibly.

Flash started as a web animation tool and remains one of the best on the market. Unfortunately, arbitrary motion graphics can repel users. Conversely, a well-thought-out and subtle animation can help make a killer first impression when it is part of a larger presentation.

Often, animation can be the key to a more engaging presentation, effective charts and graphs, and entertaining online advertisements. Flash animation has been used for everything from movie credits and DVD menus to billboards on the roofs of taxicabs. In this chapter, you'll use a few essential animation techniques to create your first animated Flash movie: a short ad for *Flash Out of the Box*. Later, you'll further your skills by morphing a graphic from one shape to another and publishing a Flash *.swf* file for use on the Web.

The animation is straightforward. We'll draw a series of colored boxes and then add the text, "Flash Out of the Box" as seen in Figure 3-1. Of course, we'll jazz it up a little by making the boxes grow and the text slide into place—just enough to catch the reader's eye without assaulting him.

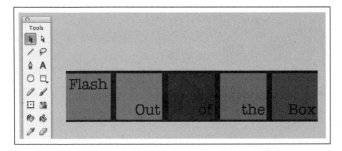

Figure 3-1. The Flash Out of the Box video.

We'll also export the Flash animation to QuickTime format. Don't confuse a Flash *.fla* source file or *.swf* published file—often called a "movie"—with the QuickTime *.mov* video format, also called a "movie." If you have QuickTime already installed, you can see the final video by running *video_complete.mov* from the *03* folder. When you're done, close the file.

We need to do a few things to prepare the animation, so let's get started.

CUSTOMIZING MOVIE PROPERTIES

The Stage's size determines the dimensions of your published Flash movie, but the default Stage size (550 × 400 pixels) is rarely the size you need, so let's set up a new file for the animation we'll create. We'll set the Stage dimensions to 500 × 100 pixels and set the background to black. Always set the Stage properties before starting the animation to avoid having to redo a lot of work.

Increasing the Stage's height adds pixels to the bottom edge of the Stage, and increasing its width adds pixels to the right edge. If you change the Stage dimensions after you create a movie, keep in mind that the content doesn't move relative to the Stage's top-left corner, (0, 0).

A *.swf* file is published for the Web by embedding it in an HTML page, just as you'd embed a GIF or JPEG image. You can resize a *.swf* file in an HTML page using the width and height attributes of the <embed> or <object> tags, but this can have unexpected results, such as an elongated or distorted appearance. Also, if your movie contains bitmap images, they can appear grainy as a result of being stretched. Bitmaps should always be brought into Flash at the largest dimensions needed for the movie. Bitmaps that are scaled down maintain a high-quality look, but enlarging a bitmap in Flash makes it look pixelated.

That said, you should try to keep your bitmaps as small as reasonably possible to reduce the download time. The best solution is to import bitmaps at the same size you want them to be in the final animation. You can scale your bitmaps using Fireworks or Photoshop before bringing them into Flash. Interestingly, designers sometimes use low-quality bitmaps and graphics intentionally to achieve a pixelated look as part of a design style, as seen in *Boy Meets Pixel* at Flip Flop Flyin' (*http://www.flipflopflyin.com/boymeetspixel*).

Changing the Stage dimensions and background color

To see the completed animation before we start, open the *animation_complete.swf* file in the *03* folder by double-clicking on the file. If you have Flash installed, the file should open in a standalone version of the Flash Player that is included with the Flash MX 2004 authoring tool. (Some *.swf* files can also be opened from inside Flash by choosing File → Open and selecting a *.swf* file. You can prevent your *.swf* file from being opened in Flash by setting the Protect from Import option in the Publish Settings dialog box. This offers only a modicum of protection, however, because SWF decompilers such as ActionScript Viewer—*http://www.buraks.com/asv*—are widely available.)

Okay, now that we know what we're aiming for, close the Standalone Flash Player and let's get to work on our animation.

Let's start by setting the Flash movie's properties:

1. Create a new, blank Flash document and save it as *animation.fla* in the *03* folder.

2. To set the Stage properties, click on the Stage's background to make sure nothing else is selected. Then, click the Size button in the Properties panel to open the Document Properties dialog box, shown in Figure 3-2.

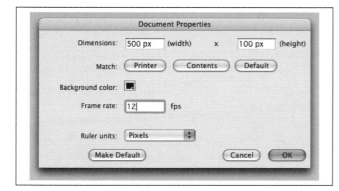

Figure 3-2. The Document Properties dialog box.

3. Set the Stage dimensions in the dialog box by entering **500** for the Width and **100** for the Height. Any part of the animation outside of the Stage does

not appear in the exported movie (using the typical export settings).

4. Click on the Background Color swatch in the dialog box, and set the background color of the movie to black. If you'd like new Flash documents to always open with a black background, you can click the Make Default button in the dialog box to change the default color, but for now, just change the background color to black.

5. Click OK to close the dialog box. This sets the Stage dimensions to 500 × 100 and the background color to black.

6. Save the file.

Customizing multiple boxes

The animation starts with boxes of different colors appearing on stage. We can keep the file size down by using multiple instances of a single box symbol.

So let's create a box in the Library and add instances of it to the Stage:

1. Create a square box symbol (using the Make a Box command we created in Chapter 2). Rename *Symbol 1* in the Library to *box_gr*. Using the "_gr" suffix makes it easier for you and other developers to identify the Library symbol as a graphic (we'll talk later about other types of symbols).

2. Create four more instances of the *box_gr* symbol. Remember, you can create a new instance by either Alt-dragging an existing instance on the Stage when using Windows (use Option-drag on the Macintosh) or by dragging a symbol from the Library panel to the Stage.

3. Line up your five instances of the *box_gr* symbol horizontally on stage, from left to right. You don't need to be exact, because we'll get Flash to align them automatically for us, but make sure they don't overlap.

Let's align and distribute the *box_gr* instances across the Stage so they look like Figure 3-3, and we'll have a good starting point for the animation. To make sure all of the boxes fit on the Stage, let's change the dimensions of each

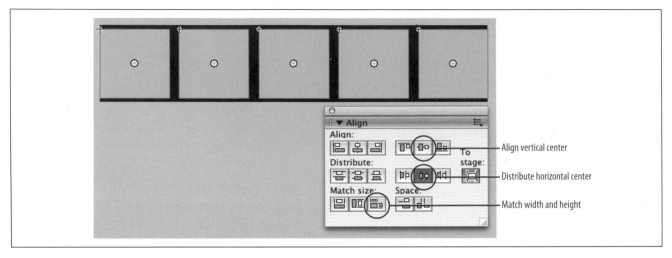

Figure 3-3. Five boxes, distributed from horizontal center.

instance to 90 × 90 pixels and then align them using the Align panel:

1. Select the leftmost *box_gr* instance and change its dimensions to 90 × 90. Remember, if you lock the padlock icon in the Properties panel, setting the width changes the height proportionately and vice versa.

2. Shift-select all five instances on the Stage.

3. In the Align panel, click the Match Width and Height button indicated in Figure 3-3. This resizes all of the *box_gr* instances to match the largest selected instance, which is the one you sized in Step 1. All five instances should now be 90 × 90 pixels. If you're having trouble with the automatic resizing, select each instance individually and change the dimensions manually in the Properties panel.

ALIGNMENT

The positioning of objects on the Stage is an important element in good design. Precise alignment and distribution makes a subconscious impression on users that your work is more professional than that of a designer who positions objects loosely.

In our *Flash Out of the Box* animation, for example, the Stage is 500 pixels wide. If the boxes are aligned so that the leftmost box instance is 5 pixels from the left edge of the Stage, and the rightmost instance is 15 pixels from the right edge, the animation appears unbalanced. The user may not be able to put her finger on why the animation looks

wrong, but it will look wrong nonetheless. If elements on the screen are meant to appear in a perfectly straight line but aren't precisely aligned, the user will notice and may feel that the site or movie is the work of an amateur. Misalignment by even one pixel can make a world of difference. This is doubly true during animations or successive scenes—if a bitmap or button shifts by a pixel, it distracts the user and undermines the illusion of continuity.

If misalignment is part of your design, make sure that items are misaligned by enough distance that the viewer knows it is intentional.

If you mastered using snap align guides in Chapter 2, the *box_gr* instances should be in a perfectly straight line. If not, let's align them and distribute them uniformly across the Stage:

1. With all five *box_gr* instances still selected, click the Align Vertical Center button in the Align panel, as indicated in Figure 3-3.

2. Click Distribute Horizontal Center, also indicated in Figure 3-3. The boxes are now evenly spaced across the Stage, as shown in Figure 3-3.

Size and position are *properties* that can be changed for any instance of any symbol on the Stage. Other properties—such as color, opacity, or brightness—can be changed as well, as we'll see later.

Managing foreground and background elements

You may have noticed in the last section, as well as in the two previous chapters, that we placed everything on the Stage within a single *layer* of the timeline. Layers are used to determine which elements appear in the foreground and which in the background, creating a visual stacking order for objects on the Stage. This is in addition to the visual stacking order of graphics within each layer that we talked about in Chapter 1. See the "Layers and the Timeline" sidebar on the next page for more information.

While using a single layer is sufficient for static graphics, animated symbols (including animated graphic symbols) require their own layer. To create multiple animations, we need multiple layers. You probably noticed that layers appear in the timeline portion of the Timeline panel, as shown in Figure 3-4.

To get ready to animate the boxes, let's move each box to its own layer:

1. With all five boxes selected, choose Modify → Timeline → Distribute to Layers. This command automatically adds five layers to the timeline and places each box instance on its own layer. It names each layer according to the name of the symbol instance that appears on the layer. In this case, all five layers are named *box_gr*.

2. *Layer 1* is now empty, and we don't need it anymore, so let's get rid of it. Select *Layer 1* by clicking on its name in the timeline and clicking the Delete Layer button (the trash can icon indicated in Figure 3-4) to remove the layer. Buh-bye *Layer 1*.

3. Select the bottom layer in the timeline. Doing so also selects the box instance on the Stage that resides on the bottom layer. Select the other layers, from bottom to top, to see which layer each instance is on.

> **NOTE**
>
> Content on the top layer is displayed in the foreground. Content on the bottom layer is displayed in the background. You can drag and drop the layers to rearrange their stacking order.

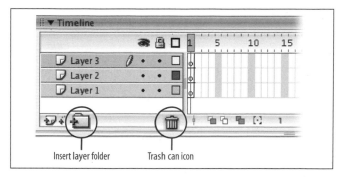

Figure 3-4. Layers in the timeline of the Timeline panel.

Having five layers with the same name makes it difficult to identify which box is on which layer, so let's rename and rearrange the layers to correspond to the positions of the boxes:

1. Determine which layer contains the leftmost box instance, and double-click on the layer's name in the timeline. Change the layer name to *box 1*.

2. Rename the remaining layers *box 2*, *box 3*, *box 4*, and *box 5*, corresponding to each box on the Stage from left to right.

3. Click on the *box 1* layer name and drag it to the top of the layer stack (i.e., the list of layers on the left side of the Timeline panel), and drop it above the other layers, moving it to the foreground.

4. Drag the *box 2* layer and position it below the *box 1* layer. Repeat for the remaining layers, in numerical order, so *box 5* is at the bottom.

The layers in your timeline should now match Figure 3-5.

We've created a more intuitive way to view the graphics by arranging the layers on which they reside. Each layer in the timeline, from top to bottom, contains a box instance

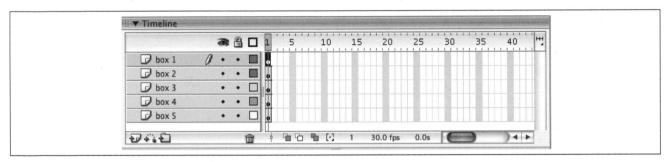

Figure 3-5. Each layer, from top to bottom, corresponds to a box on the Stage, from left to right.

LAYERS AND THE TIMELINE

The Timeline panel contains a timeline that represents the animation sequence over time. A timeline is akin to a time-based spreadsheet in which each *frame* (i.e., column) represents a moment in time. The *playhead* indicates the current frame, whose content is rendered on the Stage. Each layer (row) in the timeline represents a plane in which graphics are rendered. Content in the first layer is rendered in the foreground. Content in the last layer is rendered in the background.

Don't confuse the colored squares to the right of the layer names in the timeline with content on stage. The colored squares indicated in Figure 3-5 specify the colors used when using the Outline view mode (View → Preview Mode → Outlines). Switching to Outline view mode makes it easier to see content that might otherwise be obscured. To quickly identify the contents of a single layer, you can set the viewing mode for that layer individually by clicking the colored square to the right of its name or by using Modify → Timeline → Layer Properties → View Layer as Outlines. The Layer Properties dialog box for a layer is also accessible by double-clicking the icon to the left of the layer's name.

The Layer Properties dialog box allows you to specify other types of layers, such as Guide layers, which we'll cover in subsequent chapters. In other words, layers can be used for more than just controlling the stacking order.

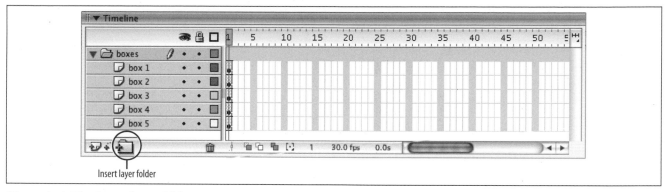

Figure 3-6. *The boxes layer folder.*

on the Stage, from left to right. For convenience, I'll refer to the boxes as *box 1*, *box 2*, and so on, as shorthand for "the *box_gr* graphic symbol instance on layer *box 1*."

We'll be adding more layers later on for the text in the animation, and the timeline will be full of layers, making it difficult to locate each one. To avoid potential confusion, let's organize the box layers in the timeline:

1. Select the *box 1* layer and then click the Insert Layer Folder button, indicated in Figure 3-6. (In the contextual menu, this command is called Insert Folder to help distinguish it from the Insert Layer command.) A *layer folder* named *Folder 1* appears above the *box 1* layer. Layer folders are used to organize layers into groups. We will use a single layer folder to keep our box layers together.

2. Shift-select the box layers and drag them on top of the *Folder 1* layer, then release the mouse (or lift your stylus if using a tablet). This moves the layers into the *Folder 1* layer folder and displays an expand/collapse arrow next to it; it also indents the layers contained within the layer folder (Figure 3-6).

3. Click the arrow to collapse the layer folder. This hides the layers, giving us room to view new layers without resizing or zooming the Timeline panel.

4. Rename the *Folder 1* layer folder to *boxes*. A custom name makes the layer folder easier to identify.

Now that our boxes are on their own layers in the timeline and stored neatly within a layer folder, let's animate them.

Changing the color of the boxes

In this animation, we'll start each box very small and increase its size over time so it appears to be growing or coming toward the viewer. Instead of using five gray boxes, let's first make the animation more colorful by changing the color of each box instance. Later, we'll change the colors to create a color-fade effect over time.

1. Open the *boxes* layer folder to see the box layers.

2. Select the *box 1* instance on stage and choose Tint from the Color drop-down list in the Properties panel, as shown in Figure 3-7. This changes the color of the graphic instance on the Stage without

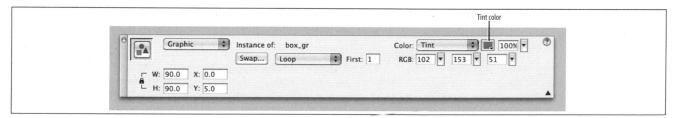

Figure 3-7. *Setting the tint color in the Properties panel.*

affecting the original symbol in the Library. Editing the symbol directly changes every instance, but here we want each instance to be a different color. (If your Properties panel doesn't contain the Color drop-down list, click on the box symbol on stage to make sure you've selected the graphic instance and not just the layer containing it.)

3. Click on the Tint Color swatch and choose any color. The instance's tint value changes to the new color. (You can set the color's intensity using the slider bar.)

4. Select each of the remaining box instances and give them new tint colors. Use any colors you like.

We'll use some of the other options available in the Color drop-down list later on to create a color-fade effect. Right now, let's animate!

ANIMATION

The tension has been mounting, and it's finally time to animate. Instead of animating each box individually, however, we'll animate all five at one time. (Shocking, isn't it?)

Why are we creating five animations at once? Well, because we can. There's no reason to create each one individually when we can do them all at once and consolidate our workload. The first thing to do is add *keyframes* to create the endpoints for the animation. Keyframes can also be used to define midpoints in animations, but for this animation, we need only two keyframes.

Your first animation

For the first part of our animation, we want the boxes to transition from one color to another over time. For now, we'll perform the animation over 20 frames.

To change the colors of the boxes:

1. Starting at frame 20 of the *box 1* layer, click and drag downward to select frame 20 on every layer in the timeline. (If you can't see all of the layers, enlarge the Timeline panel by dragging its bottom edge downward, as indicated in Figure 3-8.)

2. Choose Insert → Timeline → Keyframe. A keyframe (represented by a small black dot in the timeline if there is content on the frame, as indicated in Figure 3-8) is added to the selected layers at frame 20. A keyframe represents a point of change for a graphic or other asset in a movie. We now have an endpoint for the animation.

3. One at a time, select the layer for each box instance at frame 20 and change the tint color using the Properties panel. Use any colors you like, but pick ones that contrast with the original tint set in frame 1, so our color effect is visible. Be sure you have selected only the instance at frame 20 when setting the new tint color.

4. Press Enter or Return (or choose Control → Play) to play the animation within the Flash authoring tool, as opposed to testing it in the Flash Player.

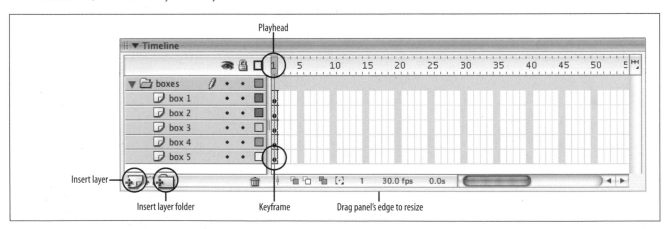

Figure 3-8. The Timeline panel.

The *playhead*, indicated in Figure 3-8, moves from frame 1 to frame 20 and stops, but nothing on the Stage changes until the keyframe at frame 20 is reached, at which point the boxes change color.

This doesn't make for a very exciting animation. We want the color transition to occur gradually over time. So let's use a *motion tween* for the color change:

1. Shift-select all the layers in the timeline. This highlights all of the frames on each layer.

2. Choose Motion from the Tween drop-down list in the Properties panel. An arrow appears on each layer in the timeline, starting at frame 1 and ending at frame 20, and the *frame span* (everything from one keyframe to the next) turns blue, indicating a motion tween has been applied, as shown in Figure 3-9. You may need to deselect the layers to see this color change in the timeline.

3. Play the animation again by pressing Enter (or Return). You should see the boxes' colors change gradually over time.

You might have assumed that a motion tween is used only to change the size or position of an object, but in fact it can be used to change any property over time, and here we've used it to change the colors of objects on the Stage.

So you've made your first animation. Before you start comparing yourself to Chuck Jones, let's see what else we can do.

We also want the boxes to grow over time, so we need to scale them to a smaller size at the beginning of the animation:

1. Move the playhead to frame 1 by dragging it across the timeline, a technique called *scrubbing*.

2. Activate the Free Transform tool, shown in Figure 3-10, and select the *box* instance on the *box 1* layer. A bounding box with eight *handles*—which allow us to

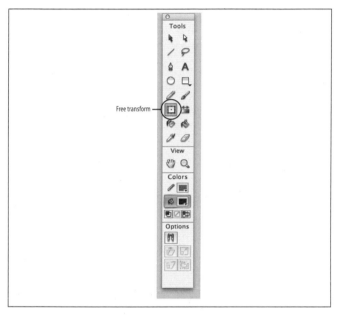

Figure 3-10. The Free Transform tool in the Tools panel.

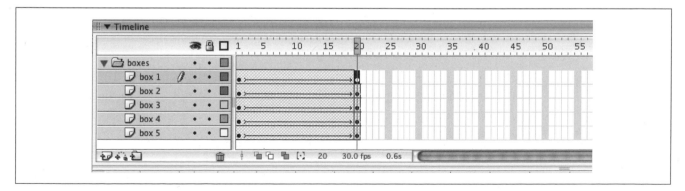

Figure 3-9. Motion tweens applied to each layer.

skew, rotate, and resize the box—appears when you select the graphic, as shown in Figure 3-11.

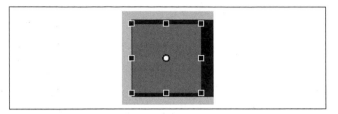

Figure 3-11. Using the Free Transform tool to scale each instance.

3. Move the cursor over a corner handle, press and hold the Shift key (constraining the dimensions of the box), and then click and drag to decrease the size of the box. Release the mouse (or lift your stylus) when the box is so small you can barely see it. When the animation is run again, the box will start small and grow over time.

4. Repeat Step 3 for the remaining boxes. Using the Free Transform tool to scale a box allows us to resize it from the center of the instance, whereas changing the dimensions via the Properties panel shrinks the instance from the top-left corner. We use the former technique to give this animation more of a 3D feel (as if the boxes are coming forward from a great distance).

5. Press Enter (or Return) to play the animation.

The boxes start small, enlarge as they appear to fly forward, and change colors.

> **NOTE**
>
> The motion tween we applied earlier automatically tweens any changing attribute from its initial values on frame 1 to its final values on frame 20. In this case, both the color and size of each box change over time.

We have created a 20-frame animation, and the movie is set to play at 12 frames per second (fps), meaning it takes almost two seconds to run. The speed of the user's computer plays a major role in the performance of Flash content, and a low frame rate is often the best option to ensure consistent playback. However, 12 fps (the default) is often not fast enough for smooth animation. A slightly higher frame rate, such as 18 fps, improves the quality of playback while still being low enough for most computers to render it smoothly.

Let's change the frame rate to improve the smoothness of the animation:

1. Click once on the Stage to deselect other items so the Properties panel shows properties for the *.fla* document itself.

2. In the Frame Rate field of the Properties panel, as shown back in Figure 3-2, enter **18** and press Enter (or Return) to commit the change.

3. Click on the Stage again to return focus to the Stage, then press Enter (or Return) again to play the animation.

The higher frame rate helps smooth out the animation. You may think that if 18 fps is good, 24 or 30 fps is even better, but higher frame rates don't always result in better playback. On some machines, higher frame rates cause the animation to appear jerky instead of smooth. Using 18 fps offers the best compromise in many cases. Test on your target machines to determine the speed at which your animation looks best.

When we increased our animation's frame rate, we indirectly shortened its duration. Now the animation occurs in about a second (20 frames at 18 fps—do the math).

Any animation that takes less than a second or so may be largely missed by the viewer. To see this for yourself, play the animation at 30 fps. Most people will notice the boxes growing, but won't notice the colors changing over time.

So how do we lengthen our animation? We simply extend the number of frames in the timeline as follows:

1. Click on any frame in the *box_1* layer and drag downward to select the frame in every layer, from *box_1* through *box_5*.

2. Press F5 repeatedly to add frames to the animation until the ending keyframe is at frame 30. Now the animation lasts almost two seconds (30 frames at 18

fps), and viewers will be able to see the effect more accurately.

3. Save and test the movie.

Always test the speed of your animation to ensure that it is paced appropriately for your goal. Usually, it should be slow enough to be seen easily but not so slow as to drag on unnecessarily. If it plays too quickly, the user will feel as if he is watching a music video with too many quick cuts. If it plays too slowly, the user is likely to be bored. The first part of the animation is finished, so let's add text to the piece to complete the ad.

PREPARING TEXT FOR ANIMATION

Text is often an integral part of an animation, drawing the eye to key terms that need to stand out in the design. In the completed version of our animation, the title of this book, "Flash Out of the Box," appears one word at a time, moving in from different directions. In this ad, the boxes serve to initially attract the user's attention, and the animated text completes the effect. A short animation such as this one serves its purpose without being gratuitous.

When choosing a font, be sure to pick one that matches the needs of the piece. If you are going to use more than one font, be mindful of the fact that designers sometimes use too many fonts or fonts that are too similar. Use no more than two or three fonts, and make sure they are dissimilar enough that the user can appreciate the difference instead of thinking she's merely viewing an inconsistent design. The same holds true for the point size of

text within a single font, or even across different fonts. If you're using more than one font, you'll generally want to use a different point size for each font. If all text is similar, you're better off sticking with a single font at a single point size. (Reducing the number of fonts also helps to keep the .swf file size down.)

Let's add the text to the movie:

1. Add a new layer folder to the timeline above the boxes layer folder. Remember, to create a layer folder, click the Insert Layer Folder button in the Timeline panel. Name the layer folder text. If necessary, drag the new folder outside the boxes folder in the layer stack (it may appear inside the boxes layer folder, depending on whether the boxes folder is open and/or selected).

2. Add a new layer by clicking the Insert Layer button in the Timeline panel, as indicated in Figure 3-8. The layer appears above the text layer folder, so drag it onto the layer folder name to move it into the folder.

3. Activate the Text tool from the Tools panel and click once on the Stage to create a static text field. Set the Field Type drop-down list in the Properties panel to Static Text, as shown in Figure 3-12. Return to the text field on stage and enter the word **Flash**. (If you click once outside the Stage before activating the Text tool, the Properties panel allows you to set the text field type before creating the text field on stage.)

4. Click once outside of the text field on a blank area of the Stage to deselect it.

5. Activate the Selection tool from the Tools panel, select the word Flash (on the Stage), and use the font drop-down list in the Properties panel to change the

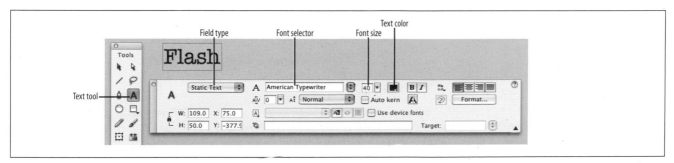

Figure 3-12. The Text tool, used to create a static text field for the word Flash.

font to American Typewriter. If you don't have the American Typewriter font, choose Times or Times New Roman (or you can simply choose _serif). Use the Font Size slider to set the font size to 30 pixels.

6. Use the Text tool to create a new text field on the same layer as the word *Flash*, and enter the word **Out** into the text field on the Stage (be sure to capitalize it).

7. Click outside of the text field and click again (on the Stage) to create another new text field and enter the word **of** into the text field.

8. Repeat Step 7 to create another text field containing the word **the**.

9. Repeat Step 7 again to create another text field containing the word **Box**, being sure to capitalize it.

10. Shift-select all five text fields and change their color to black using the Text Color swatch in the Properties panel.

11. With all five text fields still selected, use the Font Size slider in the Properties panel to set the point size for all five words to 30 pixels.

If you've followed along, the text should look something like Figure 3-13.

We now have the text we need for our animation, but we can't animate it separately if it is all on one layer. To separate the text onto five layers:

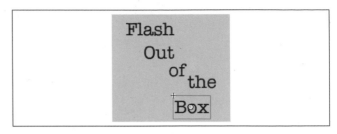

Figure 3-13. All five words on the Stage (30-point American Typewriter font).

1. Select the word *Flash* and press F8 to open the Convert to Symbol dialog box. Be sure the symbol's Behavior type is set to Graphic. Name the new symbol *Flash* and click OK.

2. Repeat Step 1 for the remaining four words, naming each symbol according to the word used on the Stage (*Out*, *of*, *the*, and *Box*). We now have five symbol instances on one layer, but each instance needs to be on its own layer before we can apply motion tweens.

3. Select the five new symbol instances and choose Modify → Timeline → Distribute to Layers to put each instance on its own layer. Automatically, each new layer uses the name of the instance that appears on the layer.

4. Delete the empty layer in the *text* layer folder (by selecting the layer and clicking the trash can icon).

5. Arrange the five text layers so that *Flash* is on top and *Box* is on the bottom, to match Figure 3-14.

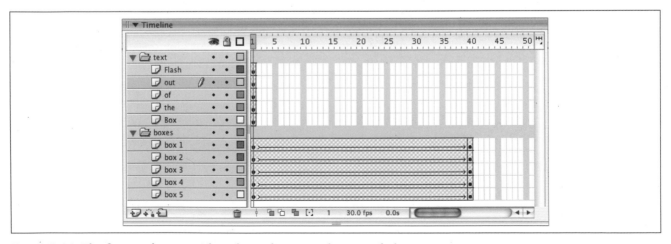

Figure 3-14. The five text layers, with each word converted to a symbol.

> Text, unlike other elements in a Flash movie, does not need to be converted to a symbol before applying a motion tween to it, because Flash converts it to a symbol automatically for you. But it is always a good practice to convert objects on the Stage to symbols before applying a motion tween. If we needed to reuse the text later on in the movie, we could create a new instance of it.

We're now ready to animate the text.

Sliding text

To complete the animation, instead of having the text resize and change colors, as we did with the boxes, we need to make each word slide onto the Stage from a different direction. There are five boxes and five words in the movie (very smart of us). To create a simple design from these elements, we can have the text on the ends slide in from the left and right edges, and we can have the text in the middle slide in from the top or bottom.

Soon, we'll tween the text animation as we did for the boxes. First, however, we need to make sure the text doesn't appear until after the box animation is finished.

To make sure the text doesn't appear until the boxes are in position:

1. Select the keyframes on frame 1 of all five layers in the *text* layer folder by clicking on the *Flash* layer's keyframe and dragging downward.

2. Click again and drag the keyframes to frame 35, and release the mouse button.

3. Now, the text does not appear until the playhead reaches frame 35. The box animation actually completes in frame 30, but we start our text animation a few frames later for effect (okay, so it isn't exactly a dramatic pause, but if you threw in a sound effect, it could be).

To animate the text:

1. At frame 55, select every layer in the *boxes* layer folder and press F5 to add frames. This ensures the

boxes continue to appear on the Stage until the end of the animation.

2. At frame 30, select every layer in the *boxes* layer folder and choose None from the Tween drop-down list. We don't need motion tweens for the boxes beyond frame 20 because they don't move or change color after that frame.

3. Select frame 35 for each text layer in turn, and position the five text symbol instances to match Figure 3-15. These positions are where the text lands at the end of the animation, but it is easier to work backward in this case. All we have to do is set the beginning and ending positions and let Flash tween between them.

Figure 3-15. The position of each word at the end of the animation.

4. Select frame 55 on all five layers and press F6 to convert the frames to keyframes.

5. Click on frame 35 in the timeline to move the playhead back to that frame. Move each text symbol instance to match Figure 3-16. This is where the text appears at the beginning of the animation.

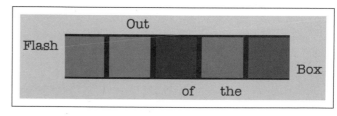

Figure 3-16. The position of each word at the beginning of the animation.

6. Select frame 35 on all five layers in the *text* layer folder and choose Motion from the Tween drop-down list in the Properties panel to apply a motion tween to each frame span.

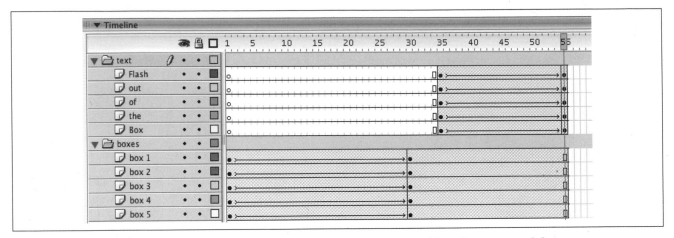

Figure 3-17. Make sure every layer extends to the end of the animation by adding frames to each layer.

7. Your timeline should now match Figure 3-17.

8. Press Enter (or Return) to play the animation in its entirety. The boxes grow and change colors, then the text slides in from different directions.

Staggering animation

We're almost done, so hang in there for just another minute or two. Remember that in the completed animation, the five words don't slide in at the same time. The word *Flash* appears first, then *Out*, and so on. To stagger the words in time (i.e., start them in succession), we need to move the frame spans for each symbol instance in the *text* layer folder:

1. On the *Out* layer, click and drag to select everything from the first keyframe in the animation to the last keyframe. Be sure to include the last keyframe in the selection. Release the mouse button after making the selection.

2. Click and drag the selected frame span 10 frames to the right so that it starts at frame 45, and release the mouse button again. The word *Out* now appears 10 frames later than the word *Flash*.

3. Repeat Step 2 for the layers containing the words *of*, *the*, and *Box*, starting the frame spans at frames 55, 65, and 75, respectively, to match Figure 3-18.

4. Again, add frames to the layers in the *boxes* layer folder so they extend to frame 95, the last frame of the text animation. Also, add frames to the *Flash*, *Out*, *of*, and *the* layers to extend each of those to 95. Now every layer extends to frame 95.

SYNCHRONIZATION

Synchronization is to animation what alignment is to static design. That is, just as you should align your graphic elements in space, you should synchronize your animation elements in time. If two elements are supposed to be synchronized, make sure they are synchronized exactly. This admonition applies whether synchronizing graphics to one another or synchronizing one or more graphics with sound or video. The canonical example of this is lip sync, in which even a small deviation in timing is very noticeable.

That is not to say you should overwhelm your viewer by doing everything at once. The companion to synchronization is timing, which is used to make sure everything isn't happening at once. For each element, decide whether it should be synchronized or spaced out in time. Avoid the ambiguous middle where your viewer won't be able to tell if you intended two events to be synchronous or discrete.

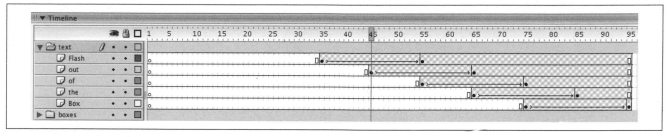

Figure 3-18. Staggered text animations, with frames added to extend each layer to the end of the animation.

5. Play the animation by pressing Enter or Return.

6. Save your work.

In the revised animation, each word moves onto the Stage at a different time. The staggered animation guides the eye from the first word to the last.

PUBLISHING YOUR MOVIE

The animation is done, but your work cannot be shown outside the Flash authoring environment without *publishing* the movie, so let's get it ready.

Publishing a Flash movie is the act of exporting the completed version of a *.fla* file (pronounced "flah," as in "rhymes with Rock the Cas*bah*") as another file type. The *.fla* format is used only for editing within the Flash authoring environment; it is too bloated with excess information (and too unprotected) to be appropriate for distribution. Another file type must be created to make the movie compatible with the various client software used to run Flash content, such as the Flash Player and Quick-Time Player. Upon publishing Flash content for the Web (for use with the Flash Player browser plugin), the *.fla* file is compiled into a self-contained *.swf* file (pronounced "swiff") for use online. You can also publish QuickTime movies (*.mov* files), static *.gif* or *.jpg* images, or Projectors (*.exe* files or Macintosh applications). Many of these published file types are discussed throughout this book.

Flash can also automatically create an HTML page in which to display your Flash *.swf* file. That is, users don't ordinarily browse directly to the URL for a *.swf* file. Instead, developers ordinarily publish an HTML file in which the *.swf* file is embedded (using the HTML `<object>` and `<embed>` tags). That allows you to publish a *.swf* as an element on an HTML page along with other content. That said, sometimes you'll want the *.swf* file to be the only thing on the page and to fill the browser window.

Publishing for the Web

The first step to getting our movie online is publishing it as a *.swf* file. Here we use the word *publishing* in the sense that Macromedia uses it—meaning "to generate a file" not "to release it on the Web."

Let's publish the movie and see how it performs:

1. With the Stage selected, choose the Settings button in the Properties panel. The Publish Settings dialog box opens to the Flash tab, as shown in Figure 3-19.

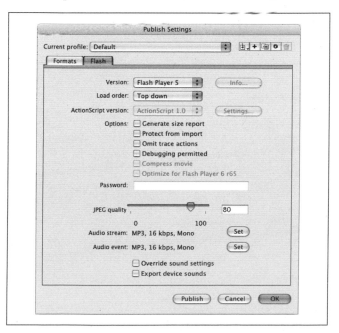

Figure 3-19. The Publish Settings dialog box.

2. Our current movie will play in older versions of the Flash Player, but realistically, most users have at least Flash Player 5 on their machines (see *http://www.macromedia.com/software/player_census/flashplayer/version_penetration.html*) so there's no compelling reason to publish our movie for a version older than that (the limiting factor in determining which version of the Flash Player can be used is ActionScript, Flash's programming language). Therefore, under the Flash tab, choose Flash Player 5 from the Version drop-down list.

> **NOTE**
>
> Be sure to set the Version back to Flash Player 7 when creating Flash movies that use features not supported in earlier versions.

3. Click the Formats tab and uncheck the HTML option. Flash can write the HTML page needed to display the movie online, but we don't need it right now.

4. Once you've specified the desired publish settings, click Publish to publish the movie. This generates a *.swf* file from the *.fla* file but doesn't literally publish the file on the Web. The *.swf* file is automatically placed in the same folder as the *.fla* file.

5. Click OK to close the dialog box. The next time you publish the movie, which you must do whenever you modify the *.fla* file, Flash will generate a *.swf* file compatible with Flash Player 5 or later.

6. Save the *.fla* file.

Running the movie in Test Movie mode creates a *.swf* as well, but the Publish Settings dialog box offers more control over the published file. A document created with Flash MX 2004, by default, will publish for Flash Player 7, which is not always necessary for your Flash content. We'll discuss the limitations of various Flash Player versions as we delve into ActionScript later on.

Now, let's view the published movie:

1. Open the *03* folder and locate the *animation.swf* file that we created in the preceding procedure. Double-click *animation.swf* to open it in the Standalone

version of the Flash Player. (The Standalone Player is installed with Flash automatically.)

2. When you're done viewing the animation, choose File → Quit to quit the Standalone Player.

Our movie plays in an endless loop. A looping animation can be a major distraction for users trying to view other content on a web page, so we want the animation to play only once. If you want the user to be able to replay the animation, a button could be added at the end that would restart the animation. We'll discuss buttons in the next chapter.

Stop looping already!

To prevent the movie from looping, we need to add an ActionScript *command* (or *action*). We'll use more ActionScript later, but for now, let's add a simple *stop( )* command and publish the movie again:

1. In the timeline for *animation.fla*, add a new layer and drag it above the *text* and *boxes* layer folders.

2. Rename the new layer *actions*. It is a good practice to keep the *actions* layer above all others in the timeline.

> **NOTE**
>
> Placing your ActionScript on the top layer and naming the layer *actions* is a convention often used by Flash developers to make it easier to find the ActionScript in a movie (some developers name the layer *scripts* or *as* instead of *actions*). To follow best practices, don't put any graphics or content other than scripts on this layer.

3. To prevent graphics from being added accidentally to the *actions* layer, lock the layer by clicking the second dot to the right of the layer name so that it turns into a padlock icon, as shown in Figure 3-20.

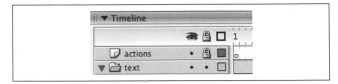

Figure 3-20. Locking the actions layer.

4. On frame 95, the last frame in the animation, add a keyframe to the *actions* layer using Insert → Keyframe. (Locking the layer prevents us from adding graphics to the Stage for that layer, but we can still add keyframes and ActionScript to the layer.)

5. With frame 95 still selected, open the Actions panel by choosing Window → Development Panels → Actions, or by pressing F9.

6. Type **stop();** into the Script pane of the Actions panel, as shown in Figure 3-21. The *stop( )* command tells the playhead to stop when it reaches the frame containing the script (in this case, frame 95).

7. Save your work and choose File → Publish to republish the movie. To see the effect of changes to a *.fla* document, you must either run a test movie or republish the movie to regenerate the *.swf* file.

8. If you haven't created the *.fla* yourself or are having trouble doing so, double-click *animation_complete. swf* from the *03* folder on the CD-ROM and watch the animation. The movie now plays only once and stops on frame 95.

Later, we'll publish HTML from Flash to create a web page for displaying our movie, but for now, let's see how Flash animations can be repurposed for broadcast use.

Publishing for QuickTime

If you're one of the many people creating homemade DVDs or doing other video work with programs such as Macromedia Director or Adobe Premiere, you may want to use Flash to create titles or other animation. Our completed animation can be modified to work with video by increasing the frame rate and exporting it as a QuickTime movie (*.mov* file). This is a good example of how Flash content can be repurposed for other types of media.

In most cases, you don't want to develop two alternative versions in parallel, so wait until you are happy with the final version before splitting off this new version. Inevitably, you may tweak things in the separate version. For example, you might decide you want the animation larger for video, or you might want to use different colors.

To prepare the movie for broadcast-quality video:

1. Open the *animation.fla* file from the previous exercise.

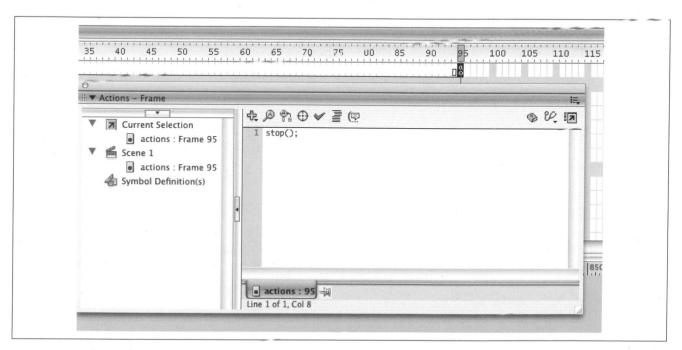

Figure 3-21. The Actions panel with a stop( ) command added to the Script pane.

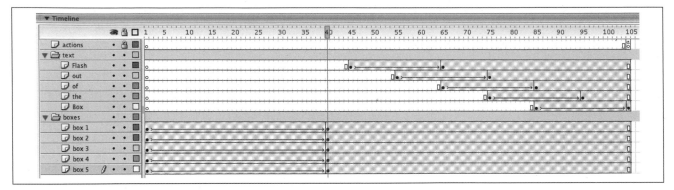

Figure 3-22. *The modified timeline.*

2. Choose File → Save As, and save the animation as *video.fla* in the *03* folder. We'll keep the *animation.fla* version for the Web and modify *video.fla* to serve as the basis for our video.

3. Close the Actions panel by pressing F9, or collapse it using the expand/collapse arrow in the top-left corner of the panel's titlebar.

4. With the Stage selected, use the Properties panel to change the frame rate to 30 fps. Video plays at approximately 30 fps—the exact rate for broadcast TV in the United States is 29.97 fps—making motion in video more fluid than our 18 fps allows.

5. Somewhere between frame 1 and frame 30, where the box animations occur, select one frame on every layer in the timeline. If clicking and dragging through layers in the timeline is awkward for you, try selecting a frame on each layer by Shift-clicking.

6. Add 10 frames to the animation by pressing the F5 key 10 times, so the keyframes on frame 30 move to frame 40. Using a higher frame rate for the movie means it takes more frames to fill one second of animation (i.e., for a given number of frames, the elapsed time is shorter), so we added frames to increase the effective duration. When you're done, your timeline should match Figure 3-22.

7. Save the *.fla* file.

With the adjustments made, we're ready to create a QuickTime movie from our Flash source, so let's do it:

1. Choose File → Export → Export Movie to open the Export Movie dialog box.

2. In the Save As field, specify **video.mov** as the filename, choose QuickTime Video from the Format dropdown list, and navigate to the *03* folder to save the file there.

3. Click Save. The Export QuickTime Video dialog box, shown in Figure 3-23, opens.

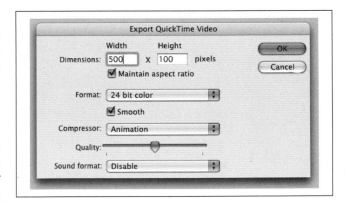

Figure 3-23. *The Export QuickTime Video dialog box on the Macintosh.*

4. Enter **500** in the Width field to match the Stage dimensions. The Height field adjusts accordingly. (If the Match Movie checkbox is checked, Flash may set the dimensions for you automatically. If necessary, you can disable the Match Movie checkbox in the dialog box and set the Height and Width manually.)

5. On the Macintosh, under Compressor, choose Animation, and set the Quality slider to 50%. The Animation *codec* (a video *c*ompression/*dec*ompression scheme) is appropriate for most video exported from Flash, assuming the only contents are graphics drawn in Flash. Our animation has no audio, so choose Disable from the Sound Format drop-down list.

6. On Windows, the export options differ from those on the Macintosh, as shown in Figure 3-24. Although you can't specify a codec on Windows, you can specify how alpha channels (transparencies) and layers are rendered. For our purposes, leave these options set to Auto. Uncheck the Streaming Sound option because there is no audio. Check the Flatten option to ensure that all necessary data is embedded within the *.mov* file. Configure the Controller and Playback options as shown in Figure 3-24.

7. Click OK to export the QuickTime video.

8. Locate *video.mov* in the *03* folder and double-click to open it in QuickTime Player. The animation plays automatically and stops at the last frame.

Pat yourself on the back; you've just created your first QuickTime movie from a Flash animation!

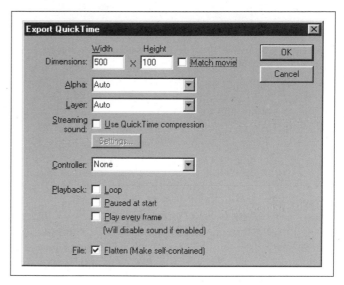

Figure 3-24. The Export QuickTime Video dialog box on Windows.

The QuickTime Player can play some *.swf* files directly. But what we've done here is export the Flash movie in a pure video format. All the ActionScript is disabled, but QuickTime movies stop automatically after playing, so our *stop( )* command is no longer necessary. If we placed a *stop( )* command on, say, frame 15, it would be ignored when we exported to QuickTime (*.mov*) format. The video would play to the end.

You can import *.mov* files into video editing applications and incorporate them into home movies and DVDs, but that is beyond the scope of this book.

GET OUT OF THE BOX

Mission accomplished! We have one animation in .*swf* format ready to be posted on the Web, and another version in .*mov* format ready to be distributed for video.

Always consider the medium via which your animations are delivered. If you're creating a spot for a broadcast commercial, you'll need to use 29.97 fps as the frame rate to conform to U.S. television (NTSC) standards. For countries that use the PAL standard, use 25 fps when exporting your video. For the Web, you should keep it down to 12 or 18 fps, so the user's computer is not overburdened by rendering work.

A computer has to draw each frame of an animation as it occurs, which can be very processor-intensive for long or complex animations, so a simplified animation not only ensures your animation is accessible to a broader audience but also serves as a challenge/opportunity to communicate your message more succinctly. The Web has more than enough useless animations. Animate responsibly. Your clients and their audiences will appreciate it.

In this chapter, we've seen how to:

- Customize Stage properties

- Change the color of symbol instances and resize them

- Use motion tweens to animate properties such as color, size, and position

- Insert and animate text

- Control the speed of an animation

- Publish for the Web and QuickTime

Frames and frame rates continue the filmmaking metaphor in Flash, but the term *keyframe* comes from traditional cel animation, not from filmmaking. Lead animators working on cartoons or movies draw two points of an animation, the beginning and end, and junior animators draw the frames between the two points, known as *tweens* for "in between." Fortunately, Flash draws the tween frames for us. Imagine how long it must take to draw each frame manually!

Flash can tween almost any property, such as color, in addition to the expected attributes such as position and size. Flash also automates shape tweens, which are used to morph one shape into another. We'll discuss shape tweens in Chapter 5 to see how they can benefit our projects.

We've already learned the basics of controlling the speed of an animation (by adjusting the frame rate or the number of frames over which an animation occurs). The pacing of an animation is key to its success, so keep it in mind as you begin new projects. A slow-paced ad for a high-speed Internet connection service, for example, would not convey the desired message to the user. Subconsciously, the user would associate a slow ad with a slow Internet connection. Therefore, you'd want to use a slow-paced animation when discussing the competing products (such as dial-up connections) and a fast-paced animation to dramatize the speed of the high-speed Internet connection.

When setting the pace of an animation, consider the commercials you see on television and how they relate to their intended audiences. MTV needs to appeal to a younger audience, so their ads are often spastic and jumpy, while an upscale department store may use midtempo or slower-paced ads to appeal to an older audience of working professionals or soccer moms. An image that appears for less than 1.5 seconds doesn't give the viewer enough time to recognize it fully, so pay attention to the duration that something is on screen as well as the speed of any motion graphics.

Try modifying other properties of the animation we created earlier in this chapter. Can you make the boxes grow from their upper-left corners instead of from the center out? Can you animate the text from a different direction? Maybe you want to use six boxes instead of five, leaving one box empty for drama. Maybe you want to use our title movie as the basis for a new animation to, say, promote your latest MP3 single.

Try changing the pace of the animation by changing the frame rate or adding or removing frames to lengthen or shorten sections of the animation. Use the Easing slider—next to the Tween drop-down list in the Properties panel when an object is selected on the Stage—to change the speed of an animation over time. A high easing value, such as 100, tells the object to start moving quickly and slow to a stop, while a low easing value, such as −100, does the opposite. Easing is a subtle way to make animations smoother and achieve a more realistic effect, such as when creating a bouncing ball animation. Easing can be used to slow the ball down as it bounces upward and speed it up as it drops to the ground.

Naturally, you can gain precise control over animation using ActionScript, but that is a more advanced topic and we don't want to get ahead of ourselves. For beginners creating simple animations, using the timeline and tweens is usually the easiest way to animate. As you become more skilled or want to create an animation that isn't fixed (such as a random animation or one under the user's control), you can explore ActionScript in more depth. Certainly, before spending hours or days on painstaking animation, ask a knowledgeable Flash developer whether it could be accomplished more easily in ActionScript. Independent animations that are always the same or animations that follow an irregular motion path are the best candidates for timeline animation. Animations that are good candidates to be performed under ActionScript control include:

- Animations that vary so they can't be predicted ahead of time, such as character movement in a game. This includes animations that have to react to user actions, runtime random events, or data received at runtime.

- Animations along paths that are easily calculable with mathematics, such as planetary motion or any physics simulation.

- Animations that must be combined with other animations or synchronized with sound rather than operating independently.

- Animations that must vary in response to runtime conditions, such as the speed or screen size of the device on which they are running.

Learning to avoid dead ends and knowing enough not to beat your head against the wall are some of the most important skills to learn as a beginner. If you're trying to create an animation by hand and it seems impossible to do, then you probably should learn ActionScript or consult a skilled scripter for help.

Returning to our discussion of timeline animation in the next chapter, you'll see how to use animations as self-contained symbols. This enables you to adjust the properties of an entire animation at once, increasing the range of effects you can achieve using Flash. In later chapters, we'll learn how to add sound to an animation and the basics of how to control animations programmatically with ActionScript.

4

INTERACTIVITY AND MOVIE CLIPS

Where do animators find
the patience to create entire
cartoons by hand using
Flash? Well, they don't.
To simplify the process,
animators use another type
of symbol in Flash called
a *movie clip*. This chapter
shows you how to use movie
clips to great advantage,
and how to control them
via ActionScript.

In Chapter 3, we created a simple animation entirely on the main timeline. But what happens when we need to create more complex animations, such as for a cartoon character? A cartoon character usually has several moving parts, such as its mouth, eyes, arms, and legs. If we had to animate the legs every time the character walks and animate the mouth every time the character speaks, it would be very time-consuming. Furthermore, to add variety would require us to create multiple permutations, such as walking while talking versus walking while not talking. In this chapter, we'll look at how *movie clips* allow us to create animations that play independently of one another. While creating Box Guy, the unofficial mascot for *Flash Out of the Box*, we'll use separate movie clips for his eyes and legs.

Before we begin animating, we need to construct our cartoon character. To do this, we'll use the Pencil tool, layers, and symbols. Once all the parts are built, we'll bring the character to life through animation.

DRAWING A CARTOON CHARACTER

The first thing we need for our cartoon character is a body. Since this character will serve as a mascot for this book, we'll make his body from a box and then add a face and legs. By doing this, we'll see how the configuration options for the Pencil tool affect the outcome of each drawn line. In more complex situations, you might sketch some character prototypes on paper and create a storyboard for the animation. But here we focus on how to use Flash rather than exploring techniques common in traditional cel animation.

Start with the body

Let's start by creating the body for the character. Later on, we'll create a background image of a street and change the Stage color to sky blue. The character will walk down the street and stop.

First, we have to create a document and configure our Pencil tool:

1. Open a new, blank Flash document and save it as *box_guy.fla* in the *04* folder.

2. Change the Stage dimensions to 550 × 200.

3. Choose Edit → Preferences (on Windows) or Flash → Preferences (on the Mac) to open the Preferences dialog box. Choose the Editing tab of the Preferences dialog box.

4. In the Drawing Settings section of the Editing tab, set the following options to Normal: Connect Lines, Smooth Curves, Recognize Lines, Recognize Shapes, and Click Accuracy. A bug in Flash MX 2004, including the 7.0.1 updater, leaves some of the drawing settings blank by default, which prevents the drawing tools from working properly. This is fixed in the 7.2 update (included on this book's CD-ROM). These options determine how the Pencil tool behaves as you draw. Click OK to close the Preferences dialog box.

5. Activate the Pencil tool. By default, the Pencil tool mode—in the Options section of the Tools panel as shown in Figure 4-1—is set to Straighten. (If it's not already set to Straighten, set it now by clicking on the current option setting.)

6. In the Properties panel, set the Pencil tool's stroke color to dark gray, set the stroke weight to 1, and choose Solid for the stroke style.

Now that we've got the Pencil tool configured, let's see what happens when we try to draw a box:

1. On the Stage, use the Pencil tool to draw a square. To do this, click and drag to draw the first line, release the mouse button (or lift your stylus), then draw the second line, and so on. Notice that each line straightens automatically after you draw it. Unless you're better at drawing connecting lines than I am, your square probably looks a little messy, so let's try something else.

2. Undo several times (or use the history slider in the History panel) to get rid of the lines you just drew.

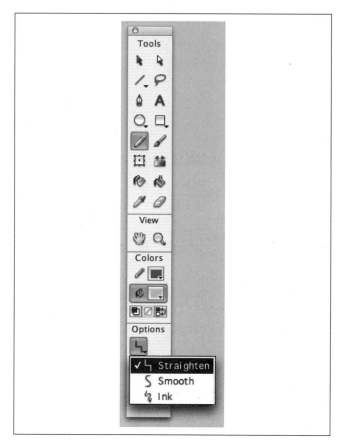

Figure 4-1. *The Pencil tool options.*

tablet. A stylus is often easier to draw with than a mouse is. You're already using a drawing tablet? Well, then, practice freehand drawing with a pencil and paper until you get better at it.

Of course, you can draw a square using the Rectangle tool, but Flash's shape recognition feature allows you to draw rectangles with the Pencil tool, too. Therefore, the Pencil tool allows you to draw shapes or sketch freehand without switching tools.

Like most men, Box Guy could use some depth if he's going to appeal to the other Box People out there. Let's fill the square with color and turn it into a cube:

1. Use the Paint Bucket tool to fill the square with the color of your choice. The stroke color is dark gray, so I chose light gray for the fill color to help define the box edges.

2. Activate the Selection tool by pressing V (not Ctrl-V or Cmd-V, just V), select the fill and stroke for the square, then resize the square to 80 × 80 using the Properties panel.

3. Alt-drag (Windows) or Option-drag (Mac) the square to duplicate it. Position the copy a little bit above and to the right, overlapping the first square, as shown in the first panel of Figure 4-2.

4. Use the Pencil tool to draw a connecting line from the upper-left corner of the first square to the upper-left corner of the second square. (To zoom in, activate the Zoom tool—the magnifying glass icon in the toolbar—and click on the Stage until the drawing is easier to see.) Notice that, even with the Straighten option enabled for the Pencil tool, it can be difficult to draw the connecting line.

   Undo. There is an easier way to draw a line.

5. Select the Line tool from the toolbar.

6. Use the Line tool to draw a connecting line from the upper-left corner of the first square to the upper-left corner of the second square.

7. Finally, draw a connecting line from the lower-right corner of one square to the lower-right corner of the other. The result is shown in the second panel of Figure 4-2.

3. Draw a square again, but this time, draw it in one continuous motion, without releasing the mouse button until the square is complete.

When you release the mouse button, your rough drawing should automatically turn into a square with four straight, connected lines. Flash automatically tries to detect what shape you have drawn, because the Recognize Shapes preference is set to Normal. Flash recognizes that you're trying to draw a square and helps you out by straightening the lines and converting the corners into right angles. (Flash also recognizes attempts to draw other shapes, such as circles, rectangles, and triangles.) If your square did not straighten, it means Flash could not recognize your drawing as an attempt at a square, so you need to undo and draw it again. It helps if your last line overlaps the first side you drew; otherwise, Flash may not close the gap or recognize the shape as a square. If you are still having trouble drawing a square, consider another career...um...I mean consider getting a drawing

Figure 4-2. Build a box from scratch.

The squares now look like a hollow cube, as seen in the second panel of Figure 4-2, but two of the corners have no fill, and two lines need to be removed to make it look like a three-dimensional box:

1. Select the top horizontal line of the first box and delete it, as shown in the third panel of Figure 4-2. Be sure not to select the entire stroke.

2. Select the vertical line on the right side of the first box and delete it as well, as shown in the fourth panel of Figure 4-2. The result is shown in the fifth panel of Figure 4-2.

3. Add the fill color to the white areas that remain using the Paint Bucket tool to create the cube shown in the final panel of Figure 4-2. Remember, if the fill doesn't

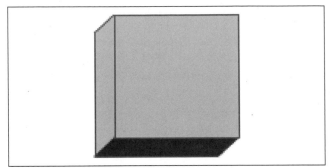

Figure 4-3. Delete the extra lines to give the cube a box-like appearance.

get applied, choose Close Medium Gaps or Close Large Gaps from the Paint Bucket tool options, and try to apply the fill again.

4. Select the fill area that represents the bottom of the box and change its color to dark gray. The box now looks as if its bottom panel is missing, as shown in Figure 4-3.

Now we have a body for our cartoon mascot. Soon, we'll add a face and legs, but the legs should appear to emerge from the bottom of the box. We can place items closer to

WHAT'S IN A NAME?

You learned earlier how to create instances on stage from symbols in the Library. Symbol names, which are assigned in the Symbol Properties dialog box, are used primarily to identify items in the Library.

Instance names, which are assigned via the Properties panel, are used to identify items on stage so they can be controlled via ActionScript.

Any ActionScript that accesses movie clips, buttons, or text fields won't work unless you first assign the item an instance name. To assign the instance name for a movie clip, button, or text field during authoring, select it on stage and enter the instance name on the left side of the Properties panel, where you see the placeholder text "<Instance Name>".

Instance names can also be assigned to instances created from a library symbol at runtime (for example, you might dynamically create 20 balloon instances, through Action-Script, from a single *balloon* library symbol). In this case, the new instance's name can be specified at the time it is created. Symbols cannot be created at runtime (they must be created in the authoring tool), but instances of symbols can.

Often, developers use the same name for both a symbol and an instance of that symbol, but you don't have to. You

the foreground or background (called *z-positioning* or the *stacking order*) using layers. So let's separate the front and back of the box, convert them to symbols, and put them on separate layers:

1. Double-click the fill area of the box in front to select its fill and stroke.

2. Convert it to a graphic symbol by choosing Modify → Convert to Symbol (F8) and setting the Behavior type to Graphic. (Hereafter, we'll simply refer to these as *graphic symbols*.) Name the symbol *front of box*.

3. Shift-select the remaining fills and strokes of the cube and convert them to a graphic symbol called *back of box*.

4. Choose Edit → Cut (or press Ctrl/Cmd-X) to cut the *back of box* instance from the Stage.

5. Add a new layer to the timeline and drag it underneath *Layer 1*.

6. Choose Edit → Paste in Place (Ctrl/Cmd-Shift-V) to paste the *back of box* instance on the new layer in the exact location from which it was cut.

7. Rename the top layer *front of box* and the bottom layer *back of box*.

8. Save your work.

Soon, we'll draw legs on a layer between the *front of box* and *back of box* layers, so that the legs appear to emerge from the bottom of the box. First, however, let's give the character a face.

Putting a face on the box

In this section, we'll create a face using separate movie clips on separate layers for each eye and the mouth.

To add the face to the character:

1. Add a new layer to the timeline, above the others, and name it *face*. Doing this first ensures that when you create the eyes and the mouth, they'll be on the *face* layer.

2. Let's create an oval for each eye. Somewhere on the Stage, use the Oval tool from the Tools panel (a.k.a. the toolbar) to draw a vertical oval about 20 pixels

---

can use any name you like for symbols, and some developers prefer to use verbose names with spaces. However, when assigning instance names, spaces aren't allowed between characters. Within instance names, it's common to use underscores (_) between words. Another popular alternative is so-called *camelCase*, in which the first word is lowercase and subsequent words are given an initial capital letter.

Regardless, the symbol name and instance name are independent (symbol names refer to assets in the Library and instance names refer to items in the timeline). If an instance

is not referred to by ActionScript, you might not bother naming it.

Be sure you understand the difference between the symbol names and instance names, although Flash documentation (including this book) often glosses over the difference in the interest of readability. For example, for brevity, if I refer to the *back of box* instance, you should understand that it is technically an unnamed, onstage instance of the symbol named *back of box* in the Library. Throughout the book, library symbol names are shown in italics and instance names are shown in constant-width text.

tall. Make sure the fill and stroke colors are both dark gray.

3. Convert the oval to a symbol and name it *eye_mc*. Instead of creating a graphic symbol, however, choose Movie Clip for the Behavior type in the Convert to Symbol dialog box. In just a minute, we'll enhance the *eye_mc* movie clip symbol to make the eyes blink independently of the animation on the main timeline.

4. Activate the Pencil tool, and choose Smooth in the toolbar's Options section. Instead of straightening the lines we draw, Flash will smooth them.

5. Draw a smile and add a laugh line to each end of the smile line, as shown in Figure 4-4.

Figure 4-4. The face of the box character.

6. Alt-drag (Windows) or Option-drag (Mac) the *eye_mc* instance to create a second instance. Arrange the smile and two eyes to make a face.

7. Select the two eyes and mouth, and position them over the *front of box* instance to give the character its face.

8. Select the two eyes and mouth, and convert them to a movie clip symbol and name it *face_mc*. We want to group them together into one symbol so they can be positioned as one entity. Frankly, we could use Modify → Group instead of creating a symbol if our only goal was to group them together. However, creating a symbol gives you the ability to control the *face_mc* clip and any clips within it in a hierarchy via ActionScript, as described in the section "Controlling Movie Clips" toward the end of this chapter. For example, you could make the eyes blink or wink randomly, or you could change the mouth position. See the "Movie Clips" sidebar for more information.

In order for the eyes to blink, *face_mc*'s symbol Behavior type must be set to Movie Clip, not Graphic. Adding the *_mc* suffix to the end of movie clip symbol names makes them easier to identify in the Library; however, the symbol's type is determined by the setting in the Symbol Property dialog box, and not by the name's suffix.

Our character is starting to get a personality, but there's still plenty to be done.

Using movie clips to create independent animations

To bring our cartoon character to life, we need to give him some human characteristics, such as blinking eyes.

MOVIE CLIPS

Movie clip symbols are the worker bees of the Flash world. You'll use them in almost every Flash project. A *movie clip instance* (or simply *clip* for short) is typically derived from a movie clip symbol in the Library. The symbol can be created from something already on the Stage, using the Modify → Convert to Symbol (F8) command, or created from scratch, using Insert → New Symbol (Ctrl/Cmd-F8). A movie clip symbol has its own layers and timeline, just like the main movie. A movie clip symbol can contain vectors, bitmaps,

sounds, or even more symbols, including Button, Graphic, and other Movie Clip symbols. The term *movie clip* is used informally to mean either a movie clip symbol in the Library or an instance of that symbol on stage. Most Flash documentation doesn't make the distinction explicit in all cases, but the difference should be clear from context.

Placing multiple elements within a movie clip is not the same as *grouping* (which can be achieved by selecting multiple

As I alluded to earlier, movie clips come in handy here because they allow the eyes to move independently of the rest of the character. Thus, Box Guy can walk and blink at the same time, or he can just blink like a proverbial deer in the headlights.

A movie clip acts like a movie within a movie. Each movie clip symbol has its own timeline. Movie clip instances play independently of the main timeline. So, if we create a 25-frame animation on a movie clip symbol's timeline and place an instance of the symbol on the Stage, it will play even if the main timeline is stopped.

We need the character's eyes to blink regardless of what is going on in the rest of the animation, so let's use a movie clip to create a blinking eye animation:

1. Assuming you are still editing the *face_mc* symbol, double-click on one of the *eye_mc* instances to edit its symbol in place. Make sure you're editing the correct symbol by checking the Edit bar, which should say *Scene 1, face_mc, eye_mc*. (If the Edit bar says *Scene 1, face_mc*, the first double-click opened the *face_mc* symbol for editing; double-click again on an *eye_mc* instance to edit the *eye_mc* symbol.) Notice that the movie clip symbol has its own timeline and can contain one or more layers.

2. Select frame 32 of the *eye_mc* clip's timeline and press F5 to add a frame. (Here, we use the term *eye_mc* clip for brevity, but it is technically an onstage clip instance of the *eye_mc* movie clip symbol from the Library. Did you notice the difference and were you able to discern its meaning in context?)

3. Add a new keyframe at frame 30.

4. At frame 30, select and delete the fill within the oval. Then, select and delete most of the stroke, leaving only a curved line at the bottom, as shown in Figure 4-5. This makes the eye appear closed, which is part of the blink sequence.

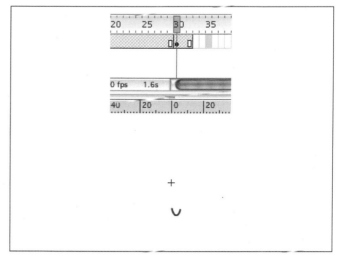

Figure 4-5. The closed eye for the blinking animation.

5. Press Enter or Return to watch the animation. When the playhead reaches frame 30, the eye closes for two frames, then stops.

6. Return to Scene 1 by clicking *Scene 1* in the Edit bar, and choose Control → Test Movie (Ctrl-Enter on Windows or Cmd-Return on Mac) to see the animation.

objects on the Stage and choosing Modify → Group). Grouped objects—such as multiple shapes or the fill and stroke for a single shape—do not have their own timeline, nor can they be targeted through ActionScript. This distinction will become clearer as you learn more about movie clips, but for now assume that for maximum efficiency, any asset you expect to reuse should be converted to a symbol.

Items nested within a movie clip behave similarly to items placed on the main timeline. The primary differences are in how they are accessed via ActionScript and how they are positioned in the movie's coordinate space. We'll see shortly how to access *nested clips* (i.e., clips arranged within other clips, creating a hierarchy) via ActionScript.

There is only one frame on the main timeline, but the eye-blinking animation takes place on the *eye_mc* clip's timeline. The *eye_mc* clips—remember there are two instances of the *eye_mc* clip symbol on *Layer 1* of the *face_mc* symbol's timeline—play in their entirety and then loop. So, no matter what the rest of the character is doing in the animation, the eyes continue to blink. This separation of character parts makes movie clips very useful for animators. Once the parts of a character are created, they can be reused whenever necessary. And they can be manipulated independently, so the eyes or mouth can animate independently of the legs. This allows you to combine them in different ways for much more variation without a lot of extra work. For example, if you're animating a dog, you might use one movie clip to create a wagging tail and a second clip for the dog's legs. You might then turn the whole dog into a movie clip that can be controlled independently of the dog's owner (another clip) on the Stage.

Next, let's draw legs and animate them so we can make the character walk across the Stage.

Drawing the legs

So far, Box Guy is a bit of a bore. All he does is stand there and blink. We want him to walk across the Stage, so let's give him some legs, as shown in Figure 4-6. We'll create a *walk cycle*—a series of character positions that, when played in sequence, makes the character appear to walk.

1. Insert a layer between the *front of box* and *back of box* layers and name the new layer *legs*.

Figure 4-6. The legs appear to emerge from the bottom of the cube.

2. Activate the Pencil tool and configure it with the Smooth option.

3. Somewhere on the Stage, on the *legs* layer, draw a leg with a foot similar to the one in Figure 4-7 and convert it to a symbol. If you prefer, you can open *box_guy_complete.fla*, located in the *04* folder, and copy and paste the drawing inside the *leg* symbol. (To enter Edit mode for the symbol, double-click on the symbol icon in the Library.)

4. Alt-drag (Windows) or Option-drag (Mac) to duplicate the leg (we want him to walk, not hop, so he'll need two legs).

5. Shift-select both legs and convert them to a graphic symbol named *legs*. Then position the *legs* instance underneath the *front of box* instance so the legs appear to emerge from the bottom of the cube, as shown in Figure 4-6.

To see our mascot in action, let's make him move from one spot on the Stage to another and stop. We'll start by

WALK CYCLES

This section's exercise demonstrates a very simple walk cycle in which Box Guy's legs move in two successive positions. A more realistic walk cycle might include swinging a character's arms or adding a bounce to its steps. Certainly, other animation cycles could be developed to show the character moving at different speeds. A horse's gallop, for example, is not simply a faster version of its walk. Observe both the physical world and existing cartoons to find animation cycles to imitate. Also, consider these cycles from different angles, allowing the character to walk or run to the left, right, foreground, and background. Of course, as a character moves from the foreground to the background, its size should change relative to its distance from the viewer.

An important part of creating cartoons is making sure a character walks and moves in a way that is appropriate for it. For example, a giraffe covers much more ground in a single walk cycle than a squirrel, so if using the two side-by-side, you might animate the squirrel running as fast as it can while the giraffe walks slowly beside it. The important part is

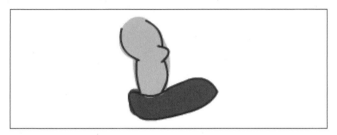

Figure 4-7. The leg for our mascot.

turning him into a movie clip symbol, which makes it easier to control him using the timeline or ActionScript:

1. Select all the parts of the character and convert them into a movie clip symbol named *box_guy_mc*. Three of the four layers in the timeline are now empty because the entire symbol is contained on one layer.

2. Delete the empty layers and rename the remaining layer *box_guy*.

3. Assign the instance of the *box_guy_mc* symbol the instance name box_guy_mc in the Properties panel. Soon, we'll use ActionScript to control this clip, so we must give it an instance name as described in the earlier "What's in a Name?" sidebar.

We want the character to walk in from offstage left and stop on the right side of the Stage. We do this by placing him at different positions in the starting and ending keyframes and then tweening the animation:

1. There is always a keyframe in frame 1, so we'll use that as the starting point for the animation. Select frame 1 and then drag the box_guy_mc clip offstage to the left.

2. Insert a keyframe at frame 60.

3. In frame 60, drag box_guy_mc to the right side of the Stage.

4. Select any frame in the *box_guy* layer, before the keyframe at frame 60, and choose Motion from the Tween drop-down list in the Properties panel, which causes Flash to tween the character from the starting position to the ending position.

5. Save your work and test the movie (Control → Test Movie).

Okay—so you saw that coming, right? The character blinks and slides from the left side of the Stage to the right, but his legs don't move and the animation loops back to the beginning. Let's fix both problems:

1. Close the Test Movie mode's Preview window and double-click on the box_guy_mc clip to edit the *box_guy_mc* symbol in place.

2. Select the instance of the *legs* symbol, which is nested inside the *box_guy_mc* symbol.

3. We converted the legs to a graphic symbol earlier, but now we want to animate them, so we need to change the *legs* symbol's type to Movie Clip. In the Properties panel, choose Movie Clip from the Symbol Behavior drop-down list. This allows the symbol instance to behave as a movie clip. Assign legs_mc as the instance name for this instance of the *legs* symbol.

that you don't have the character covering too much (or too little) ground in each part of its walk cycle. If the walk cycle covers too little ground compared to how far you move the character across the Stage, the character appears to slide across the Stage instead of walk. Likewise, if the walk cycle covers too much ground, the character appears to slip in place, like an ice skater with no traction.

After a little experimentation, you'll see that creating good-looking walk cycles can be difficult and time-consuming.

There are lots of tricks to reduce the number of positions in a walk cycle, which reduces the time required of the animator and also reduces the movie's download size. For example, you can flip the character (by selecting the object and choosing Modify → Transform → Flip Horizontal) to create a walk cycle in the opposite direction. You can also make the character hop slightly so that it doesn't appear to slide across the floor inappropriately. For more animation tips, pick up a copy of *Flash Hacks* (O'Reilly).

4. In the Library (Ctrl/Cmd-L or F11), select the *legs* symbol and click the Information icon, shown in Figure 4-8, to open the Symbol Properties dialog box.

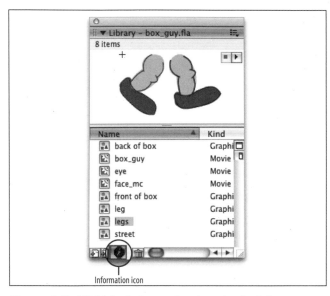

Figure 4-8. *Click the Information icon in the Library to open the Symbol Properties dialog box.*

5. In the dialog box, change the *legs* symbol's Behavior type from Graphic to Movie Clip, rename the symbol *legs_mc* (to help identify it as a movie clip in the Library and to keep names consistent for easy cross-referencing), and click OK to close the dialog box. The symbol is now a movie clip.

> **NOTE**
>
> Even though we changed the Behavior type of the instance on the Stage in Step 3, we must also change the original symbol's Behavior type for it to truly become a movie clip. A library symbol can have a different type (as set in the Symbol Properties dialog box) than an instance of the symbol on stage (as set in the Properties panel). Setting different Behavior types for library symbols and their onstage instances can become confusing, but it can also be very handy. For example, if you have a graphic instance on the Stage that you'd like to reposition via ActionScript, you can simply change the Behavior type of the instance to Movie Clip and assign it an instance name.

CODE HINTS

You may have noticed that when you type **_mc** followed by a dot (period) into the Script pane of the Actions panel, a drop-down list appears. The drop-down list is called a *code hint*. Flash recognizes the _mc suffix as indicating a movie clip instance and therefore offers a list of movie clip–related methods, commands, and properties when you add a period after the _mc suffix. Instead of typing stop( ); after legs_mc. in the script, you can scroll through the code hint drop-down list with the arrow keys to locate the *stop( )* command (or just enter **s** to jump there quickly) and press Enter or Return to add the command to the script automatically. This is a wonderful feature if you're new to using ActionScript, as it can be difficult to memorize proper syntax for every command.

Other suffixes will prompt code hints as well, and they will be mentioned as we use ActionScript throughout this book. In ActionScript 2.0, you can specify a variable's type without using a specific suffix. For example, you can declare a variable that refers to a movie clip instance as follows:

    var myClip:MovieClip;

The var keyword and the :MovieClip datatype tell ActionScript that myClip is a movie clip instance, thus providing code hints without requiring the _mc suffix.

To finish up, we must animate the legs on their own timeline to create the walking action:

1. Double-click on the legs_mc instance to edit the legs_mc symbol in place (remember, when a symbol is placed on the Stage, Flash creates a copy of the symbol, called an *instance,* but double-clicking the instance edits the original symbol from which it is derived). The Edit bar indicates you are now editing *Scene 1, box_guy, legs_mc.* In other words, you are editing the *legs_mc* movie clip symbol, an instance of which is located inside the *box_guy_mc* movie clip symbol, an instance of which is, in turn, located on the main timeline. That is, editing a movie clip in place edits the original symbol, not the onstage instance of the clip.

2. Shift-select both legs and choose Modify → Timeline → Distribute to Layers to place the legs on individual layers. Delete *Layer 1*, which is now empty, and rename the two remaining layers to *back_leg* and *front_leg,* with the back leg on the top layer (*back leg,* in this case, refers to the character's right leg, which starts in the trailing position).

3. Activate the Free Transform tool from the Tools panel and select the back leg. Eight handles appear around the bounding box of the leg, as shown in Figure 4-9. Move the cursor over the top handle and, when the cursor appears as a rotating arrow, click and drag to rotate the leg until it's in a starting position that looks natural for walking. The Free Transform tool can also be used to skew and resize an object on the Stage, which we'll talk more about later.

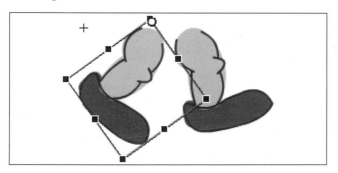

Figure 4-9. The Free Transform tool displays handles used to rotate, skew, or resize an object on the Stage.

4. With the back leg still selected with the Free Transform tool, move the center circle, or *anchor point,* to the top of the leg. When we rotate the leg again in a moment, it will rotate about its anchor point, like a construction-paper puppet with limbs held together by brass connectors at the joints.

5. Repeat Steps 3 and 4 for the front leg.

6. Insert keyframes on both layers at frame 5 and at frame 10. The legs need to rotate from frame 1 to frame 5, then return to their starting position at frame 10. Adding the ending keyframe ensures that the leg positions at frames 1 and 10 match, because a new keyframe always inherits what is on the previous keyframe. By leaving frames 1 and 10 as is, our animation loops seamlessly.

7. Select frame 5 on the *back_leg* layer and use the Free Transform tool to rotate the leg again. (You may need to first reposition the anchor point on the leg graphic because we've added keyframes since you first set the anchor point.) This time, rotate it so it appears to move from being the trailing foot to the lead foot.

8. Conversely, rotate the front leg on the *front_leg* layer so the foot goes from being the lead foot to the trailing foot (again, you may need to first reposition the anchor point). This alternation of the feet will provide the illusion of walking.

9. Create a motion tween on both layers, from frame 1 to frame 5, then from frame 5 to frame 10. To select multiple frame spans, select a frame in one of the frame spans, then press Ctrl (on Windows) or Cmd (on Mac) and select a frame in each of the other frame spans. Then choose Motion from the Tween drop-down list in the Properties panel to apply a motion tween to every frame span at once. The timeline should match Figure 4-10.

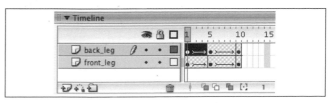

Figure 4-10. The timeline for legs_mc.

10. Save your work and test the movie.

Now the character walks his way from the left side of the Stage to the right side in a fluid motion. The movie clip for the blinking eyes plays independently of the clip for the legs, and both play independently of the main timeline. The animation on the main timeline, however, still loops, causing Box Guy to suddenly jump from the right side of the Stage back to the left side where he started. Next, we'll use ActionScript to stop the character on the right side of the Stage and stop the legs from moving. We'll leave the eyes blinking periodically.

CONTROLLING THE CHARACTER WITH ACTIONSCRIPT

As we saw in Chapter 3, we need to add a *stop( )* action to the main timeline to prevent the animation from looping. (The words *action* and *command* are often used interchangeably; both refer to an instruction programmers write in ActionScript to tell Flash what to do.) In addition, we need to tell the legs to stop moving when the character is standing still. To do this:

1. Close the Preview window and return to Scene 1 (using the Edit bar).

2. Add a new layer to the main timeline and name it *actions*. Remember, it's good practice to keep all ActionScript on its own layer so it's easy to find.

3. Add a keyframe to frame 60 on the *actions* layer.

4. Open the Actions panel (Window → Development Panels → Actions or F9).

> **NOTE**
>
> In the Script pane of the Actions panel, add the command **stop();** on frame 60. This causes the main timeline to stop animating once frame 60 is reached. As a best practice, you should include the semicolon after stop() to signify the end of the command. In simple cases such as this, the semicolon is optional because Flash can guess where the end of the command is (as indicated by the carriage return at the end of the line). But commands can be split onto multiple lines, making it harder for Flash to guess where the command ends, so it is good practice to include the semicolon at the end of each command. As a general rule, if a command is broken onto multiple lines, the semicolon belongs at the end of the last line. We'll talk more about semicolons in Chapter 7.

5. Although the main timeline will stop, the legs will keep animating because the legs_mc clip has its own independent timeline. Press Enter or Return to insert a blank line in the Script pane and add the following ActionScript to make the legs stop moving: **box_guy_mc.legs_mc.stop();**.

This last line of code, added to the main timeline, is simply another *stop( )* command, but it's targeted at the legs_mc instance located inside the box_guy_mc instance.

CONTROLLING CLIPS

ActionScript can target movie clips on the main timeline or clips nested within other clips. For example, to stop the legs from walking, we could place the following action on the main timeline: this.box_guy_mc.legs_mc.stop();

This expression tells Flash to look on the current timeline for a symbol called box_guy_mc, look for legs_mc inside of it, and tell legs_mc to stop playing. The keyword this represents the current timeline (the timeline on which the script resides), in this case, the main timeline. Specifying stop() or play()

without a preceding clip instance name stops or plays the current timeline.

When you stop or play a clip via ActionScript, nested clips do not automatically stop or play. That is, a parent clip and its nested clip have timelines that play independently.

Can you write code that causes the eyes to stop blinking? (Hint: You'll need to give instance names to the onstage instances of the *face_mc* and *eye_mc* movie clip symbols so you can target them from ActionScript. And you'll need to stop each *eye_mc* instance separately.)

Remember that clips exist in a nested hierarchy, starting from the main timeline. The dot operator (a period) is used to build the path to the intended target clip, much as slashes separate folders in a directory path. In this case, box_guy_mc.legs_mc.stop(); tells the Flash Player to look for the legs_mc clip inside the box_guy_mc clip on the main timeline and stop its playback.

> **NOTE**
>
> ActionScript can't control a movie clip instance unless you first give it an instance name using the Properties panel. Therefore, you must assign an instance name to any movie clip you intend to access or control through ActionScript.

To ensure the movie clips containing the box character and his legs are controllable via ActionScript, we assigned them the instance names box_guy_mc and legs_mc using the Properties panel when building our project.

So now Box Guy walks across the Stage and stops (and his legs stop too).

Creating the background

Before we publish the movie, let's create a background graphic, so the character appears to be walking down a street like the one in Figure 4-11.

1. Add a new layer, name it *bg* (short for background), and drag it beneath the other two layers.

2. Drag the playhead to frame 1, so the character isn't in the way as we draw the street.

3. On the Stage, draw a gray rectangle that occupies the bottom half of the Stage. Delete the right, left, and bottom lines of the stroke. We don't need them.

4. Select the remaining stroke, along the top edge of the rectangle, and change its stroke style to Ragged (the third choice in the Stroke Style drop-down list in the Properties panel). Set the stroke color to dark gray.

5. Next, we need to add yellow lane-divider markings to make it look like a street. Activate the Line tool,

set the stroke color to yellow, and set the stroke style to Dashed. Set the line thickness to 5.

6. Click the Custom button in the Properties panel to open the Stroke Style dialog box. Beneath the Type drop-down list, enter **40** into the fields that set the length of each dashed line and the distance between the lines. Click OK to close the dialog box.

7. Draw a line from one side of the Stage to the other, in the center of the rectangle. Now we have a lane divider, such as we see on a typical street, as shown in Figure 4-11.

Figure 4-11. The completed street background.

8. Shift-select all the parts of the street graphic and convert them to a graphic symbol named *street*.

9. Finally, change the background color of the Stage to sky blue. Remember, to do so, click once on the Stage and then click on the Background color swatch in the Properties panel.

10. Save your work.

11. Choose File → Publish to generate a completed *.swf* file.

12. If you have been following along (and I hope you have), *box_guy.swf*, located in the *04* folder, shows what your completed movie should look like.

Our movie is complete! The character walks from one side of the Stage to the other, blinking the whole time, and stops. When he stops walking, his legs stop moving, but he continues blinking, giving the character a lifelike quality.

Nesting movie clips within other clips is common in Flash development, as is using multiple clips within one project. Clips can be nested multiple levels deep (a clip within a clip within a clip). For example, the *face* clip can contain two instances of the *eye_mc* clip, plus a *mouth* graphic, and the entire face clip can be nested within the *box_guy_mc* clip. A movie clip can be used for an animated logo on a Flash web site, as a container for video in an interface (which we'll construct later on), and even as a menu system, similar to those made with JavaScript in traditional site design.

CONTROLLING MOVIE CLIPS

Movie clips can be assembled to create independent animations and controlled through ActionScript, as we saw in the last section, in which we used a *stop()* command to stop the animation of Box Guy and his legs. We can also allow the user to control the movie clips if we implement the necessary functionality and a user interface to control it. For example, we can tell Flash to restart the animation when the user clicks on the character. To accomplish this, we add an *event handler* to our ActionScript. An event handler tells the Flash Player, "When an event—such as the user clicking on the character—occurs, perform the following action(s)." In this case, the desired action is to replay the animation. How do we do this?

Whenever the user clicks on Box Guy, we'll send the playhead back to frame 1 and restart the main timeline and the legs. To restart the animation:

1. On frame 60 of the *actions* layer, add the following code using the Actions panel. This is our event handler. The *onPress()* event handler tells Flash to perform this action when the user clicks the mouse on the specified clip (in this case, box_guy_mc):

    ```
    box_guy_mc.onPress = function () {
        gotoAndPlay(1);
    };
    ```

2. Add a *play()* action to the event handler to restart the animation of the legs from where it last left off (changes shown in color):

    ```
    box_guy_mc.onPress = function () {
        gotoAndPlay(1);
        this.legs_mc.play();
    };
    ```

3. Save your work and test the movie.

4. When the character stops walking, click on it to replay the animation.

The script you wrote sets up a function that runs when you click on the box_guy_mc clip in the movie.

NOTE

> Note that, as a best practice, we placed this code on the main timeline, not the clip's timeline. Therefore, the clip names are relative to the main timeline. To refer to a clip nested within a clip, we can use an expression that specifies a complete path (known as *targeting*) down the hierarchy.
>
> In some situations, the best practice is to place ActionScript in external *.as* files (in fact, this is required when writing custom ActionScript 2.0 classes). For details on ActionScript 2.0 best practices, see *Essential ActionScript 2.0* (O'Reilly).

EVENT HANDLERS

In order to be interactive, a multimedia piece must react to events such as the user pressing a key or clicking the mouse button. Event handlers simply tell Flash what to do and when to do it. The *triggering event*, such as a mouse-click, executes a corresponding event handler, such as *onPress()*. Writing an event handler to react to an event is often known as *trapping* the event.

The *onPress()* event handler we wrote in the preceding exercise tells the Flash Player to send the playhead back to frame 1 and play the box_guy_mc timeline when the user clicks on box_guy_mc. In plain English, we're saying to the Flash Player, "When the user clicks on the character, go to frame 1 and replay the animation."

For each type of event you wish to trap, you should define an appropriately named event handler. You can use an

A *function* is a reusable set of actions that Flash can perform, grouped into one conveniently named command. A function in ActionScript is similar to a function in real life. For example, my brain's *getCoffee( )* function includes actions to find a coffee cup, pour coffee into it, and drink the coffee. My *getCoffee( )* function is built into my brain and I don't have to think about it (and believe me, if I had to think about it—I'd just stay in bed). The code in my brain looks like this:

```
me.getCoffee = function () {
    findCoffeeCup();
    pourCoffee();
    drinkCoffee();
}
```

My brain knows to do all these things when the *getCoffee( )* function is run, so all I need to do now is tell my brain when to run the function. To do this, I've programmed an event handler for myself:

```
me.onAlarm = function () {
    getCoffee();
}
```

When the alarm goes off, my brain runs the *getCoffee( )* function, which then performs the necessary actions to achieve the desired goal: to get caffeine into my bloodstream!

Functions can *invoke* (run) other functions by specifying the name of the function followed by the ( ) operator. Notice that *getCoffee( )* invokes several functions—*findCoffeeCup( )*, *pourCoffee( )*, *drinkCoffee( )*—whose contents are not shown.

Simplifying code

Since the *onPress( )* event handler is on the last frame of the animation, we don't actually need to tell the Flash Player to go back to frame 1. We only need to tell it to play, and it will pick up where it left off. Because the animation is already on the last frame, the playhead will automatically loop back to frame 1. Let's modify the code as follows:

1. Replace gotoAndPlay(1) with play() as follows (changes shown in color):

```
box_guy_mc.onPress = function () {
    play();
    this.legs_mc.play();
};
```

2. Save and retest the movie. When the character stops walking and you click on it, the animation replays.

onRelease( ) handler to make Box Guy respond when the mouse button is released instead of when it is clicked (using *onRelease( )* instead of *onPress( )* allows the user to change her mind by rolling off Box Guy before releasing the mouse button). Of course, you're not limited to trapping mouse events.

For example, to detect when the user presses a key (i.e., to trap keypresses), define an *onKeyDown( )* handler. The following handler causes our Box Guy animation to restart whenever the user presses a key:

```
box_guy_mc.onKeyDown = function () {
    gotoAndPlay(1);
    this.legs_mc.play();
};
```

We'll use other event handlers later in the book to react to other events, such as the loading of data or the user clicking a button.

GET OUT OF THE BOX

In this chapter, we've worked with the Pencil tool, movie clips, and ActionScript to create a cartoon character and control it in an animation. We've seen how:

- The Pencil tool can be configured to recognize shapes and smooth or straighten lines after we draw them

- Movie clips allow animations to be played independently from one another and from the main timeline

- ActionScript can be used to control movie clips

- Event handlers can be used to add interactivity, effectively letting the user control the animation

Before moving on to the next chapter, try using your new ActionScript knowledge to make the character's eyes stop blinking. Also, flip the character horizontally (by selecting the movie clip instance and choosing Modify → Transform → Flip Horizontal) and make him walk from right to left. Can you make him walk offstage and then start over automatically?

Movie clips are arguably the most powerful objects in Flash. They can be used for independent animation, such as we created in this chapter, or as self-contained pieces of functionality and logic for a movie. For example, later on in this book, we'll use a movie clip to create a preloader for external assets that load into a Flash movie while it's running. (Preloaders give users a visual way to see that an external asset is being loaded.) The preloader clip contains nothing but Action-Script and a text field. (Later still, we'll turn the same clip into a reusable *component*, but that's a different story altogether.)

Another great benefit to using movie clips instead of animating everything on the main timeline is that clips can be used in more than one project. If you plan to create an entire series of cartoons using the same characters, for example, you might create walk cycles for each character and simply import them into each new movie. In the next chapter, we'll see how to import external assets, such as bitmaps and symbols from other Flash documents, and work with them.

5

USING IMAGES AND VIDEO

Flash can be thought of as a multimedia construction kit. This chapter shows how images and videos can be imported from external sources and combined into an elegant Flash piece. Along the way, you'll learn a lot about optimization while improving your design skills.

Flash's drawing tools are primarily vector-based, and so aren't ideal for editing bitmaps. We'll cover a few bitmap-related tricks in Chapters 6 and 7, but meaningful bitmap editing requires a program designed for that purpose, such as Adobe Photoshop or Macromedia Fireworks. In this chapter, we'll look at how integrating Flash with other applications helps us meet our design needs for a project.

While Photoshop and Illustrator are the standard tools for graphics editing and creation, Macromedia has done a lot to ensure that Fireworks and Flash work well together. As a result, Fireworks is a viable alternative for web-based graphics development. If you purchased Studio MX 2004, Fireworks is likely already installed on your machine and dying to be put to use. If not, go install the trial version now from the CD-ROM included with this book...I'll wait.

In addition to bitmaps, video is a wonderful way to offer high-quality content to users through Flash, and Flash is actually quite powerful when it comes to compressing and deploying video online. We'll explore video in Flash as we create an online ad for a pet adoption event. Throughout this chapter, and indeed the entire book, we use the term *movie* to refer to a compiled *.swf* file, and the term *video* when referring to QuickTime *.mov* files or other video formats.

WORKING WITH OTHER SOFTWARE

Locate *scrappy_complete.swf* in the *05/complete* folder and open it to see what we'll be creating. The movie features a bitmap, text, a semi-opaque box (of course, there had to be a box in there somewhere), and a video. Each element, whether created in Flash or another program, must be imported into our Flash document to complete the project. Let's see how it's done.

Importing Fireworks artwork

To get our Adopt-a-Dog-athon ad started, we'll import an image to use as a background. I've captured a PNG image

> **NOTE**
>
> If need be, you can install Fireworks or FreeHand from this book's CD-ROM. If you don't want to install them, you can skip the exercises that require them and use the *.fla* and *.swf* files provided on the CD-ROM instead. To work with the video, you'll need QuickTime. If you do not already have QuickTime, visit *http://www.apple.com/quicktime* to download and install it. Don't worry—although QuickTime Pro costs $29.99, the free version is sufficient for our needs. Leave your credit card in your wallet.

from the video we'll use later on in this chapter. To set up our Flash movie and import the PNG image:

1. Create a new, blank document and save it as *scrappy.fla* in the *05* folder.

2. Change the Stage dimensions to 500 × 400. Leave the background white, but change the frame rate to 18.

3. Rename *Layer 1* to *bg* (short for background). As we add elements to the project, we'll keep this as the bottom layer to ensure the background image appears behind everything else. (If you're familiar with Macromedia Director, the order in which Flash displays layers in the timeline is the reverse of the order in which Director displays sprites in its score. You'll get used to it.)

4. Choose File → Import → Import to Stage (Ctrl/Cmd-R) and locate *still.png* in the *05* folder. Select it and click Open. Flash's Fireworks Import PNG Settings dialog box opens.

5. Check the Import as Single Flattened Bitmap option and click OK. The image imports and is placed on the Stage. Note that frame 1 of the *bg* layer, where the image was imported, is now a keyframe because it contains content. (Flash always converts frame 1 to a keyframe the first time content is added to it.)

When we start adding other elements to the project, the background will be too distracting, so let's lighten it using Fireworks:

1. With the image selected, click the Edit button in Flash's Properties panel. Fireworks launches and the *still.png* file opens. (This is the so-called *round-trip editing* feature, which makes Flash and Fireworks workflow a snap.) If the Edit button in the Properties panel is not active, you forgot to check the Import as Single Flattened Bitmap option when you imported *still.png*. To select a different editor, you can right-click (Windows) or Cmd-click (Mac) the item in the Library and choose Edit With from the contextual menu.

2. In Fireworks, select the image (by clicking on it) and choose Filters → Adjust Color → Brightness/Contrast to open the Brightness/Contrast dialog box.

3. Set the Brightness slider to 70 and the Contrast slider to −70. Now the image is light enough that other elements can appear clearly in front of it.

4. Click OK to close the dialog box, then click the Done button in the top-left corner of the open file, as shown in Figure 5-1. The Fireworks image closes and you are returned to Flash.

Figure 5-1. The still.png file opens in Fireworks using round-trip editing, and the changes are reflected in Flash.

Although you edited the image in Fireworks, the image is updated automatically inside Flash as well. This process is called *round-trip editing* and is a tremendous time-

saver when working with programs in the Macromedia Studio MX 2004 suite.

> **NOTE**
>
> Flash uses JPEG compression on every bitmap image in a Flash document when a movie is published. Because of this, it's a good idea to import bitmaps as PNG files, which are not already compressed. If you import a JPEG, which is a compressed format, Flash compresses it again, which can adversely affect the quality of the image in the final movie.

Bitmaps compressed in Fireworks often have smaller file sizes than those compressed in ImageReady or Photoshop, so I highly recommend using Fireworks to create the smallest possible web graphics. I'm going to duck and run now, before Adobe diehards come after me.

Importing FreeHand artwork

Macromedia FreeHand—included as part of the Studio MX 2004 suite and included on this book's CD-ROM—is a wonderful illustration tool for vector artwork (it competes with Adobe Illustrator). For this project, I've used FreeHand to create a logo for Canine Solutions, the company sponsoring the Adopt-a-Dog-athon.

To import the FreeHand file into the Flash project:

1. With *scrappy.fla* open in Flash, choose File → Import → Import to Stage (or press Ctrl/Cmd-R), locate *canine_solutions_logo.fh11* in the *05* folder, and choose it. Flash's FreeHand Import dialog box opens.

2. Your settings should match Figure 5-2:

   a) We need to import the logo to a keyframe, so enable Keyframes in the Pages section of the dialog box.

   b) In the Layers section of the dialog box, choose Flatten so the image imports onto a single layer. (If you choose Layers or Keyframes, the logo imports onto multiple layers or keyframes.)

c) Under Options, uncheck Include Invisible Layers, and check the Include Background Layers and Maintain Text Blocks options.

3. Click OK to close the dialog box. The logo imports into a keyframe on *bg*, the same layer containing the background image.

4. Save your work.

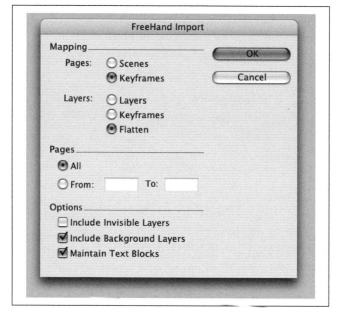

Figure 5-2. The FreeHand Import dialog box.

Note that if you attempt to import artwork that uses a font not installed on your system, you will see a warning dialog box that asks you to choose another font or use a default font. This warning can be avoided by using system fonts or by using outline fonts in the original artwork.

When we import the logo artwork, two folders are created in the Library, each of which contains several graphic symbols we don't need. Symbols don't add file size to a published movie unless they are used on the Stage (or if the Export for ActionScript option is activated under their Linkage properties), but they do take up space in the Library unnecessarily, so let's delete them:

1. Open the Library (Ctrl/Cmd-L).

2. Select the Brush Tips and FreeHand Objects folders and delete them by clicking the trash can icon in

the Library. Click OK when asked to confirm the deletions.

It's always a good idea to convert a graphic in Flash to a symbol (so we can reuse and animate it), so let's do that. Also, let's move the logo to its own layer—we need to add another element between the logo and the background, so they must be on separate layers:

1. With the logo still selected, convert it to a graphic symbol named *cs_logo*.

2. Choose Edit → Cut to remove the logo from *bg*.

3. Insert a new layer named *assets*, and choose Edit → Paste to add the logo to the new layer, as shown in Figure 5-3. Since nothing in this project requires a motion tween, several elements can be placed on one layer. (Remember that a motion tween can be applied only when a layer contains only one object.)

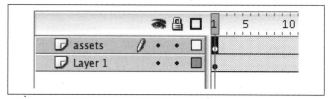

Figure 5-3. Cut and paste the cs_logo instance to a new layer named assets.

Now that we have imported artwork from Fireworks and FreeHand, we are ready to move on. The next major element in the project is the text, and we'll grab that from another Flash file. First, however, let's set up a space for the text to appear, using a white box to make it easier to read.

Setting opacity for symbol instances

The final version of this project includes a semi-opaque white box that appears behind the text. The box makes the text more readable but is partially transparent so the background image shows through, unifying the design elements. To create the semi-opaque box:

1. On the *assets* layer, draw a white rectangle with no stroke, such as the one in Figure 5-4. Select and delete the stroke if necessary.

2. Convert the rectangle to a graphic symbol named *box*. The Properties panel now shows properties for a graphic symbol (refer back to Figure 3-7).

3. Choose Alpha from the Color drop-down list in the Properties panel and drag the Alpha slider to 65% to make the *box* instance semi-opaque.

The box looks less harsh when it is semi-transparent, and being able to see through it helps unify the design. Now we just need to move the logo we imported from Free-Hand into this area of the Stage:

1. With the logo selected, choose Modify → Arrange → Bring to Front, then move the *cs_logo* instance over the *box* instance, toward the bottom of the Stage, to match Figure 5-4.

2. Resize the logo using the Free Transform tool so it looks like Figure 5-4. Hold down the Shift key while resizing to maintain the original aspect ratio of the instance.

Figure 5-4. Position the cs_logo instance over the box instance.

Using shared assets

I've created two symbols in another *.fla* file that we need for this project, so let's import them:

1. Choose File → Import → Open External Library, locate *scrappy_lib.fla* in the *05* folder, and select it.

The Library of *scrappy_lib.fla* opens, and we now have two Library panels, one for each open *.fla* (assuming your Library is still open from the last section). The two Libraries appear identical except for the title bar, which provides the name of the *.fla* file with which each Library is associated. The *scrappy_lib.fla* Library contains two symbols, as shown in Figure 5-5.

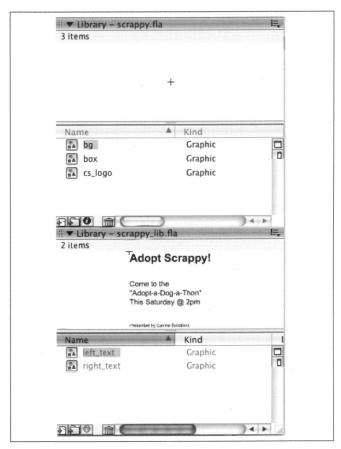

Figure 5-5. The Library panel's title bar indicates the file with which the Library is associated.

2. Select the *assets* layer in the timeline, drag the *right_text* symbol from the Library of *scrappy_lib.fla* to the Stage, and position it in front of the *box* instance.

3. Drag *left_text* to the Stage and position it on the left side of the Stage, as shown in Figure 5-6.

4. Save your work.

Figure 5-6. Position left_text on the left side of the Stage.

Using assets from one *.fla* file in another *.fla* file is called *author-time sharing*. Opening the library of one *.fla* file and pulling assets from it to the Stage of another *.fla* file creates copies of the symbols in the destination file's Library. This is convenient when working with a team of Flash designers or multiple projects for the same client, as assets can easily be shared between projects. After you complete the preceding procedure, the Library for *scrappy.fla* contains the *right_text* and *left_text* symbols.

IMPORTING, COMPRESSING, AND USING VIDEO

Now that we have the background image, logo, and text we need for our project, it's time to prepare the video. As with bitmaps, we can simply import the video and use the Flash Player to display it. However, video files are usually too large to post online without some sort of compression. Flash to the rescue!

Flash MX and Flash MX 2004 have a video *codec* built into them, courtesy of a software developer named Sorenson. Sorenson's commercial product, Squeeze, is a powerful tool used by many video gurus to compress video. A lite version of the codec, named Spark, is built into Flash. What does this mean to you? It means you can dramatically decrease the file size of video through Flash

while maintaining high-quality playback. However, you need to take a few steps that I've never seen covered in any other tutorial I've read, online or in books. In the following sections, you won't just learn to use video in Flash, you'll learn to use it efficiently.

Prepping video for use in Flash

We want to add a video of a dog to our ad. The raw video is too large for online distribution, but we'll tackle compression shortly. For now, we'll simply import the external video as follows:

1. Insert a new layer between the *bg* and *assets* layers, and name it *video*.

2. Choose File → Import → Import to Stage, locate *SniffingForCats.mov* in the *05* folder, and select it. The Video Import Wizard opens.

3. From the first screen of the wizard, choose Embed Video in Macromedia Flash Document and click Next. (Alternatively, you can choose to link to an external video file, but this works only if you publish a QuickTime movie instead of a *.swf*.)

4. From the second screen of the wizard, choose Import the Entire Video and click Next.

5. Choose DSL/Cable 256 Kbps from the Compression Profile drop-down list. This option determines how much the video will be compressed to play within the bandwidth requirements. Do not click Next yet.

6. From the Advanced Settings drop-down list, choose Create New Profile. This opens the Advanced Settings dialog box.

The Advanced Settings dialog box, shown in Figure 5-7, is used to adjust attributes of the video, such as color, contrast, and brightness. We'll use this screen to make sure Scrappy the dog looks as good as he can. We'll adjust the image quality and then crop off the edges of the video:

1. Set Hue to –10, Saturation to +10, and Contrast to –30. This adjusts the entire video to balance out the colors and make Scrappy look better by improving the contrast.

2. In the Crop section of the Advanced Settings screen, the four fields—for top, left, bottom, and right margins—are arranged in a diamond as shown in Figure 5-7. Set the Top to 21, the Left to 62, the Right to 57, and the Bottom to 43. These settings tell the Sorenson codec how to crop the video clip during import.

Notice that white lines appear in the Preview area of the screen, as shown in Figure 5-7, indicating how the video will be cropped. The grass in the background to the left and right is not an important part of the video, so we crop it out.

Let's complete the import process:

1. In the Track Options section of the Advanced Settings screen, set the Import Into option to Movie Clip, and set the Audio Track option to None. There is no sound in the video, and there is no point in forcing Flash to figure that out on its own. We'll import the video into a movie clip so that we can control the video via ActionScript.

2. Compare your settings with those in Figure 5-7. Click Next if everything matches.

3. Enter a name for the import profile, such as **Adjusted Color and Cropping**, and an optional description if you'd like. Click Next, then click Finish. Click OK if Flash prompts you to add enough frames to display the entire video.

If you're working on a slow computer, your processor may have a small heart attack right about now. The Quick-Time video we're importing is 55 MB! A file this large can take quite a while to import, so feel free to go make a sandwich while it's importing. Hey, make me one too, would ya?

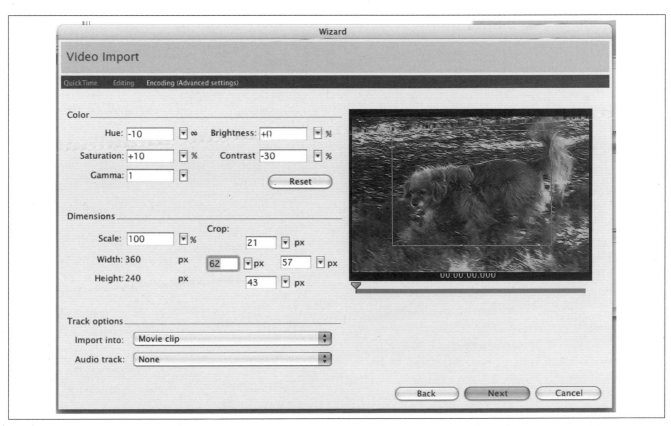

Figure 5-7. The Advanced Settings screen of the Video Import Wizard.

Sorenson Spark compresses the video quite a bit during the import process, so when it's complete, let's see how much Spark compressed it:

1. Test the Flash movie.

2. In the Preview window, check the size of the .*swf* movie. It's around 13 MB, which is a substantial improvement considering we imported a 55 MB video.

3. Close the Preview window.

Sorenson Spark was able to squash the 55 MB Quick-Time movie down to a 13 MB .*swf* file, but 13 MB is still unrealistically large for online distribution. Most people are still using 56 Kbps modems, and it could take an hour or more for a user to download this file. In short, if you want to deploy video through Flash, you'll need to be a little more creative than the average Flash geek. Let's see what we can do.

Using video in Flash MX 2004

We need to get our Flash movie down to a reasonable size. To further compress the video for use in Flash:

1. Select the *SniffingForCats.mov* video clip icon in the Library and choose Edit → Copy. (Be sure to select the *SniffingForCats.mov* video clip in the Library, not the movie clip of the same name.)

2. Create a new Flash document, and change the Stage dimensions to 241 × 176 to match the dimensions of the video.

3. Choose Edit → Paste to paste the video into the new Flash document and position it at (0, 0).

4. Choose File → Export → Export Movie. The Export Video dialog box opens.

5. Set the export file type to QuickTime, set the export filename to *scrappy.mov,* and click OK. Flash's Export QuickTime Video dialog box opens. Set the dimensions to 241 × 176.

6. On the Macintosh, set the Compressor option to Sorenson Video 3. Also, set Sound Format to Disable, as shown in Figure 5-8. On Windows, use the default settings as shown back in Figure 3-24.

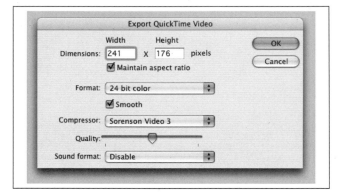

Figure 5-8. Flash's Export QuickTime Video dialog box.

7. Click OK to export the video. Flash saves *scrappy. mov* in the *05* folder with a much lower file size, approximately 4 MB.

8. Close the Flash document without saving it.

COMPONENTS

Components are prebuilt user-interface elements that were introduced by Macromedia in Flash MX to alleviate the time-consuming task of creating common pieces of functionality, such as a scrollbar for a text field or a preloader for larger files, and also to standardize the look and feel of the elements. Designers and developers have been creating their own Flash widgets like these for several years, and it is often frustrating to users to have to learn how each one works.

A scrollbar on one site may have a sliding bar that you drag with your mouse, while another may include up and down arrow buttons.

Having a standard set of these types of components cuts down on development time, as you no longer have to write the ActionScript necessary to create the elements, and also improves usability for end users across multiple web sites by standardizing some of the UI interactions.

9. Open *scrappy.mov* in the QuickTime Player and play the movie. The playback is still high quality, despite having shaved 51 MB (more than 90%) from the original file size.

Importing the original video into Flash and exporting it as a new QuickTime video lowered the file size substantially, but there is a catch: importing the QuickTime video back into Flash increases its file size somewhat (the amount of increase varies depending on the original size of the video clip). We'll explore other compression techniques later to circumvent the problem.

Let's take a look at how Flash MX Professional 2004 (a.k.a. Flash Pro) and its included MediaDisplay component make video more usable in Flash.

Using video in Flash Pro

Flash Pro includes some video features not included in the standard edition of Flash MX 2004. Even if you're not using Flash Pro, you should still read this section so you understand the benefits it offers. Flash Pro's Media components make the job of deploying video in Flash almost as easy as dragging a symbol from the Library to the Stage. In addition, the video is kept external to the *.swf* file and is streamed at runtime, meaning the user does not have to load the entire 13 MB video of Scrappy before it starts to play.

To use the MediaDisplay component, we must first create a version of the video file that can be streamed into Flash. The Sorenson Spark codec built into Flash compresses

video as it's imported into Flash, but we need to then export it as a compressed Flash Video (*.flv*) file to stream it. To do this:

1. Open the Library (Ctrl/Cmd-L).

2. Right-click (Windows) or Cmd-click (Mac) on the *SniffingForCats.mov* video clip in the Library and choose Properties from the contextual menu. The Embedded Video Properties dialog box opens.

3. In the dialog box, choose Export. Name the file *scrappy.flv* and navigate to the *05* folder. Click OK to export the video.

4. Click OK to close the dialog box.

5. Locate the *05* folder on your hard drive and make sure *scrappy.flv* is now in the folder.

NOTE

You do not have to own Flash Pro to complete the preceding exercise. You can also export *.flv* files from Flash MX 2004.

The *.flv* file is around 14 MB, which is larger than the *.swf* we created earlier from the test movie (a *.swf* file is generated every time you run a test movie), so it doesn't help much. A 14 MB file is still too large for most users to stream online, so let's try creating a smaller *.flv* file from *scrappy.mov* using the FLV exporter in the QuickTime Player.

Flash MX 2004 ships with many components, including the Label, Button, ProgressBar, and RadioButton components. Flash Pro ships with about twice as many components, including a set of Media components (discussed in this chapter) and Data components, for connecting easily to databases and web services.

The prebuilt components can be large to download, as discussed in Chapters 10 and 11, and cumbersome to modify. Skilled developers often create their own components to handle all kinds of tasks within Flash, and many of these components can be downloaded free of charge through the Flash Exchange (*http://www.macromedia.com/exchange/flash*). The Flash Exchange is discussed in Chapter 6.

TIP

If you haven't already installed the FLV Exporter that comes with Studio MX 2004 Pro, locate your installation CD-ROM. Double-click the *Flash_Video_Exporter.exe* file (Windows) or *Flash_Video_Exporter.dmg* (Mac) in the Flash MX 2004 Installer folder to run the FLV Exporter Installer. (If you're a DevNet Pro subscriber or if you purchased Studio MX 2004 online, log into your Macromedia account and download the installer from there.)

The FLV Exporter is a plugin that works within several video editing applications, such as Quick-Time, Apple's Final Cut Pro, and Adobe Premier, to enable the creation of *.flv* (Flash Video) files. Flash Video files can be streamed into the Flash Player via ActionScript or by using any one of the Media components that ship with Flash Pro.

1. Open *scrappy.mov* in the QuickTime Player again.

2. Choose File → Export, name the file *scrappy.flv*, and set the Export format to Movie to Macromedia Flash Video (FLV).

3. Click the Options button to open QuickTime's Flash Video Exporter dialog box.

4. In the dialog box, your settings should match Figure 5-9.

   a) Set the Encoding Method to Baseline, and set the Frames per Second to Same as Source.

   b) Set Quality to Custom, and enter **1000** into the Limit Data Rate To field.

   c) Set the Keyframes option to Custom, and enter **18** into the Keyframe Every __ Frames field.

   d) Set the Motion Estimation option to Better to maintain high quality for the video.

   e) Set the Resize To option to None, and set the Width and Height fields to 100%. This means

Figure 5-9. Settings for the Flash Video Exporter.

the exported *.flv* file will be set to the same dimensions as the current movie.

f) Depending on your version of QuickTime, the chosen codec, and what platform you're on, the dialog box may also prompt you for the kilobits/sec. Choose the highest value that still keeps the video small enough for web use or the lowest value you can get away with without degrading quality. The optimal setting also depends on the source video, length of the video clip, and expected bandwidth of your users, so feel free to experiment.

5. Click OK to close the dialog box, and click Save to perform the export.

Unless your computer is newer and has a superfast processor, the export process could take several minutes and possibly cause another small heart attack for your computer. When the export is complete, quit QuickTime and locate the *.flv* file in the *05* folder. *Scrappy.flv*, which began as a 4 MB QuickTime movie, is now only 2 MB! Although a 2 MB file is still too large to conveniently download over a 56 Kbps modem, now at least we have a video we can consider streaming. There will be a noticeable delay on a 56 Kbps when buffering the initial portion of the video. If the delay is unacceptable, you can lower the size or quality of the video or offer a low-bandwidth version of your site that uses animation or still images instead of video.

Now we can go back into Flash Pro and use the Media-Display component to stream the *.flv* file into our *.swf* movie:

1. In *scrappy.fla*, delete the video clip from the Stage and from the Library. We don't need it anymore.

2. Choose Window → Development Panels → Components to open the Components panel, shown in Figure 5-10. (See the earlier "Components" sidebar for information on components.)

3. In the Components panel, expand the Media Components set of components by clicking on the + sign (Windows) or arrow (Mac) to the left of the name Media Components. This displays a set of three Media components, also shown in Figure 5-10.

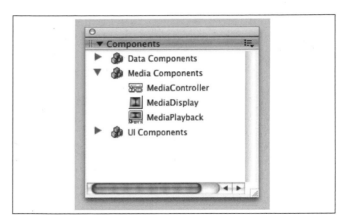

Figure 5-10. The Components panel.

4. Click and drag the MediaDisplay component from the Components panel to the Stage and position it in the upper-left corner of the Stage, a few pixels from the top and left edges.

5. Resize the component to 241 × 176.

6. With the component still selected, select the Parameters tab in the Properties panel, then click Launch Component Inspector to open the Component Inspector panel, shown in Figure 5-11. Alternatively, you can open the Component

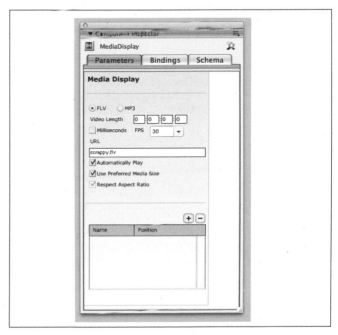

Figure 5-11. The Component Inspector panel.

Inspector using Window → Development Panels → Component Inspector.

7. Choose the Parameters tab of the Component Inspector panel, choose the FLV radio button, and enter **scrappy.flv** into the URL field. Also, check the Automatically Play and Use Preferred Media Size options.

8. Now for the fun part: test the movie.

The Preview window opens, the *.flv* loads into the MediaDisplay component, and the video plays automatically. Most importantly, however, is the size of the Flash *.swf* movie, which is now an incredibly low 83 KB. The external video clip is still 2 MB, but since it's being streamed by Flash, it can begin to play while it is still loading.

To recap, we:

- Started with a 55 MB QuickTime movie

- Imported it into Flash using the built-in Sorenson codec, while cropping the video and adjusting the contrast

- Exported it as a new QuickTime movie (less than 4 MB) using the Sorenson Video 3 compressor option

- Used the FLV Exporter to create a *.flv* file (approximately 2 MB) so we could stream it into Flash at runtime

- Streamed the movie into Flash using the Media-Display component

We've gone from a 55 MB QuickTime movie to a Flash movie that's less than 90 KB, and our video has better cropping and contrast than the original!

Impressive, no?

There's only one thing left to do now: publish the movie. The Media components included with Flash Pro have been created to work with Flash Player 6 or later, and many end users still have Flash Player 6 installed, so let's change the Publish Settings to publish to that older file format:

1. Click on the Stage to display Document properties in the Properties panel and click the Settings button to open the Publish Settings dialog box.

USING VIDEO IN FLASH

Dial-up Internet connections are still the majority of the installed base, as compared to DSL and cable connections. Web content needs to load fast, render correctly, and be flexible to accommodate the user's needs.

Flash is well known for its ability to generate small files. But video, with its larger file size, disrupts that trend, which means Flash is not usually the best option, unless you have taken additional steps to compress the video.

The best ways to use video in Flash are as follows:

- Macromedia Flash Communication Server MX (Flash-Com) is a server application that allows multiple connections to Flash content and streams audio, video, and other data. FlashCom is supported by Flash Player 6 and later, but it is not covered in this book. Visit Macromedia's web site *(http://www.macromedia.com/ software/flashcom)* for more information. Prior to Flash Player 7, FlashCom was the only method available for streaming video into Flash.

- Flash MX 2004 supports ActionScript that can be used to stream *.flv* files into a *.swf* running in Flash Player 7, as discussed in Chapter 9.

2. Under the Formats tab, check the Flash option and uncheck all the other options.

3. Under the Flash tab, choose Flash Player 6 as the Version (Flash Player 6 or higher is required when publishing a movie that contains video), Top Down for Load Order, and ActionScript 2.0 as the ActionScript Version. ActionScript 2.0 is new to Flash MX 2004, but much of it is backward compatible with Flash Player 6.

4. Enable the Compress Movie and Optimize for Flash Player 6 r65 options in the dialog box as well. Flash Player 6 r65 (revision 65 of Flash Player 6) featured enhancements and bug fixes that allow improved performance.

5. Click Publish to publish the movie, then click OK to close the dialog box.

6. Save and close *scrappy.fla*.

7. Open *scrappy.swf* (located in the *05* folder) to see the completed movie.

It's done! With a *.swf* file that's less than 90 KB, we're able to stream a 2 MB video clip that plays beautifully, and we did it without writing a single line of code. This is why Flash Pro's Media components are so useful. Convinced?

- Flash MX Professional 2004 (Flash Pro) includes a set of three Media components, each of which allows for quick setup and streaming of Flash Video files into Flash Player 7 at runtime. This chapter covers the MediaDisplay component.

If you haven't yet purchased the newest version of Flash and plan to use video in your Flash content, I highly recommend purchasing Flash Pro instead of the standard edition. Flash Pro costs $100 more than Flash MX 2004, but the Media Components alone can justify the increased cost.

See the earlier section "Using video in Flash Pro" for an example of how its included Media components make video deployment easier and more user-friendly by enabling you to deploy video in your Flash movies without writing any ActionScript.

The most important thing to do when using video online, whether with Flash or another media player (such as Quick-Time), is to make sure the file has a streaming rate that can be achieved without falling behind on the connection. This chapter revealed how to make sure your video looks great, loads fast, and plays well.

As you can see, Flash is capable of importing files from many graphics and video programs, and incorporating external assets is often necessary to accomplish our goals with Flash. In this chapter, we've seen how to:

- Import assets from other programs, such as Fireworks and FreeHand

- Store those assets in the Flash Library and manipulate them in useful ways

- Compress video to an astounding degree without severe loss of quality

- Use streaming video effectively within our presentation

- Use components to save time when building application UIs

In later chapters we'll explore additional techniques to gain more confidence in Flash and enrich to our designs.

6

BUILDING AN ANIMATED AD

In this chapter we continue our exploration of Flash animation, including text effects, shape tweens, visual transitions, and timeline effects. You'll see how understated animation can contribute to an effective and compelling design.

Despite the fact that Flash is not a powerful bitmap editor, it is capable of creating some cool effects. All it takes is a little creativity and some know-how. In this chapter, we'll take a look at the techniques used to create text, graphic, and bitmap effects. What you learn here will prepare you for Chapter 7. The two chapters together give you a glimpse of the skills used to create sites like the over-the-top 2Advanced Studios (*http://www.2advanced.com*) and many others, so get ready to use some cool Flash design techniques.

By the way, I don't necessarily recommend designing Flash sites like the 2Advanced Studios site. While the effects and transitions are visually very cool, many users will find the heavy use of eye candy intrusive when trying to acquire information from the site. That said, you can create many effects in Flash that not only support your content, but can bring it to life via the art of motion and graphic design.

REVEALING OBJECTS OVER TIME

First, we'll use Flash to create two more animations and increase our ability to bring our ideas to life. We'll start by creating a typewriter effect, which will give us practice using text animation. Many of the same principles apply to motion graphics, but it is easy to create the text so we can focus on the animation. Text effects can be used in the most conservative sites (such as PowerPoint-like presentations) to the most extravagant (say, modeled after the famous green text waterfall in *The Matrix*).

> **NOTE**
>
> To perform certain text effects, such as rotating text, the outline of the font must be available at runtime. In such a case, embedding the font is necessary but will also add to the *.swf* download size. Such text effects won't work with device fonts (those available on the system at runtime) because the outline information isn't available.

To embed the necessary font information in the *.swf* file:

1. Create a text field.

2. Use the Properties panel to set the text field's type to Dynamic Text.

3. Click the Character button in the Properties panel to open the Character Options dialog box (if you don't see the Character button, make sure your text field's type is set to Dynamic Text, not Static Text).

4. In the Character Options dialog box, under Embed Font Outlines For, select the Specify Ranges radio button.

5. Choose the character ranges, such as Uppercase [A.Z], to embed from the scrolling list. To select multiple contiguous items, hold down the Shift key when clicking. To select discontiguous items hold down the Ctrl key (Windows) or Cmd key (Mac) while clicking.

The typewriter effect

To create a typewriter effect, letters in a line of text are revealed in succession instead of all at once. To do this:

1. Create a new Flash document and save it as *frame_ by_frame.fla* in the *06* folder.

2. Change the Stage dimensions to 300 × 50 and set the frame rate to 10 fps. Slowing down the frame rate often improves playback performance on slower machines, and in this case, a higher frame rate is not necessary.

3. Activate the Text tool and choose the _typewriter font from the Properties panel's font drop-down list. If you don't have this font, choose any font you like.

4. Set the font size to 50.

5. On the Stage, using the Text tool, create a text field and enter **FLASH FX**, in all capital letters.

Now we have one line of text on one layer in a single frame. To generate the typewriter effect, the letters need to appear over time, so each letter needs to appear on its own frame. We'll use Flash's Break Apart command to split the text into individual letters that can be manipulated as separate elements:

1. Position the line of text at the center of the Stage using the Align panel.

2. With the text still selected, choose Modify → Break Apart to separate the letters in the text. Each letter now has its own bounding box and can be treated as an individual graphic, as shown in Figure 6-1.

Figure 6-1. Break apart the line of text.

3. Click on frame 7 of *Layer 1* and drag left to select all the frames, back to frame 1.

4. Choose Modify → Timeline → Convert to Keyframes. A keyframe appears on every frame, from frame 1 to frame 7.

5. On frame 1, delete every letter of the text except for the *F* in the word *FLASH*. On frame 2, leave only the letters *FL*. On frame 3, leave only *FLA*, and so on.

6. When we broke apart the text in Step 2, the space between *FLASH* and *FX* doesn't become its own graphic (Flash can't create a shape for it, because it is just whitespace). To simulate the spacebar being pressed between *FLASH* and *FX*, select frame 5 and press F5 to insert a frame between frames 5 and 6.

7. Press Enter (or Return) to see the animation. Each letter appears in succession. The extra frame inserted between frames 5 and 6 takes time to display, causing a small pause between words.

We've just created a *frame-by-frame* animation in which each frame contains a new image in a sequence, similar to a flip book. Notice, though, that the *F* in *FLASH* appears on frame 1, so it is present at the start of the movie rather than appearing to be typed. To remedy this:

1. Select frames 1 through 8 by clicking and dragging on the frames.

2. Drag the selected frame span to the right, so that the span starts at frame 5 and ends at frame 12.

3. Test the movie to see the completed animation. Now there is a momentary pause, during which the Stage is empty, before the text appears.

The *.swf* file is only about 427 bytes, which is less than 1 KB. There is no reason to be concerned about file size with this animation, but now is a good time to learn about an issue that you'll need to keep your eye on when you start creating complicated animations. Here's the scoop.

A published *.swf* file stores information about the contents of each keyframe in the movie. In this animation, each keyframe stores redundant information. Frame 1 contains the letter *F*, but frame 2 contains *F* and *L*, and so on, so information about the letter *F* is stored in the file seven times. On each keyframe in the animation, the Flash Player has to read information from the *.swf* file about the font, color, size, and position of the letter *F*. In this particular animation, it shouldn't make a difference, because the file is so small and not much is happening on stage. But in more complicated movies, redundant information like this can adversely affect download time and playback speed.

To reduce the amount of redundant information in this movie, we must first move each letter of the text to its own layer, then we'll stagger them in time:

1. Choose File → Save As, name the file *frame_by_frame_2.fla*, and save it in the *06* folder.

2. Undo repeatedly until you are left with the seven characters in the text on one frame. If you used the History panel to undo, instead of Ctrl/Cmd-Z, give yourself a gold star.

3. With the first frame selected, choose Modify → Timeline → Distribute to Layers. Each character moves to its own layer, and each layer is named according the letter that resides on it. *Layer 1* is empty, but we'll use it in a minute, so don't delete it.

4. Select the keyframe at frame 1 of every layer (except *Layer 1*) and drag it to frame 5.

5. Select frame 5 of the *L* layer and drag it to frame 6.

6. Select frame 5 of the *A* layer and drag it to frame 7.

7. Continue this process until each letter appears in succession. Leave an extra frame between the words

FLASH and FX. (To do this, move the F in FX to frame 11 instead of frame 10 and move the X to frame 12.)

8. Add a frame to each layer including *Layer 1* (using F5) at frame 12, except for the X layer. When you're done, your timeline should match Figure 6-2.

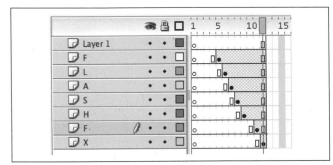

Figure 6-2. The timeline for the typewriter effect.

9. Play the animation by pressing Enter (or Return).

With each letter on its own layer, Flash needs to store information about each letter only once. Each letter is rendered once instead of being re-rendered on every keyframe in the animation. This is more efficient when rendering the movie in the Flash Player, as evidenced by the fact that we've cut the file size approximately in half (about 215 bytes).

Now we just need a *stop()* command on the last frame so we don't annoy users with a looping animation:

1. Change the name of *Layer 1* to *actions* and insert a keyframe at frame 12, the last frame of the animation.

2. Open the Actions panel (F9).

3. With frame 12 still selected, enter **stop();** into the Script pane of the Actions panel and save your work.

4. Publish the movie.

Before moving on, change the frame rate for the movie a few times to see how it affects the animation. What does a slower frame rate communicate? What is communicated by a higher frame rate? If this animation is used in a cartoon, a slow frame rate might imply that a character

is a slow typist. By varying the interval between the appearance of letters, you can create a more realistic typewriter effect in which the letters are not uniformly spaced in time. You could even add mistakes to imply that the typist is a beginner, or perhaps drunk.

When you get tired of thinking, let's move on.

ANIMATED TRANSITIONS

Creating frame-by-frame animation by hand can be extremely time-consuming, particularly when creating transitions such as shapes that morph into other shapes or illustrations that sharpen over time into photographs. But transitions such as these are an intriguing way to introduce graphical elements to a movie or carry the user from one page, or state, to another. In this section, we'll explore animated effects that can give your movie a professional touch and help maintain a unifying theme throughout a Flash project.

Shape tweens

An oft-seen transition technique is one in which an interface appears to draw itself, line by line, until it is complete and filled with content. An example of this can be seen at the American Splendor site (*http://www.americansplendormovie.com*), where a set of panels for a comic strip is drawn right in front of you and filled with images. This can be done with motion tweens, but it would involve using *masks*, which we'll talk about in Chapter 10, and would be more complicated than it needs to be. The solution? *Shape tweens*.

Let's see how it's done by creating line art of a house with a gradient background. First, we'll make a vertical line that appears to extend upward over time:

1. Create a new Flash document and save it as *shape_tweens.fla* in the *06* folder. Change the frame rate to 18 fps. Use the default Stage dimensions.

2. Activate the Line tool and set the stroke color to black with a stroke weight of 1.

3. Draw a very short and straight vertical line at the bottom of the Stage, toward the right side.

4. Convert frame 5 to a keyframe (by pressing F6).

5. At frame 5, activate the Selection tool and move the cursor over the top end of the line you drew in Step 3. The cursor displays a small right angle icon next to it. This means you are hovering over the endpoint of a line.

6. Click and drag upward to extend the length of the line to the vertical center of the Stage.

7. Select a frame on *Layer 1* between frames 1 and 5. Choose Shape from the Tween drop-down list in the Properties panel. The frame span turns light green and an arrow appears between the two keyframes, as shown in Figure 6-3.

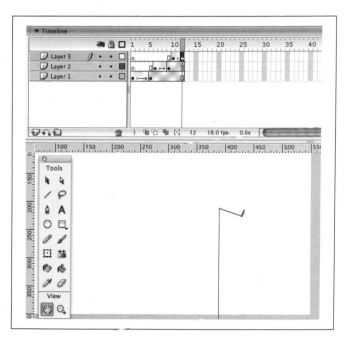

Figure 6-4. Add more lines to make a house.

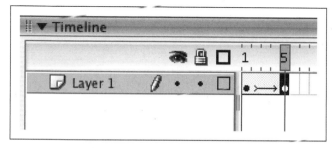

Figure 6-3. A shape tween as it appears in the timeline.

8. Press Enter (or Return) to play the animation.

The line starts short (in frame 1) and gets longer, ending at frame 5. Instead of creating the animation one frame at a time, the shape tween changes the length of the line for us. This is similar to a motion tween, but with shape tweens, we do not need to convert the line to a symbol.

Let's continue our animation by drawing the remainder of the house:

1. Insert a new layer, named *Layer 2* by default, and add a keyframe at frame 6 of the new layer.

2. Add frames to *Layer 1* so you can see the previously drawn line to know where to continue drawing. Starting in frame 6 of *Layer 2*, draw a short, diagonal line from the top end of the vertical line to about 20 pixels to the right, to match Figure 6-4.

3. Add a keyframe to frame 9 of *Layer 2* and, in that keyframe, stretch the new line so it's about an inch long.

4. Add a shape tween to the frame span between frames 6 and 9.

5. Add a new layer, *Layer 3*, insert a keyframe at frame 10, and draw another short, diagonal line.

6. Add a keyframe at frame 12, stretch the line, and add a shape tween to the frame span, as shown in Figure 6-4.

7. Repeat Steps 5 and 6 until your timeline and Stage match *shape_tween_1.fla*, located in the *06* folder. (If necessary, add frames so that each layer extends to frame 12.)

8. Test the movie to see the animation.

Now we have a line drawing of a house that appears to draw itself over time.

Let's finish up our animation by adding the background and a *stop( )* command:

1. Insert a new layer named *bg* and drag it to the bottom of the layer stack.

2. Lock the other layers in the timeline by clicking the black dot in the padlock column next to each layer name. A padlock icon indicates that a layer is

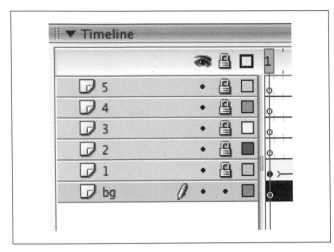

Figure 6-5. Lock the layers.

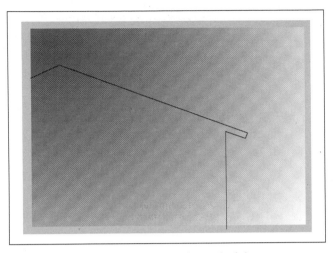

Figure 6-6. Apply a gradient to the end of the animation on the bg layer.

locked, as shown in Figure 6-5. A locked layer, again, prevents elements from being added to the layer and prevents elements already on the Stage for that layer from being selected or edited.

3. At frame 26, insert a keyframe on the *bg* layer and use the Rectangle tool to draw a box that covers the entire Stage. You can resize and reposition it with the Properties panel for accuracy.

4. Add another keyframe to frame 40 of the *bg* layer, select the box, and open the Color Mixer panel (Window → Design Panels → Color Mixer).

5. In the Color Mixer, set the Fill style to Radial, and change the gradient color on the left side to sky blue.

6. Using the Paint Bucket tool, click once in the upper-left corner of the Stage. The radial gradient is centered where you clicked the mouse, making the background look like sunlight that fades to darkness, as shown in Figure 6-6.

7. Add a shape tween to the frame span on the *bg* layer to tween the radial gradient.

8. Insert a new layer, above the others, named *actions*. ActionScript can be added to layers even if they are locked. Therefore, you can lock your *actions* layer to prevent graphic elements from being added to it while still allowing scripts to be added as needed.

THE DRAWING API

This chapter demonstrates some relatively straightforward animation, such as using shape tweens to draw the outline of a house. Throughout this book we've created animations at authoring time, and you might be wondering by now how to handle more complex line drawings and animations, particularly at runtime. For example, suppose you wanted a drawing to appear in response to the user's mouse movement, so the artwork could not be created at authoring time.

Luckily, ActionScript offers the Drawing API (which stands for *application program interface*). It isn't as scary as it sounds, because the Drawing API is really just a way to imitate a simple pen plotter (like the Hewlett-Packard plotters used to create CAD drawings). Furthermore, the Drawing API is really just a group of commands, such as *lineStyle( )*, *moveTo( )*, and *lineTo( )*, that can be executed on movie clips. A simple example to draw a three-pixel-wide, black line dynamically might look like this:

9. In the *actions* layer, add a keyframe to the last frame of the animation (frame 40) and add a *stop( )* command using the Actions panel (don't forget the semicolon).

10. Save your work and test the movie.

The movie, at this point, looks like a good beginning for an ad for a company that builds houses, so let's add some text to the movie:

1. Create a new layer named *text*. Flash inserts the layer above whatever layer was selected at the time. If necessary, drag the *text* layer higher in the layer stack to ensure it is in the foreground. Add a keyframe at frame 40.

2. Activate the Text tool, choose Verdana from the font drop-down list in the Properties panel, and set the font size to 16. Also, activate the Bold option by clicking on the B icon in the Properties panel.

3. To set the font color, click on the color chooser in the Properties panel, and then click on the sky blue color in the background gradient. Choosing the color from the gradient ensures you choose the correct shade of blue, as opposed to choosing it from the color chooser.

4. Click once on the Stage to create a text field and type **Flash Builds Homes Faster than Anyone**. Press Enter (or Return) after the word *Homes* so the text appears on two lines.

5. Convert the text to a graphic symbol named *text_gr* and position it where you think it looks good in relation to the background gradient and the house.

6. Add another keyframe to frame 50 of the *text* layer.

7. At frame 40, select the instance of the *text_gr* symbol and use the Properties panel to set its alpha value to 0. Then add a motion tween to the frame span.

8. Drag the keyframe on frame 40 of the *actions* layer to frame 50. This moves the *stop( )*; action from frame 40 to frame 50. Therefore, the playhead won't stop until it reaches frame 50.

9. Save and test. To compare your animation with mine, see *shape_tween_complete.fla* in the 06 folder.

The animation is complete, and you've mastered the basics of shape tweens (hopefully). If you make a mistake with a shape tween, you can undo it by using Edit → Undo, or you can select the tween and set the Tween option in the Properties panel to None (or choose Insert → Timeline → Remove Tween). The techniques you've learned here can be applied throughout a larger Flash project, such as a web site or series of ads, to unify a design and improve the user experience.

For example, if a project involves guiding users through a virtual tour of a house, you might use the self-drawing-UI approach from this chapter to draw the wireframe (blueprint-like outline) of a room. When going to the next room you could "undraw" the room by reversing the drawing sequence and segue into a new section by building the next room (perhaps changing directions along the way, to give the illusion of going upstairs). From this, users would be able to build a mental map of the house based on where the line takes them. All this can be built using shape tweens.

```
// Create a new empty clip to act as the drawing canvas
var clip = this.createEmptyMovieClip("canvas_mc",
    this.getNextHighestDepth());
// Create a 3-pixel, black stroke, with 100% alpha
canvas_mc.lineStyle (3, 0x000000, 100);
// Start at origin (upperleft of Stage or center of
// parent clip)
canvas_mc.moveTo(0, 0);
// Draw a horizontal line 100 pixels long
canvas_mc.lineTo(100, 0);
```

For many more details on the Drawing API, see Flash's online documentation or *ActionScript for Flash MX: The Definitive Guide* (O'Reilly).

Next, we'll look at how *shape hints* can help us control the animation of a more complicated shape tween to create another type of transition.

Improving tweens with shape hints

The preceding section shows a simple example of shape tweening. It is easy for Flash to figure out how to tween the animation from a short line to a long line (it simply extends the line over time). But suppose we want to morph between two shapes that aren't as similar to each other as a short line is to a long line. One common technique is to use *shape hints* to guide a shape tween, perhaps to morph one letter into another.

For example, you might want to morph the letter *e* into the letter *c*. Flash cannot always morph letters gracefully on its own—sometimes we need to help it out. Regardless, letters first need to be converted to vector shapes using the Modify → Break Apart command (applying Modify → Break Apart once to a multiletter text field breaks it into individual letters, in which case you must apply the command again to break each letter into a vector shape).

Although the shapes of the letters *e* and *c* seem similar to us, when Flash tweens complex shapes, the results are often unpredictable. Flash works best when two shapes have the same number of perimeters, but the lowercase letter *e* has two perimeters (the outside and the eye in the middle) whereas the letter *c* has a single continuous perimeter. This disparity in the number of perimeters is more apparent if you temporarily view the content in outline mode (a.k.a. wireframe mode) using View → Preview Mode → Outlines.

When faced with such a situation, Flash performs the transformation in whatever way it can, which can end up looking, well, ugly. A workaround is to use an invisible hairline gap to essentially make the lowercase *e* have a single continuous perimeter, which Flash can more easily correlate to the perimeter of the letter *c*. This hack is described in detail in *Flash Hacks* (O'Reilly).

Even when the two shapes have the same number of perimeters, Flash doesn't automatically perform the morph in the way we might consider most sensible or graceful. To remedy this, we use shape hints, which are small dots added to a shape tween to guide its transition. To see this in action, let's use shape hints to help morph the capital letter *C* to the capital letter *E*:

1. Create a new Flash document and save it as *shape_hint.fla* in the *06* folder and change the Stage's dimensions to 200 × 200.

2. At frame 1 of *Layer 1*, type a giant *C* on the Stage (using the Text tool and the Properties panel) and then center it (relative to the Stage) using the Align panel.

3. Convert frame 20 of *Layer 1* to a keyframe, delete the letter *C* from the Stage, and type the letter *E* in its place. Center it as well.

4. Select frame 20, which simultaneously selects the letter *E* on the Stage, and press Ctrl/Cmd-B to break it apart. Instead of being static text, the letter is now raw vector art, as shown in Figure 6-7.

5. Break apart the letter *C* on frame 1 using the same technique.

Figure 6-7. Break apart each letter so a shape tween can be applied to it.

6. Select the frame span on *Layer 1* and choose Shape from the Tween drop-down list in the Properties panel.

7. Press Enter/Return to view the animation.

The letter *C* morphs into an *E* as we requested, but the animation looks bad. Let's add some shape hints to guide the shape tween:

1. At frame 1, choose Modify → Shape → Add Shape Hint. This adds a small circled *a* to the Stage.

2. The animation will look better if the middle line for the letter *E* emerges from the center of the letter *C*. So drag the *a* shape hint to the center of the letter *C*, as shown in Figure 6-8.

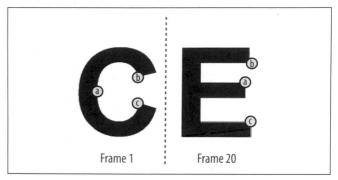

Figure 6-9. Add two more shape hints at frames 1 and 20 and position them to guide the animation.

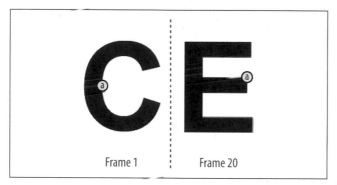

Figure 6-8. Add a shape hint to frames 1 and 20 of the animation.

3. At frame 20, drag the *a* shape hint to the right end of the middle line for the letter *E*.

4. Play the animation again.

Now, the shape hint pulls the center of the letter *C* to the right until it becomes the center line for the letter *E*. Much smoother, don't you think? Let's add more shape hints to make the tween look even better:

1. At frame 1, add two more shape hints. Drag the *b* shape hint to the end of the top curved line for the letter *C*, then drag the *c* shape hint to the end of the bottom curved line, as shown in Figure 6-9.

2. At frame 20, drag the *b* and *c* shape hints to the ends of the top and bottom straight lines in the letter *E*.

3. Save your work and play the animation.

Now *that's* a smooth animation. The letter *C* very gracefully turns itself into the letter *E*.

Shape hints can be used to guide the transition of any vector shape into another. In the context of our imagi-nary home-builder client, a shape tween of a capital letter *A* morphing into a wireframe house (or vice versa) might be in order.

When using this morphing style of animation, keep in mind that shape tweens and shape hints can be applied only to vectors that have not been converted to a symbol. Therefore, to apply a shape tween to a symbol instance, you must first break apart the symbol instance using Modify → Break Apart (this effectively separates the in-stance from its source symbol).

Tracing bitmaps

Flash is capable of much more than simple shape morphs, and in this section, we'll look at another way to achieve engaging visual transitions in our movies.

An increasingly common transition style is that in which a cartoon- or illustrative-style image sharpens itself, over time, into a photograph. But if you're like me, your abili-ties as an illustrator are, well, lacking, and creating the initial image for a transition like this is not so simple. So what's a boy (or girl) to do when in need of a nice, artful illustration? Trace the same photograph with which you plan to end the transition using the Trace Bitmap feature! The effect is configurable and the result can be quite el-egant. Let's see how it's done by importing a photograph and tracing it.

We'll start with a *.png* file and create an illustration from it. You can obtain a starting photograph from commer-cial art libraries (such as Comstock.com or other stock sites), by scanning in a photograph, or by using a digital camera. For this exercise, we'll use a photo of a house and continue building Flash content for our imaginary home-builder client.

To create our starting illustration:

1. Create a new Flash document and save it as *trace_bitmap.fla* in the *06* folder.

2. Change the Stage dimensions to 315 × 500.

3. Import *house.png*, located in the *06* folder, by choosing File → Import → Import to Stage. Import it using the Single Flattened Bitmap option.

4. Align the upper-left corner of the image to (0, 0) on the Stage. If your image is larger than the Stage, with the Stage effectively cropping the photograph, it gives the sense that the image cannot be contained and has taken over the screen. This look is often used in magazine ads and television commercials to convey a larger-than-life feeling.

5. With the image selected, choose Modify → Bitmap → Trace Bitmap to open the Trace Bitmap dialog box, shown in Figure 6-10.

6. In the dialog box, set Color Threshold to 120, Minimum Area to 40, Curve Fit to Normal, and Corner Threshold to Normal.

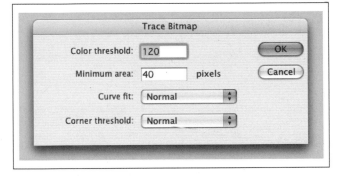

Figure 6-10. The Trace Bitmap dialog box.

7. Click OK to close the dialog box and run the process. Flash traces the bitmap image with strokes and fills, replacing the original image with a vector illustration (which means Flash is a better artist than I am). The final illustration appears as a meshed collection of dots, as shown in Figure 6-11.

Figure 6-11. The traced house image converted to vectors.

8. Deselect the image to see how it looks.

9. Test the movie.

The file size is only 5 KB. The original bitmap image was 633 KB, so tracing the bitmap made a substantial difference. However, the bandwidth savings comes at a price. Much of the detail is lost and many of the colors bleed into one another.

Let's adjust our settings to see if we can create a cleaner version:

1. Undo twice to return the bitmap image to its original state. Be careful not to undo too many times—if you undo the import, you'll be left with a blank Flash document.

2. Choose the Trace Bitmap menu option again to reopen the dialog box.

3. Set Color Threshold to 40. The Color Threshold option determines how much a color can change before Flash sees it as a new color. A lower number results in more colors.

4. Set Minimum Area to 10. This option determines how much space a color must cover, so a lower number results in a greater amount of detail.

5. Set the Curve Fit option to Very Tight. This results in more curves, which, although it provides more detail, also creates a less optimized image. A high number of curves results in a larger file size, but this image is small enough that it won't be a problem.

6. For Corner Threshold, choose Many Corners. This results in more defined edges within the image, again providing greater detail, as seen in Figure 6-12.

7. Click OK to trace the bitmap. Deselect the image when the trace is complete.

8. Test the movie.

Although the file size is now a bit larger than before, about 42 KB, it still represents a substantial savings over the original image size of 633 KB. And this version of the image has much more detail and makes a nice illustration.

Now that the bitmap has been traced, we can use it as the basis for further work. Let's integrate it into our design as follows:

1. Click on the Stage to display Stage properties in the Properties panel.

2. Select the area of sky that appears in the image without selecting parts of the house itself, as shown in Figure 6-12. Hold down the Shift key while doing this to select multiple fill areas. Delete them when you're done. You may want to zoom in on the Stage while doing this to avoid deleting anything you want to keep (press Z to activate the Zoom tool).

3. When you're done, click and drag (or use Edit → Select All) to select the entire image, then convert it to a graphic symbol named *house*.

4. Save your *.fla* file.

Figure 6-12. Select the fill areas that comprise the sky and delete them.

When using a bitmap image as part of a symbol, the original bitmap must be kept in the Library because it is referenced by the symbol, and this can increase file size. A traced bitmap, however, is an independent vector graphic that does not reference the original bitmap in any way (despite having been created from it), so it's not necessary to keep the original bitmap. This results in lower file size. In this case, though, we'll use the bitmap again, so don't delete it.

If you do not need the original bitmap for other purposes, you can delete it from the Library. (This is not mandatory, as unused library assets are not exported into the published *.swf* file, but it helps keep the Library organized and the file size for the *.fla* file down, taking up less hard drive space.)

UNIFYING A DESIGN

Good design often involves a unifying element, or "character," such as the thematic use of color. One element or effect often becomes the basis of the design style for an entire project, used to unify disparate design elements.

A Flash site, for example, might have 10 different sections of content, each with its own look and feel, making it impossible to use color as a unifier. In cases like this, a transition effect or graphic might be used to unify the design instead. For example, renowned Flash designer Hillman Curtis used a soccer ball as a unifying theme for the site to support the movie *Bend it Like Beckham (http://www2.foxsearchlight. com/benditlikebeckham)*. Each section of the site involves at least one soccer ball, lending a sense of continuity throughout the site.

Similarly, this book, as you may have noticed, features a box as its main character. The purpose of the book is to help you get out of your proverbial box by learning to use Flash to help you accomplish your goals, so the obvious graphical theme is to use a box in almost every exercise, push its limits, and eventually bust out of it.

The house image we just completed will serve as a good beginning for the illustration-to-photograph transition.

To create the transition in which the vector image of the house appears to sharpen into a photograph, follow these steps:

1. Position an instance of the *house* symbol, hereafter referred to as the *house* instance for brevity, with its upper-left corner at (0, 0).

2. Rename *Layer 1* to *house_anim* and add a keyframe at frame 10.

3. Select the image at frame 1 only and set its alpha to 0 (leave the alpha in frame 10 at 100 percent). Then, click inside the frame span and choose Insert → Timeline → Create Motion Tween (which does the same thing as choosing Motion from the Tween drop-down list in the Properties panel). This causes the house to fade in over 10 frames.

4. Add a new layer named *bitmap_anim*, drag it to the bottom of the layer stack, and insert a keyframe at frame 10.

5. With frame 10 selected, drag *house.png* from the Library to the Stage. Position it to (0, 0) so the vector house in the *house* instance lays perfectly in front of the bitmap house in the original image.

6. Convert the bitmap to a graphic symbol named *bitmap*.

7. On the *bitmap_anim* layer, insert a keyframe at frame 20.

8. At frame 10, select the *bitmap* instance, set its alpha to 0, and apply a motion tween to the frame span. Now, the *house* instance fades in, and then the *bitmap* instance fades in behind it.

9. Add keyframes at frames 20 and 30 of the *house_anim* layer.

10. At frame 30, select the *house* instance and set its alpha to 0, then apply a motion tween to the frame span from frame 20 to frame 30.

11. At frame 30 of the *bitmap_anim* layer, press F5 to add frames.

12. Change the frame rate for the movie to 18 fps.

13. Save your work and test the movie.

If you've followed these steps correctly, your timeline should look like the one shown in Figure 6-13.

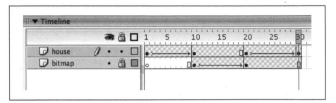

Figure 6-13. The timeline for the illustration-to-photograph animation.

Can you guess what I'm going to say next? Yup. We need to add a *stop( )* command to keep the movie from looping:

1. Close the Preview window.

2. Add a new layer named *actions*.

3. Insert a keyframe at frame 30, and attach the *stop( )*; command using the Actions panel.

4. Save and test the movie again.

If each section of a project involves images of houses, but each image has different colors and backgrounds, a transition effect like the one you just completed could be an excellent unifier. Each section could start as an illustration that sharpens into a photograph. Other unifying elements, such as font and font style, color, and perhaps a distinctive graphic style can—and usually should—be used to unify a design as well.

To explore this concept further, visit any of your favorite web sites. Try to locate one or more design elements that unify the site as a whole. On the Bend it Like Beckham site (*http://www2.foxsearchlight.com/benditlikebeckham*), it was a soccer ball. On Macromedia's web site (*http://www.macromedia.com*), it's a collection of elements, such as muted colors, a newspaper-style layout, organization of content into panels, and the use of a shadow on each panel.

TIMELINE EFFECTS

Speaking of shadows, Flash MX 2004 has the built-in ability to automate the creation of several effects, such as a drop shadow. (Nice segue, huh?)

Let's get familiar with timeline effects by quickly adding a drop shadow to a graphic. After this, we'll take a look at a custom timeline effect.

Adding a drop shadow in 30 seconds or less

To implement the drop shadow effect, we'll use the same process I use any time I want to test out a new effect very quickly. I draw a box on the stage, convert it to a symbol, and apply the effect to it. In fact, this process is what sparked the idea for *Flash Out of the Box*.

To create the shadow:

1. Create a new Flash document and save it as *drop_shadow.fla* in the *06* folder.

2. Draw a box on the Stage, and convert it to a graphic symbol named *box*.

3. Double-click on the *box* instance on the Stage to enter Edit mode.

4. In Edit mode, select the box shape (select both the stroke and fill) and choose Insert → Timeline Effects → Effects → Drop Shadow. The Drop Shadow dialog box, as shown in Figure 6-14, opens.

5. Change the color of the shadow by clicking on the Color chooser. Select dark gray.

6. For Shadow Offset, enter **5** for the X and Y fields.

7. Click the Update Preview button in the upper-right corner of the dialog box to see how the effect will look.

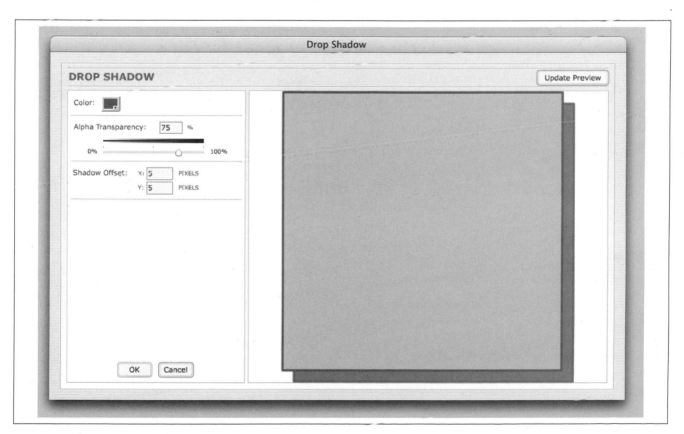

Figure 6-14. Dialog box for the Drop Shadow timeline effect.

8. Click OK to close the dialog box and apply the effect.

9. Save and close the file. We'll use it again later.

Every box instance on the Stage now has its own drop shadow. See? I told you it would be quick. We've just made use of a new feature in Flash MX 2004 and Flash Pro known as *timeline effects*. A timeline effect is kind of like a graphical macro—one command can create a graphical effect. Without the built-in drop shadow timeline effect, we'd have to add a layer in Edit mode, copy and paste the box onto the new layer, change its color, position it, and manually leave Edit mode. Using a timeline effect is much faster.

Custom timeline effects

Arguably, the coolest thing about timeline effects is that you can create your own or download effects created by other developers from the Macromedia Flash Exchange. Creating a timeline effect from scratch requires JSFL (Flash JavaScript—I know, the acronym is backward), a full discussion of which is beyond the scope of this book (if you want more information, JSFL is covered in the Flash Help documentation and in the *FL_JSAPI.pdf* file on the book's CD-ROM). Here's a look at an effect created by another developer to give you an idea of the power of timeline effects. Special thanks go to Ron Haberle (*http://www.giantproblems.tv*) for whipping up this effect on a moment's notice.

First, we need to install the effect:

1. Quit Flash.

2. Locate the *Giant_Problems* folder inside the *06* folder, Shift-select all of the files in the folder, and press Ctrl/Cmd-C to copy the items.

3. Copy the files into the *Effects* folder in the Flash install directory on your hard drive, which is found in a path similar to one of the following locations, depending on your operating system and your software configuration. In each of the following paths, substitute your user account name for *USER* and your Flash language code for *LANGUAGE_CODE*, which is "en" for English:

Windows 2000, Windows XP
```
C:\Documents and Settings\USER\Local Settings\
Application Data\Macromedia\Flash MX 2004\
LANGUAGE_CODE\Configuration\Effects
```

Note that the *Local Settings* folder is hidden by default but can be revealed in Windows File Explorer using Tools → Folder Options → View → Advanced Settings → Files and Folders → Hidden Files and Folders → Show Hidden Files and Folders.

Windows XP, Windows 98 single-user systems
```
C:\Windows\Application Data\Macromedia\Flash MX
2004\LANGUAGE_CODE\Configuration\Effects
```

Windows 98 multiuser systems
```
C:\Windows\Profiles\USER\Application Data\
Macromedia\Flash MX 2004\LANGUAGE_CODE\
Configuration\Effects
```

PLUGINS FROM RED GIANT

Red Giant, a software developer of plugins for video professionals, has released a set of timeline effects that I find incredibly useful. The set—which includes Distort FX, Pixel FX, and Text FX—enables Flash nerds everywhere to create text animations, Photoshop-like bevel and emboss effects, and a slew of other timesaving effects that give Flash extra graphic editing and automation powers it never had before. In other words, the effects are freakin' cool.

The effects set costs $149 and can be purchased online at *http://www.redgiantsoftware.com/flash.html*.

I have no affiliation with Red Giant, so this plugin plug is sincere despite appearing shameless.

Macintosh OS X

```
Macintosh HD/Users/USER/Library/Application
Support/Macromedia/Flash MX 2004/LANGUAGE_CODE/
Configuration/Effects
```

The preceding steps install the effects where Flash can find them. The custom effects appear under the Insert → Timeline Effects menu in Flash.

To use the new timeline effect in Flash:

1. Launch Flash.

2. Create a new Flash document and save it as *giant_problems_effect.fla* in the *06* folder.

3. Enter the words **Falling Text** into a static text field on the Stage, with a font size of 40, using any font you like. Position the text at the center of the Stage.

4. With the text still selected, choose Insert → Timeline Effects → Giant Problems → Falling Text. The Falling Text Effect dialog box, as shown in Figure 6-15, opens.

5. In the Horizontal Options section of the dialog box, set the Offset to 100 and choose Left. This makes the text fall from 100 pixels to the left of the ending position for each character. The preview of the animation will not update until we click the Update Preview button, which we'll do in a moment.

6. In the Vertical Options section, choose 70 and Top for the Offset options.

7. In the Misc. Options section, choose 8 for the Speed, Left to Right for Text Orientation, and uncheck the Show Falling Trails option.

8. Click the Update Preview button. The animation in the preview pane updates and we see how the effect looks.

9. Click OK to close the dialog box and apply the effect.

The timeline effect automatically adds frames to the timeline, which now contains 85 frames. Timeline effects automatically generate graphic symbols (every timeline effect does this), which also have their own internal timelines. The important difference for this discussion between animated graphic symbols and movie clips is that movie clips require only one frame on the main timeline to play in the published movie. A graphic symbol must be present on its parent timeline long enough to play its own timeline in its entirety. In other words, if a graphic symbol contains an animation on its internal timeline that is 40 frames long, its parent timeline (the timeline on which an instance of the symbol is placed) must contain at least 40 frames; otherwise, the graphic's animation won't play in its entirety.

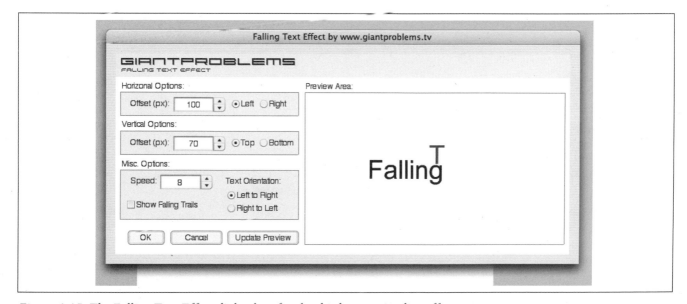

Figure 6-15. The Falling Text Effect dialog box for the third-party timeline effect.

There is no benefit to creating animation on a graphic's internal timeline unless you need to:

- Reuse the animation (in which case, you could use a movie clip symbol instead and gain the ability to control the animation via ActionScript)

- See it animate on the main timeline during authoring (animations in movie clips do not display while scrubbing the playhead of the clip's parent timeline)

Flash can use *easing* to create a more natural-looking animation. Easing increases or decreases the size of successive animation steps to create the illusion of acceleration or deceleration. Let's edit the effect to change the easing values for the motion tweens inside of the graphic symbol's timeline:

1. In the Library, locate the symbol named *Falling Text 1*. Notice that there are 11 other symbols in the Library, each of which is one of the letters used in the text animation.

2. Double-click on the graphic symbol icon in the Library for *Falling Text 1* to enter Edit mode. Click OK to bypass the warning message that appears. The warning message tells us we will lose the ability to edit the settings for the effect if we continue, but it's not entirely true. We can edit the symbol in Edit mode as much as we want and still edit the effect settings later.

3. In Edit mode for *Falling Text 1*, notice that all the characters have been converted to graphic symbols and placed into position, and motion tweens have been applied to create the effect. All of this was done automatically when we applied the timeline effect.

4. Expand the Timeline panel enough to see all of the layers. To do this, click on the bottom edge of the Timeline panel and drag down.

5. Press the Ctrl key (Windows) or Cmd key (Macintosh) and select one frame in each motion tween in the animation.

6. Change the Ease value in the Properties panel to 100 (Ease Out). This makes each letter start fast and then slow to a stop.

7. Save and test the movie.

The effect is complete.

From here, you can add a *stop( )* command to the end of the animation, but you'll have to change the Behavior type for the symbol instance to Movie Clip. Movie clips can have ActionScript nested inside of them, but graphic symbols cannot.

Knowing how to create a few effects in Flash can take you a long way. The methods used to create each one can be applied to many others, and as you get more experience designing these elements, your arsenal will grow. In this chapter, we've seen how:

- Frame-by-frame animation, though time-consuming, can be used to create text effects

- Shape tweens create the illusion of drawing over time

- Shape hints can be used to morph one shape into another without a lot of manual effort

- Bitmaps can be traced to appear as vector illustrations that are easily editable in Flash

- Effects, used in conjunction with other design elements, can unify a design

- Timeline effects can speed up the process of creating effects with Flash

Where do you go from here? You go on to the next chapter, of course. But first, take some time to experiment.

Draw a box on the Stage and apply some timeline effects to it. The timeline effects that generate animations result in looping animations, but if you've followed the exercises in the previous chapters, I bet you can figure out how to (hint, hint) change the symbol's Behavior type to Movie Clip and add a *stop( )* command. When the box gets boring, create a line of text and apply various effects to it, such as the timeline effect named Explosion. When you're done, enter Edit mode for the effect (by double-clicking on the symbol in the Library) and study how the animation was made. Is every character in the text converted to a symbol? Does it need to be? Why?

Also, while you're looking for design unifiers at other sites, take a look at the Bend it Like Beckham site (cited earlier) and other animated sites to see if you can dissect how they were done. Flash sites usually involve a lot of ActionScript, and you'll certainly learn more about ActionScript in later chapters, but you've already learned everything you need to create the animations on a site like Bend it Like Beckham.

If you want to see some Flash work worthy of nightmares, turn up the volume on your computer (better yet, use headphones and crank it) and check out the haunting Conclave Obscurum (*http://conclaveobscurum.ru*), which gets my vote for Most Artistically Disturbing Site on the Web. You now know some of the same things this site's designer knows, so good luck trying to sleep tonight.

When you're ready to digest some more, move on to Chapter 7.

7

EFFECTS AND BEYOND

As with animation, effects are often overused in Flash. So the goal of this chapter is to teach you not only some effects but how to use them wisely. The key is to use effects to advance or convey the Flash movie's purpose and not merely as eye candy. This chapter covers animation paths and motion design, and gives you more practice in achieving effects with ActionScript.

The preceding chapter introduced animation and text effects, including motion tweening and shape tweening. This chapter goes into effects in greater detail. Excessive use of effects will repel the very users you want to attract. So when is it best to use effects? As in most things, less is more—the best effects don't necessarily jump out at the user as an effect. For example, you might use effects to create variation without increasing the file download size. Or you might use a subtle effect, such as sliding in text when the user rolls the mouse over a hotspot. In this case, the effect is a useful feedback indicator. It says in a subtle way, "I am adapting the interface to your needs. What can I do for you next?" Contrast that with the case in which an effect is merely there so the designer can show off, which ends up assaulting instead of assuaging the user.

So let's look at some techniques for creating effects and their prudent use. We'll look at how to animate text, which can be used to highlight a particular item or add a subtle professional polish to an otherwise mundane design. Text can be a great way to convey information. For example, you can use text effects for titling over video.

In the second half of the chapter, we'll look at some motion effects. Again, motion should be used prudently. For example, in a physics simulation, realistic motion can be a vital teaching tool. This chapter also gives us another opportunity to use ActionScript—in this case, to animate programmatically—and see how it compares to using timeline-based animation.

Of course, all these techniques will also help you become more familiar with Flash and its possibilities.

TEXT EFFECTS

Remember the typewriter effect we created in Chapter 6? Well, that's nothing compared to what's possible with Flash if we employ a little more creativity. Remember, though, that while text effects are a powerful way to make text pop in any design, they should be used in moderation. The last thing most users want to see is a bunch of letters flying around the screen arbitrarily (most Flash pieces shouldn't be performance art).

Cascading text

First, we'll create the ever-popular cascading text effect, as shown in Figure 7-1, in which the text appears to soar into position from close up to far away. An effect like this one is often used to make a particular word or term the focus of an animation so its importance is communicated to the user. Text effects might be applied to a company or product name to help brand it, or to something as simple as a step number in a tutorial to segue to the next section.

Figure 7-1. Cascading text effect.

To create the cascading text effect:

1. Create a new Flash document and save it as *cascading_text.fla* in the *07* folder.

2. Change the Stage dimensions to 190 × 85, and set the frame rate to 18 fps.

3. Activate the Text tool and use the Properties panel to set the font to Verdana, set the font size to 24, set the text color to black, and make the font boldface. If your text effect doesn't work at runtime, you probably used a device (system) font or forgot to embed the font using the Character button in the Properties panel, as described in Chapter 6. Embedding the font is necessary for text effects, such as rotation, for which Flash needs the font outline information.

4. On the Stage, enter the word **CASCADE**, in all capital letters, in a text field.

5. Position the word at the horizontal and vertical center of the Stage.

6. Break apart the word into individual letters (by selecting the word and pressing Ctrl/Cmd-B), as shown in Figure 7-2.

Figure 7-2. Break apart the word CASCADE.

Now some tweaking is necessary. Unlike the frame-by-frame typewriter effect we created in the preceding chapter, each letter in this animation starts large and ends small, so a motion tween must be applied to each frame span. Motion tweens, again, can be applied only to symbols on a timeline, so each letter must be converted to a symbol before it can be animated. By this point, you should know how to do that, but there is a catch: two of the letters appear more than once (the letters *C* and *A*). It would not be efficient to turn both occurrences of the letter *C* into separate symbols, and we can't use duplicate symbol names in the Library, so we'll consolidate by reusing the letters *C* and *A*.

To do this:

1. Select the letter *C* on the Stage and press F8 to convert it to a graphic symbol named *C*.

2. Delete the second letter *C* (in the middle of the word *CASCADE*)

3. Select the first letter *C* and copy it to the clipboard.

4. Right-click (Windows) or Cmd-click (Mac) on the Stage and choose Paste in Place from the contextual menu. A second instance of the *C* symbol is pasted onto the Stage directly atop the first one.

5. Without deselecting, press the right arrow key on your keyboard to move the new instance into position in the center of the word. You can speed up the process by holding down the Shift key while pressing the arrow, which moves the instance in 10-pixel increments. For finer control, release the Shift

key and continue using the arrow keys to nudge the instance into position.

6. Repeat Steps 1–4 for the letter *A*, naming the symbol *A*, and move the second instance into the appropriate place in the word.

Now we have a more efficient movie, using multiple instances of the *C* and *A* symbols. Let's continue converting the rest of the letters to symbols and distributing them to their own layers:

1. Convert the remaining letters to symbols, naming them *S*, *D*, and *E*.

2. Using the Selection tool, click and drag on the Stage to select all of the symbol instances at once, then choose Modify → Timeline → Distribute to Layers to place each instance on its own layer at frame 1. Then delete *Layer 1*, which is now empty.

3. For convenience, reorder the layers so they appear in the same order as in the word *CASCADE*.

4. Select frame 20 on every layer (by clicking and dragging downward from the top layer to the bottom) and press F6 to convert each frame to a keyframe, as shown in Figure 7-3.

5. Move the playhead back to frame 1 by clicking on frame 1 in the timeline.

Next, we need to define the look of each symbol instance at the beginning of the animation (frame 1). For this effect, we'll increase the size of each instance individually:

1. Choose View → Rulers, if the rulers are not already visible. We'll use a guide to make sure each instance on the Stage at frame 1 is scaled to the same dimensions.

2. Click on the top horizontal ruler and drag downward to add a guide to the work area (the gray area surrounding the Stage). You may need to zoom out (using View → Zoom Out, the Zoom tool in the Tools panel, or the percentage zoom drop-down list in the Timeline panel) to see the work area around the Stage. Position the guide approximately 35 pixels above the top edge of the Stage. Use the numbers in the rulers to help you.

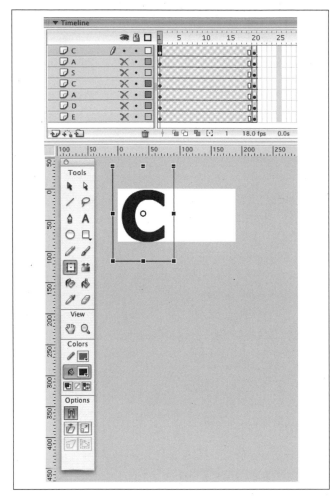

Figure 7-3. Select frame 20 on every layer at once and press F6 to add keyframes.

3. Select the *C* instance on the far-left side of the Stage, then activate the Free Transform tool.

4. Press Shift, then click and drag any corner of the *C* instance's bounding box to increase its size. Drag until the top edge of the bounding box covers the guide above the Stage, as shown in Figure 7-3. (The green line of the guide turns pink when the bounding box is directly on top of it.) Pressing Shift constrains the proportions of the instance and ensures the instance scales from its center point.

5. Repeat Step 4 for each instance on the Stage. To help you differentiate instances as they begin to overlap each other, toggle the Show/Hide Layer option on each layer by clicking the black dot shown in the eye

Figure 7-4. Resize each letter at frame 1 using the Free Transform tool.

column next to each layer, as shown in Figure 7-3. A red *X* appears when a layer is hidden.

6. When each instance has been scaled, reveal all the layers by clicking the Show/Hide All Layers button (the eye icon) in the Timeline panel. When you're done, your Stage should match Figure 7-4 at frame 1.

To complete the effect, we need to make the instances on frame 1 invisible and apply motion tweens so the instances fade in. After that, we need to stagger the tweened frame spans, so each letter appears in succession. Let's perform the fade-in portion first:

1. Select all the instances on frame 1, choose Alpha from the Color drop-down list in the Properties panel, and drag the Alpha slider to 0. All the instances are now invisible.

2. Select a frame on every layer, somewhere between frame 1 and 20, and choose Motion from the Tween drop-down list in the Properties panel (if you haven't been using Ctrl/Cmd-F3 to open the Properties panel, now is a good time to start). Motion tweens are applied to every layer at once.

3. Save your work and test the movie.

The animation starts with large, invisible letters and ends with each letter in place, but every instance appears at once, so we still need to stagger the animation:

1. Close the Preview window.

2. On the top layer (the first *C* layer), click and drag from frame 1 to frame 20 to select the entire frame span. Drag the frame span to the right so it starts at frame 5.

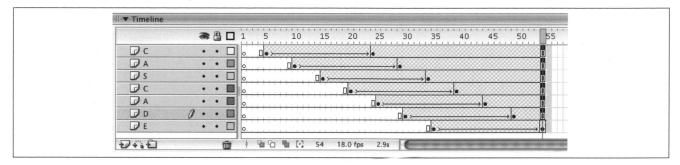

Figure 7-5. Drag the first animated frame span to frame 5 and stagger the remainder of the animation.

3. Repeat Step 2 until the frame span on each layer starts five frames later than the one above it, as shown in Figure 7-5.

4. Add frames to each layer to extend them to frame 54. To do this, select frame 50 on every layer and press F5 several times.

5. Save your work and test the movie.

Now, each letter in the animation appears in succession, and our text effect is complete. Notice, though, that the animation does not loop seamlessly. When the playhead reaches frame 54, it returns to frame 1 where the text disappears abruptly. This reminds me of those awful, blinking "CLICK HERE" animated banner ads that never end, and that's not good. Let's give the animation a smoother ending:

1. Select frame 70 on every layer (by clicking and dragging vertically down the layers) and press F6 to insert keyframes.

2. Also, add a keyframe to every layer at frame 80.

3. At frame 80, click and drag to select all the instances on the Stage, then set their alpha values to 0.

4. Apply a motion tween to every layer between frames 70 and 80.

Now, each instance fades out completely before the animation loops, but this doesn't maintain the appearance of cascading text. In the beginning of the animation, the instances fade in and scale one at a time, from left to right. To end the animation, the instances should fade out the same way. To accomplish this:

1. Stagger the frame spans at the end of the timeline so each one starts five frames later than the previous one, as shown in Figure 7-6.

2. At the ending keyframe of each layer, use the Free Transform tool to scale each instance down so it's almost invisible. Use the Zoom tool on the area of the Stage on which you want to zoom in.

3. Save your work and test the movie again.

Notice that we didn't add frames to the layers at the end of the animation. Because the instances disappear at the end of the animation, it's not necessary to keep them on the Stage. When the playhead passes frame 80, for example, the letter *C* can be removed from the Stage, as it is

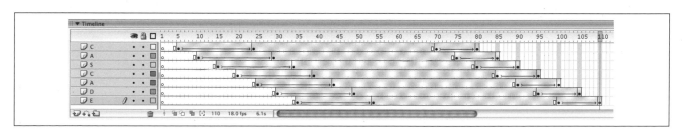

Figure 7-6. Stagger the frame spans at the end of the animation so the letters fade out one-by-one.

no longer needed. This is another way to make sure your movie is built efficiently.

Remember, the Flash Player stores information about the size, color, and position of every instance on the Stage, so even if an instance is invisible, the Flash Player still has to calculate its size and position, which is not efficient. Whenever a symbol instance does not need to appear on the Stage, it's good practice to remove it.

> **NOTE**
>
> One way to remove the instance is to simply let the frame span end without adding more frames to the layer. The other way is to insert a *blank keyframe*.

Let's see how blank keyframes affect the look of our animation:

1. Select frame 25 of the top layer in the timeline. This is the frame immediately following the end of the fade-in sequence for the letter *C*.

2. Press F7 (or choose Modify → Timeline → Convert to Blank Keyframe) to convert frame 25 to a blank keyframe. The gray between frames 25 and 70 disappears, indicating that nothing appears on the layer during those frames.

3. Insert a blank keyframe after each frame span in the beginning of the animation, so that your timeline matches Figure 7-7.

4. Save your work and test the movie.

Now, after each letter fades in and scales, it disappears abruptly. Then, at the end of the animation, each letter reappears and fades out. Adding just a few blank keyframes changed the animation dramatically.

There is quite a bit of time between the fade-in sequence and fade-out sequence, so let's shorten the gap:

1. Click and drag upward from the blank keyframe on the bottom layer (frame 55) to select that frame in every layer.

2. Press Shift-F5 to remove frames, one frame at a time, until the fade-out sequence begins on frame 56.

3. Save and test.

Now, as soon as the fade-in is complete, the fade-out starts. This creates a very different effect than when we started. Quite stylish.

There are millions of possible ways to animate text (don't forget to embed the font as discussed in Chapter 6). Your imagination is the only limitation, so be sure to eat your Wheaties. You'll need the energy.

MOTION EFFECTS

Filmmakers communicate in myriad ways. Themes are communicated through dialog, character action, staging, pacing, and even color. The movie *The Cooler*, for example, communicates the current mental state of the protagonist (played by William H. Macy) through his clothes. When his luck is bad, his suit is loose and frumpy. When his luck starts to turn around and he falls in love, his suit fits perfectly and he looks like a million bucks. At one point during the metamorphosis he stands in front of a sign inside a casino that says "Change" in bright, neon letters. The sign is just part of the background, but the way it integrates into the scene helps capture the moment.

Motion design can have an equally powerful effect. Convoluted intros on web sites are virtually extinct now

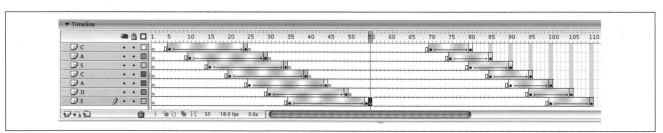

Figure 7-7. Insert blank keyframes to remove objects from the Stage when they are no longer needed.

(fortunately), but motion design is still alive and well, as it should be. If you were a site-hopper back in the early days of the Web, you remember page after page of static text. Today's web technology is capable of much more, and a little motion can dramatically improve the online experience. Can you imagine Donnie Darko (*http://donniedarko.com*), for example, without Flash?

Let's explore the use of motion effects to help us communicate.

Realistic motion

If you read the Preface of this book, you know how much I loved the legendary bouncing ball tutorial that was included with Flash 3. Part of the reason I loved it is that it showed me how to create realistic motion. When a ball bounces, it doesn't simply go straight up and down; it falls quickly, slows as it bounces upward, drops quickly again, bounces upward more slowly and not as high, and so on, until it rests on the ground.

Realistic motion isn't just handy for a bouncing ball, though. The effect can be applied to anything you animate. A sliding panel in an interface, for example, could be designed to slide quickly at first, slowing gradually to a stop, which helps make an interface more elegant. Instead of just plopping into position, it comes to rest gracefully like an airplane pulling into the gate.

To create the deceleration effect:

1. Create a new Flash Document and save it as *easing.fla* in the *07* folder.

2. Change the Stage dimensions to 550 × 100, and set the frame rate to 18 fps.

3. Run the Make a Box command we created in Chapter 2 by choosing Commands → Make a Box.

4. Position the box at (5, 5) and size it to 90 × 90.

5. Insert a keyframe at frame 40.

6. Hold down the Shift key and press the right arrow key to move the box to the right edge of the Stage in a straight line.

7. Apply a motion tween to the frame span.

Now we've got an animated box, created the same way as the animations in previous chapters, but let's take the additional step of adjusting the easing value and see how it affects the animation:

1. Select any frame in the motion-tweened frame span and drag the Ease slider in the Properties panel to −100 (Ease In), as shown in Figure 7-8.

2. Play the animation. The box starts moving slowly and speeds up.

3. Change the Ease slider to 100 (Ease Out) and play the animation again. The box moves quickly at first and slows to a stop.

4. Save and publish the movie. (This movie works for any version of the Flash Player.)

Easing in means the object on the Stage speeds up (accelerates), and *easing out* means it slows down (decelerates).

An example of this effect is included in the *07* folder. Open *bouncing_ball.swf* to see how easing affects the motion of a bouncing ball. Easing is applied to each motion tween in the animation to give the ball realistic movements.

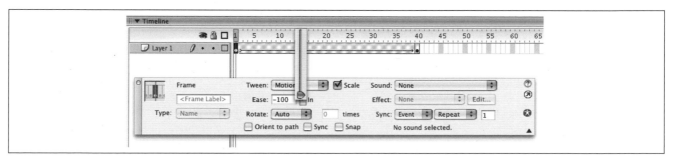

Figure 7-8. Set the easing value for motion tweens using the Ease slider.

Combinations of long and short animated frame spans can put a cool twist on reality. In *The Matrix*, for example, bullets are shown moving at an incredibly slow pace while our protagonist, Neo, moves at regular speed, creating the illusion that Neo is moving faster than the bullets.

In Flash, a similar effect might be achieved by moving one object very slowly while a background image moves at high speed (using a movie clip as a looping background animation). A looping illustration of a street may move quickly in the background while a superhero, perhaps The Flash (my personal favorite, for obvious reasons), runs in place to make it seem he is racing through a city to save the day.

You can also use motion to convey a sense of depth. In the real world, objects close to the viewer appear to move more quickly than objects that are far away. How might you use this fact to make, say, an animation of falling snow appear more realistic?

High-speed blur

Continuing with the high-speed motion concept, the show *Smallville* (WB) often features moments of slow-moving reality while Clark Kent races through the scene in a blur. In reality, we can't move Flash graphics fast enough to appear blurred (the graphics end up looking choppy, not blurred). It is possible to simulate a blur using alpha channels in Flash, but runtime performance is often better if you apply a motion blur effect ahead of time in a program such as Fireworks or Photoshop. The blurred images can then be imported into Flash and used as part of an animation.

Let's create a motion blur of our own:

1. Open Fireworks and create a new file (File → New) that is 250 × 250 pixels with a white background.

2. In Fireworks, activate the Text tool and change the font to Webdings using Fireworks' Properties panel (the Properties panel is common to all Studio MX 2004 applications). Set the text point size to 96.

3. Click once in the Fireworks document's image area and type a lowercase **b**. The Webdings font creates

symbols instead of letters, and the lowercase *b* is a line drawing of a bicycle.

4. With the bike selected, choose Filters → Blur → Motion Blur to open Fireworks' Motion Blur dialog box, shown in Figure 7-9.

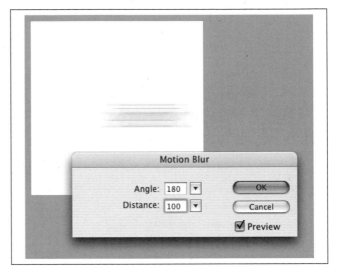

Figure 7-9. The Motion Blur dialog box in Fireworks.

5. Change the Angle option to 180 degrees. You can either enter **180** or use the circular slider that appears when you click on the triangle.

6. Enter **100** for the Distance option and click OK. The dialog box closes and a motion blur is applied to the bike image.

7. With the bike still selected, copy it to the clipboard.

8. Undo twice to return the bike to its original appearance. We'll need to repeat Steps 4–8 several times, lowering the amount of blur each time, but first, we need a Flash document to create the animation.

9. Return to Flash and create a new Flash document with dimensions 160 × 46. Save it as *blur.fla* in the *07* folder.

10. Paste the bike image onto frame 1 of *Layer 1* in Flash. (Any image can be copied and pasted from Fireworks to Flash using the clipboard.)

11. Align the blurred bike image to the horizontal and vertical center of the Stage.

12. Add a keyframe to frame 2 of *Layer 1* and delete the bike image. Each frame in the animation needs a new version of the bike so that it starts blurry and comes into focus over time.

13. Return to Fireworks and repeat Steps 4–8 ten more times, each time lowering the Distance value in the Motion Blur dialog box by 10 pixels (90, 80, 70, and so on). For the last image in the sequence, choose 1 for the Distance value. As you create each new version of the bike, paste it into Flash onto a new keyframe on *Layer 1*. You'll end up with 11 keyframes.

14. Save *bike.fla* and play the animation by pressing Enter or Return.

The bike starts as a blur and gradually comes into focus. Notice, though, that the blur in frame 1 stretches from one side of the Stage to the other, but the focused bike in the last frame is positioned in the center of the Stage. This looks a bit awkward, so let's adjust the position of the bike in each frame:

1. In Flash's Timeline panel, activate the Edit Multiple Frames button, shown in Figure 7-10. This feature allows you to see an item over time, somewhat akin to the way onion skinning allows you to see multiple images overlaid in space.

2. The starting and ending frames to edit are determined by the *frame markers* indicated in Figure 7-10. The frame markers (a.k.a. *onion markers*) appear when the Edit Multiple Frames button is toggled on if the Always Show Markers option is set using the Modify Onion Markers button.

3. Drag the lefthand frame marker to frame 1 and the righthand frame marker to frame 11.

4. Click and drag to select frames 1–11. Every frame in the sequence is displayed at once.

5. Click the Align Right Edge button in the Align panel. The image on each frame aligns to the right edge of the Stage.

6. Disable the Edit Multiple Frames option by clicking it again.

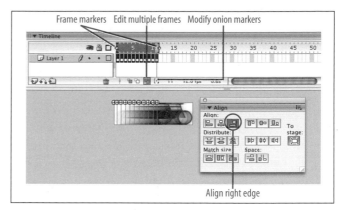

Figure 7-10. Editing multiple frames.

Now, the bike appears to come into focus on the right side of the Stage. To see it in context, open *blur_complete.swf*, located in the *07* folder. In the example animation, the bike stays in one place and comes into focus gradually, while the background moves quickly and slows to a stop.

What does this effect communicate? Speed, man, speed. To illustrate the point even more, kick the frame rate up to 24 or 30 fps, or decrease the number of frames used in the animation. A fast blur effect communicates fast action. Used in an animation about an Internet Service Provider (ISP), potential customers would be more prone to believe the service can deliver a high-speed connection.

Animating along a path

You saw in Chapter 6 how to use easing to create more realistic motion tweens. Easing can be used with motion tweens to animate a ball that bounces straight up and down. But what do we do if we need it to bounce while moving from left to right across the Stage? A straight-line motion tween will not suffice; we'd have to create multiple keyframes at different points to approximate a curve and tween between them, which makes it hard to achieve smooth, continuous motion. To move the ball along an arbitrary path, we can instead use a *motion guide*.

Let's first simplify the existing bouncing ball movie in preparation for a new animation:

1. Open *bouncing_ball.fla*, located in the *07* folder, and save it as *bouncing_ball_on_path.fla*, also in the *07* folder.

2. Click and drag to select frames 30–170 on both layers and delete them by right-clicking (Windows) or Cmd-clicking (Mac) on the selected frame span and choosing Remove Frames from the contextual menu.

3. Right-click or Cmd-click on frame 20 of the *ball* layer and choose Clear Keyframe to remove the keyframe there. You should be left with only a dashed line on the *ball* layer, as shown in Figure 7-11.

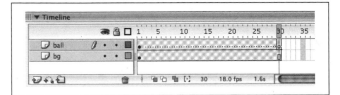

Figure 7-11. Delete frames 30-170 and clear the keyframe on frame 20 of the ball layer.

Now we can prepare the timeline and motion guide for the bouncing ball animation:

1. Add a new layer named *path*.

2. Activate the Pencil tool, choose Smooth from the Options section of the Tools panel, and draw a line across the Stage similar to the one in Figure 7-12. This line is the motion guide. When we're done, the ball will animate along this path.

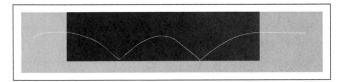

Figure 7-12. Draw a line to use as the motion guide.

3. Right-click or Cmd-click on the layer name for the *path* layer and choose Guide from the contextual menu. This converts the layer icon to a dotted arc, indicating it is now a guide layer.

4. Click and drag the *ball* layer (by dragging the layer name at the left of the timeline, not the content of the layer's frames) onto the *path* layer.

The *ball* layer is now nested underneath the *path* layer, as shown in Figure 7-13, indicating that the motion guide

(which we drew in the previous step and will configure in a moment) on the *path* layer will be used to guide the object on the *ball* layer. If you don't understand this right now, don't worry—it will become clear in just a minute.

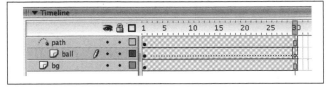

Figure 7-13. Nest the ball layer underneath the path layer.

To move the *ball* instance along the motion guide:

1. At frame 1, select the *ball* instance with the Free Transform tool and drag the anchor point (the small circle in the center of the instance) to the center of the bottom of the ball, as shown in Figure 7-14. I'll explain this in a moment.

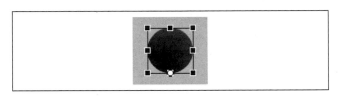

Figure 7-14. Reposition the anchor point for the ball instance using the Free Transform tool.

2. At frame 1, drag the *ball* instance to the left end of the motion guide and position the anchor point on top of the curve.

3. At frame 30, add a keyframe to the *ball* layer and position the ball over the top of the right end of the motion guide. The anchor point, again, should be on top of the curve.

4. Save and test the movie.

The ball animates along the motion guide, which is now invisible, making it look as though the ball were thrown by someone offstage and is bouncing across the Stage.

Flash uses the anchor point for the *ball* instance to determine the position for the ball on the motion guide. Since the motion guide touches the bottom edge of the Stage, the anchor point must not go beneath the bottom edge of the Stage, or else it will look as though the ball is going underground before it bounces. Therefore, we position the anchor point at the bottom of the ball.

Aside from bouncing a ball across the Stage, motion guides can be used to guide a bird through the sky, a car down a winding road, or even a drunk cartoon character down a blurry sidewalk. (Drunk cartoon characters? For shame!)

NOTE

Guide layers not used for motion tweens are not exported when you publish a movie; therefore, content on an otherwise unused guide layer does not affect the file size of a movie. You can use guide layers to store design notes—text or graphics to describe how a file works—to help document the process or specify future enhancements under consideration. You can also temporarily convert a normal layer into a guide layer to hide its contents during testing.

ACTIONSCRIPT EFFECTS

Throughout the remainder of the book, we'll use Action-Script more and more to add interactivity and logic to our Flash content. For now, though, let's start small and use it to loop an animation.

Many of the same effects we create using motion tweens, such as the bouncing ball, can also be created using Ac-tionScript, and scripting the effects often results in a more efficient movie. Keyframes add to file size, and in complicated projects, those keyframes add up fast. Also, when animating an object on the Stage, ActionScript is smoother. For example, a motion tween used to rotate a hand on a clock will come to an end and must start over. If the hand rotates exactly 360 degrees, there will appear to be a split-second pause at 12 o'clock because the hand appears in that position at both the end and beginning of the looped animation. Although it can be fixed by changing the position of the hand at the last keyframe, there is often a slight pause as the playhead loops back to frame 1. Therefore, in many cases, it is easier to create smooth motion using ActionScript.

Scripted motion allows for infinite (even random) varia-tions, whereas timeline-based motion is always fixed. Likewise, scripted animation can respond to user actions (such as following the mouse) in ways that timeline-based animation cannot. This opens up new possibilities for games, physics simulations, and animations that are impractical to create by hand. Therefore, scripted anima-tion can be used when timeline-based animation is not possible or is possible but is prohibitively difficult or time-consuming.

Motion tween versus ActionScript: The battle begins

In this section, instead of using a circle as a bouncing ball, we'll use it as a clock face and see how scripted ani-mation improves the fluidity of the hand's rotation. To start preparing our clock's hand animation:

1. Open *clock.fla*, located in the *07* folder. It contains two layers: *assets* and *hand on left*. The hand inside the clock on the left is on the bottom layer. A motion tween will be applied to it, so it must be on its own layer. The hand on the left is a graphic symbol and the hand on the right is a movie clip.

2. On the *hand on left* layer, insert a keyframe (F6) at frame 60.

3. Apply a motion tween to the frame span on the *hand on left* layer.

4. Click anywhere on the motion tween, choose CW from the Rotate drop-down list in the Properties panel, and enter **1** for the value, as shown in Figure 7-15. This causes the hand to rotate clockwise once every 60 frames. If you, like me, never seem to have enough time, choose CCW from the Rotate drop-down list. The clock will run backward and more accurately reflect our wishes.

5. Insert a keyframe at frame 60 of the *assets* layer (by pressing F5) so that the other graphics appear throughout the animation. (Otherwise, they'd disappear when their frame span terminated.)

6. Test the movie.

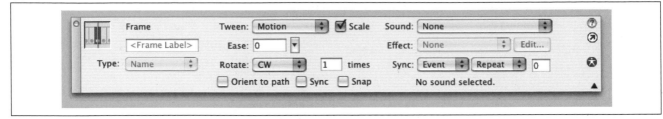

Figure 7-15. Set the clockwise rotation of the clock hand.

When the hand rotates clockwise and returns to 12 o'clock, there is a small pause before it moves again because the first and last frames of the animation are the same. Let's see if we can fix it by ending the animation with the clock hand a little short of 12 o'clock:

1. At frame 60, select the clock hand on the left.

2. Activate the Free Transform tool and use a corner handle to rotate the hand slightly to the left about 1/8 inch (as little as possible), as shown in Figure 7-16. The cursor appears as a circular arrow when the cursor is over the corner handle. If you prefer, use the Transform panel (Window → Design Panels → Transform) to set the rotation to –6 degrees.

3. Save and test the movie.

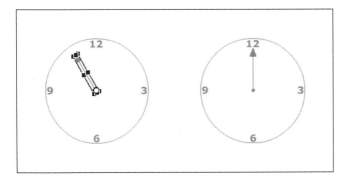

Figure 7-16. Rotate the hand using the Free Transform tool.

We've rotated the hand slightly so that it doesn't complete its rotation cycle by the last frame. The idea is that if the hand is slightly left of its starting point on the last frame of the motion tween, there will be no duplicate to cause a pause when the animation starts over. But, as you can see, there is still a pause. It's almost unnoticeable, but it's there. Also, the animation seems a bit choppy, as a result of being rotated on a per-frame basis. Let's see if ActionScript can make the animation smoother:

1. Select the clock hand on the right side of the Stage. The Properties panel shows it is a movie clip with an instance name of hand_mc.

2. Open the Actions panel (F9).

3. With the hand still selected, attach the following script using the Actions panel:

```
onClipEvent (enterFrame) {
    this._rotation += 12;
}
```

Here, we're telling Flash that as soon as the playhead enters frame 1 of the main timeline (which happens immediately upon running the movie), it needs to start rotating the hand (the current clip, as indicated by this) in 12-degree increments. Just as a movie clip on stage has alpha and tint properties, it also has a _rotation property. (Many built-in movie clip properties, such as _rotation, start with an underscore, although many do not. The older properties that have been supported since Flash 4, including _x and _y, usually start with an underscore, but properties added in later versions usually don't. Consult the online documentation or *ActionScript for Flash MX: The Definitive Guide* (O'Reilly) for a list of movie clip properties. Those beginning with an underscore are also listed at the beginning of the code hint drop-down list.)

The preceding ActionScript simply says, "For each tick of the frame rate, rotate the movie clip another 12 degrees clockwise from its current position." (Because there are 360 degrees in a circle and 60 minutes in an hour, there are 6 degrees of rotation for each minute. So 12 degrees rotation is equivalent to two minutes time.)

When you save and test the movie, the clock on the right runs smoothly and there is no pause in the animation.

Why? Because it's not dependent on the playhead advancing through the timeline. For the clock on the left to work, the playhead must play all 60 frames in the timeline and then start over. The clock on the right, however, simply rotates the clip 12 degrees at a time, regardless of what else is going on in the movie. ActionScript wins!

Conditional animation

In the preceding example, the hand on the clock rotates 12 degrees per frame in an endless circular path, because if the rotation is greater than 360 degrees, it simply wraps around. For example, setting a movie clip's _rotation property to 390 is the same as setting it to 30. But what if the object we're animating is moving on a linear path? How would the Flash Player know to start over?

Scripting an object to move from one side of the Stage to the other is similar to scripting the clock hand, but if we don't reset its position at some point, the object will move off the Stage, never to be seen again.

To remedy this, we must alter the animation under certain conditions. Let's see how this works:

1. Open the *easing.fla* file we created earlier under "Realistic motion," located in the *07* folder, and save it as *actionscript_animation.fla* in the same folder.

2. Select frames 2–40 and delete them by pressing Shift-F5.

3. Select frame 1 and choose None from the Tween drop-down list in the Properties panel (or use Insert → Timeline → Remove Tween) to remove the motion tween.

4. Drag the instance of *Symbol 1* (the box) offstage to the left. To drag it in a straight line, hold down the Shift key while dragging it.

5. With the instance of *Symbol 1* still selected, choose Movie Clip from the Symbol Behavior drop-down list on the left side of the Properties panel. (As discussed in Chapter 4, this changes the symbol type of the instance on stage but not of the original symbol in the Library.) Give the instance an instance name of box_mc.

Why are we destroying a perfectly good animation? We're going to create a new animation using ActionScript. Doing this will better prepare you for the coding we'll use later on the book, so play along for a few minutes—it'll be worth it.

Let's add the ActionScript to animate the box:

1. Create a new layer and name it *actions*.

2. Using the Actions panel, attach the following event handler to frame 1 of the *actions* layer:

```
box_mc.onEnterFrame = function () {
};
```

The *onEnterFrame( )* event handler is similar to the *onClipEvent(enterFrame)* event handler used in the preceding section, but in this case, we're targeting the movie clip from the main timeline instead of attaching code directly to the movie clip. When code is written on a separate timeline rather than attached to the movie clip itself, we must tell ActionScript how to target the clip we wish to control. (You remembered to give the clip the instance name box_mc using the Properties panel, right? Without an instance name, the clip can't be controlled by ActionScript.) Here, we're saying, "Locate box_mc on the main timeline, and then perform these actions on every frame." Conversely, when we attach code directly to a movie clip, Flash assumes we're targeting the clip to which the code is attached. Therefore, it isn't necessary to explicitly specify a target by its instance name. The keyword this represents the current clip to which the code is attached.

What's the difference between the two coding styles? As far as the end result is concerned, there really isn't a difference; the code will work either way, so it's a matter of preference to some degree. However, many Flash developers—myself included—prefer to write all the ActionScript for a movie in one place or, at the very least, on one layer (usually named *actions*). When passing files among multiple developers, or while trying to deconstruct a file you created a long time ago and since forgot, it's helpful to have all the code in one place.

If code is attached to buttons, movie clips, and movie clip timelines throughout the file, it can become frustrating to try to find all of it. Centralizing the code makes it much easier to locate. Centralized coding also tends to lead to more understandable code because references are *fully qualified* (i.e., they include the instance name of the movie clip or button). When using fully qualified references, the code tells the whole story because the code's effect is less dependent on where the code is placed. Contrast this with attaching code to a movie clip in which, even if you read the code, you still need to see where it is attached in order to understand its effect on the program's operation and build a mental model of the file.

> **NOTE**
>
> You can use the Movie Explorer (accessible under Windows → Other Panels → Movie Explorer and shown in Figure 7-17) to locate scripts or to find a particular text string within a script.

The Movie Explorer is very useful when trying to understand a *.fla* file someone else programmed. You can use the Scripts button in the Movie Explorer to show all scripts in the *.fla* file. That said, the Movie Explorer doesn't show scripts from external *.as* files (which are often used as code repositories, which are incorporated into the *.swf* at compile time).

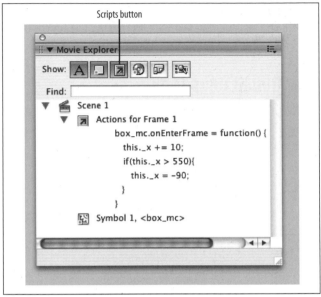

Figure 7-17. The Movie Explorer.

ACTIONSCRIPT OPERATIONS

ActionScript can be difficult to grasp at first, particularly if you don't know the terminology. Let's see what the following code means in plain English. The lines starting with // are comments to help you understand the code, as described in the "Comments" sidebar in Chapter 8.

```
// onEnterFrame() executes once for each frame
box_mc.onEnterFrame = function () {
  // Add 10 to the current horizontal position
  this._x += 10;
  // Check whether the clip has moved off the Stage
  if (this._x > 550) {
    // If so, return it to the left side of the Stage
    this._x = -90;
  }
};
```

In this script, we're saying to Flash, "In each frame, I want you to move box_mc, 10 pixels at a time, across the Stage. If box_mc moves beyond 550 pixels on the X axis (off the right edge of the Stage), put it back at –90 (offstage left) and start over."

And because Flash can do only what we tell it to do, it obeys.

The += operator simply adds the number on the right, in this case 10, to the item on the left, in this case this._x, which represents the x position of the current movie clip (box_mc).

```
  this._x += 10;
```

An *operator* simply performs some calculation on one or more *operands*. For example, the familiar addition operator (+) simply adds two numbers. The += operator is just a shorthand way to add a number to an existing value. Adding 1 to a number is so common that there is an even shorter

Let's continue with our scripted animation. Add the following command to the *onEnterFrame( )* event handler (additions to the code are shown in color):

```
box_mc.onEnterFrame = function () {
  this._x += 10;
};
```

This statement, which adds 10 pixels to the horizontal position of the movie clip every time the command is executed, is similar to the one used in the clock example. However, instead of changing the movie clip's _rotation property, we're changing its _x property, which represents the clip's horizontal position. (Again, note the initial underscore, which is part of the property name, _x, and is therefore mandatory.)

If you've written the script correctly, when you test the movie, the box moves from the left side of the Stage to the right. We've essentially created a motion tween using ActionScript. There is one big problem, though: the box goes offstage and does not come back. As the box's _x property increases indefinitely, it simply floats off into cyberspace, never to be seen again, like the monster in the movie *Aliens*. (Well, the alien explodes, but you get the idea.) We need to add an *if* statement, which is a *conditional*, to the script to tell the box to go back to its original position and start over when it gets too far to the right.

Add the following *if* statement to the *onEnterFrame( )* event handler (additions shown in color). Note the placement of the semicolon at the end of the second line of the *if* statement, in the statement body between the curly braces. Do not put semicolons immediately after either curly brace used in the *if* statement:

```
box_mc.onEnterFrame = function() {
  this._x += 10;
  if (this._x > 550){
    this._x = -90;
  }
};
```

Resave the movie and test it.

The new code checks whether the movie clip has disappeared from the Stage by testing whether its horizontal position is greater than 550 pixels (the width of the Stage). Now, when the box moves past the 550-pixel mark, the Flash Player moves it back to −90 on the X (horizontal) axis. (The box is 90 pixels wide, so we must move it to −90 to start it offstage left.) Once the box is repositioned,

---

shorthand for it, the *increment operator* (++). The following three lines of code are equivalent:

```
this._x += 1;
this_x++;
this._x = this._x + 1;
```

All three expressions tell Flash to take the old value of this._x, add 1 to it, and store the new value back into this._x.

Don't confuse the equals sign operator (=) with the algebraic equals sign you learned about in school. It does not test whether two values are equal. Instead, it calculates the value on the right side and stores it in the property or variable on the left side.

To test a value, use a double equals sign (==), as follows. It is a *comparison operator*, which tests the value of this._x without changing it:

```
if (this._x == 500) {
  trace ("The box is at the right side of the Stage");
}
```

The following is wrong. The code is missing an equals sign, so it sets this._x to 500 instead of testing whether it is already 500:

```
if (this._x = 500) {   // WRONG!
  trace ("The box is at the right side of the Stage");
}
```

Other common comparison operators include greater than (>), less than (<), greater than or equal to (>=), and less than or equal to (<=).

the script continues and the box keeps moving 10 pixels at a time from left to right.

Wanna see a neat trick? It takes only a few small adjustments to reverse the animation. First, though, open the Options menu in the Actions panel and select View Line Numbers.

To reverse the animation:

1. Change the addition sign (+) in line 2 of the ActionScript to a subtraction sign (-) so it reads this._x -= 10;.

2. Change line 3 to if (this._x < -90).

3. Change line 4 to this._x = 550;.

4. The script should now look like this (changes in color):

```
1   box_mc.onEnterFrame = function () {
2     this._x -= 10;
3     if (this._x < -90) {
4       this._x = 550;
5     }
6   };
```

5. Save and test the movie.

The animation is now the reverse of the original. Increasing the value of the _x property of a movie clip moves it to the right, and decreasing the value moves the clip to the left.

Are you finding yourself suddenly more interested in ActionScript? Check out the sidebar "ActionScript Operations" for clarification on the terms and operators used in the preceding exercises. The sidebar touches on some ActionScript basics. For many beginners, writing their own code is easier than understanding someone else's. Both skills are much easier if you understand ActionScript's basic syntax. When trying to program your own ActionScript, my best advice is to write down in plain English what you want Flash to do, and then translate your notes into ActionScript. I've been programming for years and I still do this. It's a great way to organize your thoughts about how a project works and avoid time-consuming mistakes.

As we progress through the rest of the book, we'll focus increasingly on ActionScript. I'll show you how to do some really cool things and also how to debug code to determine what's wrong when a script is not working.

Understanding the basics will help you to better take advantage of the resources cited in Chapter 13.

We've covered a lot of ground in this chapter. If you aren't thinking outside your proverbial box yet, I hope the box has at least expanded to the point where you have more choices within the box.

Whether you're using Flash with other programs or all by itself, the effects you create can be an integral part of your designs and projects. A drop shadow could be just the professional touch your client is looking for, and the right text effect, such as a motion blur, could make your next online ad more effective than the last. To review, in this chapter we've seen how:

- Staggered animations are used to make up text effects

- Timeline effects can speed up the design process

- Easing provides the illusion of realistic motion

- Motion guides can be used to animate along an irregular path

- Integrating Flash with other graphic programs enables us to create effects that are difficult or impossible when using Flash alone

- ActionScript can be used to smoothly animate objects on the fly

- ActionScript can be used to create animations that would be time-consuming, difficult, or even impossible to do by hand

Now that you've seen how to use ActionScript to move a box across the Stage, can you figure out how to move it diagonally? Hint: change the movie clip instance's _y (vertical position) in addition to its _x position. Note that, unlike the Cartesian coordinate system, _y increases as you move down the Stage.

Also, try moving the box faster by changing the incremental value. Instead of moving the box 10 pixels at a time, move it by 20. How large can the increase in _x be before the animation looks bad? Would this be different if using a smaller or larger box? What happens if you increment _x by a very small number such as 1? What if you use a decimal value such as 0.75 or 1.5?

If you're up to the challenge, try to create a bouncing ball animation of your own and see how realistic it is. The ball itself is made using the Oval tool with a radial gradient and no stroke. After converting it to a symbol, you might choose to animate it manually in the timeline. If so, use a motion tween to make it "drop in" from above the Stage, then incrementally add keyframes, leaving less space between keyframes each time, and animate the ball so it moves up and down. Remember, each time the ball bounces upward, it travels a shorter distance than it did on the previous bounce. Apply easing to each tween to speed it up and slow it down. To make your bouncing ball more like an episode of the Twilight Zone, reverse the easing values so that the ball speeds up while ascending and slows down while descending. Then show it to your mother as an example of how strange you truly are.

Truth be told, creating the animation manually is a royal pain in the neck. Using a motion guide certainly can simplify the process somewhat. However, you can also create the bouncing ball animation using a movie clip and ActionScript. If you take the time to learn some basic ActionScript, you'll recoup the investment quickly in the time saved by no longer having to create animations manually. You don't need to learn much ActionScript at first, because you can usually find an existing code example. Chapter 5 of *Flash Hacks* provides the code to implement bouncing balls, acceleration, inertia, and more. The code is downloadable from *http://www.oreilly.com/catalog/flashhks*.

To experiment with other motion effects, try creating a looping background image as a movie clip, and draw a bullet or superhero that sits in place. Remember to make the object look blurred, as though it's moving at high speed.

When you're ready to move on, we'll start working with buttons to add interactivity to Flash movies. From here on out, our Flash movies will be even more exciting and powerful.

8

BUTTONS AND INTERACTIVITY

It's time to get interactive! Animation alone doesn't enable the user to control anything. The Web isn't about *seeing*, it's about *doing*. Its real power is in the user's ability to interact with content to buy and sell merchandise, learn something new, and communicate with people all over the world.

We touched very briefly on interactivity in Chapter 3, in which we let the user restart the animation by clicking on Box Guy. But that is just the beginning. In this chapter, we'll learn more about making Flash movies interactive through the use of buttons and ActionScript.

The easiest way to add interactivity to Flash is to use a button to run some ActionScript. One button might run a script that opens a web page, while another triggers the loading of a product catalog listing from a database. The ActionScript executed by a button can display help information for the user, add a product to a shopping cart, or send the user to any page in an online catalog. You may be saying, "Big deal. I can do those things with HTML." True, but buttons can be much more powerful than a link in HTML. Buttons can contain animation and sound, react to rollovers, be activated or dimmed dynamically, or be repositioned automatically when, say, the browser window is resized.

Of course, buttons are just the beginning. There is really no limit to the interactivity you can create with Action-Script, and it can be implemented in a variety of ways. A great example of this is pixeltees (*http://pixeltees.com*), where you can design a T-shirt from scratch and order it online—all from within a Flash interface.

Flash can also be used as a learning tool, and later on in this chapter, we'll see an example of that when we implement a quiz. But let's start by getting familiar with buttons.

BUTTONS AS SYMBOLS

In earlier chapters we learned about graphic symbols and movie clip symbols. Let's see how to create the third type of symbol, a button symbol, and add ActionScript to make it launch a web page.

Simple buttons

Soon, we'll see how to create complicated buttons (and even an invisible button), but let's start with a basic button symbol.

To create a button with the word *Button* on it:

1. Create a new Flash document, set the Stage dimensions to 200 × 25, and save the file as *simple_button.fla* in the *08* folder.

2. Draw a rectangle (choose any color you like), resize it to 200 × 25, then position its upper-left corner at (0, 0) so it covers the Stage.

3. Use the Text tool to enter the word **Button** and position it at the vertical and horizontal center of the Stage. The word appears in front of the rectangle.

4. Delete the stroke of the rectangle.

5. Click and drag to select everything on the Stage, then press F8 to convert the image to a symbol.

6. In the Convert to Symbol dialog box, name the symbol **btn** and choose Button as the Behavior type, as shown in Figure 8-1. Click OK to close the dialog box.

7. Test the movie.

Figure 8-1. Convert the image to a button symbol.

The Preview window opens, and when you drag your cursor over the instance of the *btn* symbol, the cursor displays as a hand, just as it does when you roll over a link on a web page. Flash knows that, even without any ActionScript associated with the button, it needs to display the hand icon instead of your cursor.

Let's continue by making the button respond to mouse-clicks:

1. Close the Preview window.

2. Select the button and assign it an instance name of my_btn. The *_btn* suffix triggers code hints in the Actions panel, which you'll see in a moment.

3. Create a new layer named *actions* and open the Actions panel (F9).

4. In the Actions panel, create an event handler. In this case, we want something to happen when the user releases the mouse button, so we create an *onRelease( )* event handler.

```
my_btn.onRelease = function () {
}
```

5. When you type the dot after my_btn, a code hint appears. Instead of typing the script in its entirety, you can choose *onRelease* from the code hint menu.

6. Add a *getURL( )* command to the event handler to launch a web page (additions shown in color):

```
my_btn.onRelease = function () {
    getURL(
}
```

Notice that as soon as you type the opening parenthesis after getURL, another code hint appears. This code hint informs you that you must enter a URL, followed by a comma, then enter the window type, followed by a comma, and finally, enter a method, which we'll discuss later on. The three things the code hint asks for are called *parameters*, or *arguments* (the terms are largely interchangeable). Each parameter is passed by the command to the Flash Player to tell it what to do when you click the button.

> **NOTE**
>
> Parameters in ActionScript are often optional. In the *getURL( )* command, the URL and window parameters are required information, but the method parameter is optional.

Let's finish the script to launch the desired URL when the user clicks the button:

7. After the opening parenthesis of the *getURL( )* command, enter a URL and a window type, completing the command as follows (additions shown in color). Be sure to use quotes around the URL and window type:

```
my_btn.onRelease = function () {
    getURL("http://www.flashoutofthebox.com",
                    "_blank");
}
```

8. The "_blank" parameter, just as in HTML, tells Flash to open the URL in a new browser window.

9. Save your work, then choose File → Publish Preview → HTML. (If the File → Publish Preview → HTML option is disabled in your menu, first check the HTML (.html) checkbox in the Publish Settings dialog box under File → Publish Settings.)

The Publish Preview command opens your default browser and displays the Flash button embedded in an HTML page. This also creates *simple_button.html* and saves it in the *08* folder (the same directory as the *.swf* file). Later on, we'll see more about embedding Flash content in HTML pages.

When you click the button, a new browser window opens and goes to my new favorite web site, *http://www.flashoutofthebox.com*.

As is often true, there is an easier way to create the same functionality, as explained next.

Using behaviors

Behaviors are new to Flash MX 2004 and Flash Pro. They largely supersede the menu-driven Normal mode, which was available in the Actions panel available in Flash MX. Behaviors are somewhat similar to commands (in a second-cousin sort of way), which we used earlier, but instead of being used to repeat tasks within the Flash interface, they are used to help write the ActionScript used in your published movies. Here's how to use a behavior so you don't have to write a script yourself:

1. Close your browser.

2. Back in Flash, close the Actions panel and delete the *actions* layer by clicking the trash can icon in the Timeline panel.

3. Select the my_btn instance and choose Window → Development Panels → Behaviors to open the Behaviors panel.

4. In the Behaviors panel, click the Add Behavior button and choose Web → Go to Web Page. The Go to URL dialog box, shown in Figure 8-2, opens.

Figure 8-2. The Go to URL behavior dialog box.

5. In the dialog box, replace macromedia.com with **flashoutofthebox.com** and choose "_blank" from the Open In drop-down list.

6. Click OK to close the dialog box. The Behaviors panel now lists On Release, Go to Web Page as a behavior attached to the button.

7. Open the Actions panel again. You see the following script:

```
on (release) {
  //Goto Webpage Behavior
  getURL("http://www.flashoutofthebox.com",
"_blank");
  //End Behavior
}
```

The preceding script, which Flash wrote for you, does the same thing as the one you wrote earlier—it opens *http://www.flashoutofthebox.com* in a new browser window. Note that the *on (release)* handler in the preceding script is attached to the button itself, so it doesn't need to refer to the button by name. Contrast this with the earlier version attached to the *actions* layer, as reiterated here:

```
my_btn.onRelease = function () {
  getURL("http://www.flashoutofthebox.com",
"_blank");
}
```

Since that script wasn't attached to the button directly, it refers to the my_btn instance by name to make Flash associate the script with the button. Furthermore, that script declared (a 50-cent word for *created*) a function and stored it in the onRelease property of my_btn, which is equivalent to the *on (release)* handler created automatically by Flash.

Let's test the script that Flash wrote for you:

1. Save and choose File → Publish Preview → HTML again to see the button in a web page.

2. Click the button.

COMMENTS

Notice that lines 2 and 4 in the code generated by the Go to Web Page behavior include two forward slashes (//) at the beginning. The two slashes indicate a *comment* in ActionScript—a line that is not executed as part of the script. Comments can be used to write notes about your code (so you or someone else can easily discern the operation or purpose of the code). Comments initiated with // are automatically terminated by the next carriage return.

In this case, when Macromedia developed the Go to Web Page behavior, they added the two comment lines as notes about how the script was created and where it ends. Since the code is attached directly to the button and the script is brief, a developer could interpret the code easily without the comments. However, as scripts become more numerous and lengthy, comments make the code more discernible.

As a best practice, you should add comments to your code. When working with a team of developers or even alone, use comments to explain what each part of a script does, when it was created, and who created it.

Comment marks can also be used to temporarily or permanently disable a line of code (simply precede the line of code with // to "comment out" the code, and remove the slashes to re-enable it). To disable multiple lines of code or

Again, flashoutofthebox.com opens in a new window, but this time, you didn't have to create an *actions* layer or write any ActionScript to make it happen. Efficient, huh? Um…yeah. The major downside to using behaviors is that you can't depend on them too much. Only a few behaviors are built into Flash, so often you'll need functionality that isn't provided by a built-in behavior.

On the upside, however, with a little practice, you'll be able to write scripts yourself instead of relying on behaviors. Behaviors' extra level of user interface simply allows them to prompt the developer for parameter values. If you have a little knowledge of XML, you can write your own behaviors and build up an arsenal to handle your most common needs (or provide them to coworkers who don't know how to program ActionScript). To learn more about the "XML-to-UI" extensibility of Flash MX 2004 and Flash Pro, see the existing *.xml* files in the *Behaviors* folder of your Flash install directory.

Button states

Now that you've constructed your first button, let's take a peek inside a button symbol to see what else we can do with it. A big factor in the usability of buttons is user feedback. HTML links are usually indicated by underlined text (often blue) and the cursor changing to a hand when the user's mouse rolls over the link. Some links change colors after being clicked, and many include other indicators, such as tool tip–like help text.

Macromedia.com's home page, for example, displays a light blue highlight when the user rolls over link text. This type of feedback tells the user that he is hovering over a link even though the link text is not underlined. So how we do this in Flash?

Each frame in a button symbol's timeline is known as a *button state*. The Up state represents the button's appearance when the cursor is not over it, the Over state is displayed when the user rolls over the button, and the Down state displays when the user clicks the button.

Let's create the Up, Over, and Down states for our button symbol:

1. In our existing *simple_button.fla* file, double-click the my_btn instance to edit the *btn* symbol in place. The button symbol's timeline has four frames, labeled Up, Over, Down, and Hit (we'll get to the Hit state

write a long comment, start the comment with /* and terminate it with */, such as:

```
/* This is a
   multiline comment
*/
```

Your comments should always be descriptive and not simply reiterate what is obvious from the code. This comment is not very helpful:

```
// Add 5 to _x
_x += 5;
```

This comment explains the code at a higher conceptual level:

```
// Move clip 5 pixels to the right with each iteration
_x += 5;
```

Naming your variables appropriately greatly aids readability and reduces the need for comments. (If you don't know what a variable is, don't worry. Variables are simply named containers for temporarily holding data, such as the user's current score. For more details, see the "Variables" sidebar in Chapter 9.)

```
// This is hard to understand without further
explanation:
p = q / r;

// This hardly requires a comment:
averageScore = totalScore / numStudents;
```

later). There is a keyframe in the Up frame, as shown in Figure 8-3.

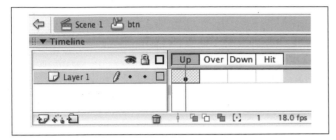

Figure 8-3. Timeline for a button symbol.

2. Select the Up frame and press F6 to add a keyframe to the Over frame (pressing F6 while a keyframe is selected adds a keyframe to the frame immediately following the one selected). The rectangle and text are both selected.

3. Deselect the text on the Over frame by Shift-clicking on the word *Button* (Shift-clicking enables you to select multiple objects or deselect individual objects). The rectangle remains selected and the Properties panel shows the editable properties for the shape.

4. In order to visually distinguish the button's Over state from its Up state, while in the Over frame, change the fill color for the rectangle.

5. Add a keyframe to the Down frame and change the fill color there as well (again to distinguish the Down state from the other button states).

6. Save and test the movie.

When you roll over it, the button displays its Over state, which in our case changes the button's color. When you click it, the button displays its Down state, which causes it to change colors again (oh, and that pesky flashout-ofthebox.com home page opens, too).

So now we know how to create the Up, Over, and Down states, but what does the Hit state do? Let's find out by first testing what happens when we do not use the Hit state in a button symbol containing only text:

1. Choose File → Save As, and save this file as *hit_state. fla* in the *08* folder.

2. On each frame of the button timeline, delete the rectangle, leaving only the word *Button* on stage.

3. On each frame, change the color of the word *Button* so the different button states are apparent as you roll over and off them.

4. Save and test the movie.

Unfortunately, the user must roll over the text to activate a change of button state; the whitespace between letters does not activate the change of button state. The pixels that make up the text can be quite difficult to roll over with your cursor. To solve the problem, make the text REALLY BIG! Okay, I'm kidding. Let's use the Hit state of the button instead:

1. Add a keyframe to the Hit state of the *btn* symbol.

2. At the Hit frame, draw a rectangle as shown in Figure 8-4 over the word *Button*. The rectangle can be any color you like—content on the Hit frame does not appear in the published movie.

3. Save and test the movie.

Figure 8-4. Use the Hit state to define a hit area for the button.

Now, when you roll over the area defined in the Hit state of the button, the button is activated and the button state changes. The hit area is now the entire rectangle and not just the pixels occupied by the text.

Whenever the hit area for a button doesn't correspond directly to the button's assets, such as in a disjointed roll-over (in which a button rollover affects a graphic somewhere else on the Stage), add a keyframe to the Hit state and define the hit area.

Navigating through a movie

The Web wouldn't be what it is today without having some interactivity built into it. The basic ability to link from one page to another is so ingrained in our heads that it's difficult to imagine the Web without it.

In many Flash projects, the ability for the user to navigate through a series of screens is also essential. In Chapter 11, we'll create a presentation that makes use of linear navigation to advance through several screens, but let's look now at how to jump from place to place within a Flash movie, on a nonlinear path, as you'd do within a web site. In this section, we'll create three buttons, each of which will make a different shape appear on the Stage.

The first thing we need is a button, so let's grab the one we made earlier and add a stroke to it. We'll line up three instances of the button horizontally, and the stroke will make the edges of the button visible:

1. Create a new Flash document with Stage dimensions of 600 × 200, and save it as *navigation.fla* in the *08* folder.

2. Choose File → Import → Open External Library and open the Library of *simple_button.fla* (located in the *08* folder). The Library contains the *btn* symbol we created earlier.

3. Drag an instance of the *btn* symbol to the Stage. Then, double-click on the instance to edit the symbol in place.

4. In Edit mode for the *btn* symbol, activate the Ink Bottle tool, which adds a stroke (analogous to the way that the Paint Bucket tool adds a fill). Set the stroke color to black and set the stroke weight to 1, then click once near the edge of the rectangle to add a stroke to the shape.

5. Repeat Step 4 for the Over and Down frames of the button.

6. Return to Scene 1 (by clicking *Scene 1* in the Edit bar).

7. If the Library for *simple_button.fla* is docked with another panel, click and drag the dots at the left side of the titlebar of the Library panel to undock it. Then close it.

8. Save your work. This time, saving is very important. You'll see why in a minute. (And don't save the file again until I say, "Simon says.")

Now we have a button, but we didn't change the text inside it. Let's do that now:

1. Enter Edit mode for the *btn* symbol again, and replace the word *Button* with the word *Box* on each frame. Before you replace the word, select it and click the Align Center button in the Properties panel to align the text to the center of its text field. This way, you don't have to reposition the text after you type the new word.

2. Return to Scene 1.

The first button is complete, but we still need two others, so let's make those as well:

1. Open the Library panel of *navigation.fla*.

2. Double-click on the symbol name for the *btn* symbol to make it editable and change the name to *box_btn*.

3. Click on the Options menu in the upper-right corner of the Library panel and choose Duplicate. The Duplicate Symbol dialog box appears.

4. Enter *circle_btn* for the name of the new symbol and click OK to close the dialog box.

5. Drag *circle_btn* to the Stage and double-click to edit it in place.

6. On every frame of the *circle_btn* timeline, change the word *Box* to the word *Circle*.

Okay, this isn't any fun; it's a lot of redundant work just to make a few buttons. There has to be a better way, and, alas, there is:

1. Rather than undoing a bunch of times, return to Scene 1 and choose File → Revert. This option reverts the file back to the condition it was in the last time you saved. See? I told you saving was important. If you didn't save when I told you to earlier, you'll have to start from scratch. Don't say I didn't warn you.

2. Double-click the *btn* instance to edit the *btn* symbol in place.

3. Delete the word *Button* from every frame in the button symbol's timeline.

Next, instead of embedding the text within the *btn* symbol, we'll keep it separate so that the button is generic

Box	Circle	PolyStar

Figure 8-5. Align the text in front of the btn instances.

(that is, the text appears atop the button on stage, but the text is not part of the button symbol):

1. Return to Scene 1.

2. Alt-drag (Windows) or Option-drag (Mac) the *btn* instance to create a second instance and align the new instance directly to the right of the first one. Repeat this process for a third box. There are now three buttons lined up at the top of the Stage in a horizontal row.

3. To make sure the *btn* instances are aligned perfectly, Shift-select the three boxes and choose Align Top Edge and Distribute Horizontal Center in the Align panel.

4. On *Layer 1*, activate the Text tool and type **Box** in the work area (outside the Stage). Click in the work area twice to create another text field and type the word **Circle**. Then, click twice again and type the word **PolyStar**.

5. Position the word *Box* in the center of the first *btn* instance on the left. Position *Circle* in the center of the second *btn* instance, and *PolyStar* in the third, as shown in Figure 8-5.

6. Simon says, "Save the file."

7. Test the movie.

Now we have three buttons, made from only one button symbol. Not only is this easier to create than duplicating buttons and changing the text inside them, but using only one symbol decreases the file size for the published movie (which, as I've said a couple of hundred times already—and may keep saying, just to bug you—is important).

Now we'll create the content for the three screens in the project:

1. Draw a square on the Stage, then draw a circle. Convert both to graphic symbols, naming them *box*

and *circle*, and delete both instances from the Stage. (The symbols remain in the Library.)

2. In the Tools panel, click on the Rectangle tool and hold the mouse button down until a menu appears, as shown in Figure 8-6. Choose the PolyStar tool from the menu.

3. Draw a polystar on the Stage, convert it to a symbol named *polystar*, and delete the instance from the Stage.

Now, we need to divide the movie into three different screens. We'll do this by using frame labels to name

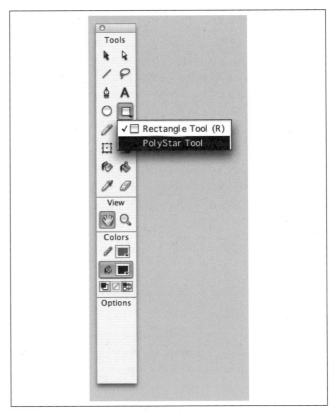

Figure 8-6. Choose the PolyStar tool from the Rectangle tool menu in the Tools panel.

several frames, and placing the various shapes we created a moment ago at separate points:

1. Rename *Layer 1* to *btns*.

2. Create a new layer and name it *screens*. It doesn't matter if it's above or below the *btns* layer.

3. Create another layer named *actions* and drag it to the top of the layer stack.

4. Select frame 40 on every layer and press F5 to insert frames.

5. Select frame 1 on the *screens* layer and, in the Frame Label field in the Properties panel, enter **home** and press Enter (or Return) to commit the name to the selected frame. The frame label home appears in the timeline, as shown in Figure 8-7. Just as we place all our ActionScript on a layer named *actions* created for that purpose, so too we can create all our frame labels on a layer named *screens* (some developers name this layer *labels*, and others put labels on the *actions* layer).

6. Choose Anchor from the Label Type drop-down list in the Properties panel. Named anchors (which have no relation to the anchor point of a graphic) are a type of frame label that enables a browser's Back and Forward buttons to work properly when navigating through Flash movies (Windows only). This is important for usability, because the most commonly clicked button in a browser is the Back button.

7. Insert a keyframe at frame 10 of the *screens* layer and assign the label box to the frame as a named anchor.

8. Repeat Step 7 on frame 20 using the label name circle.

9. Repeat Step 7 again at frame 30 using the label name polystar.

Now we have four destination frames—home, box, circle, and polystar—that will serve as different states in the published movie.

> **NOTE**
>
> We're using the timeline's playhead position to reflect the current state of the Flash application. Each frame label constitutes an application state, which we can jump to simply by using *gotoAndStop( )* or *gotoAndPlay( )*. The *application state* represents where the user is in the application.

In a simple case, the application state may be simply one of the screens in a multiscreen presentation (that is, a four-screen presentation can be thought of as having four possible application states). In a more complex case, such as a game, the application state would include the user's score, his list of possessions, his current location in the virtual world, and so on. In the case of a multipage fill-in form, the application state would comprise the user's current page and data entry so far.

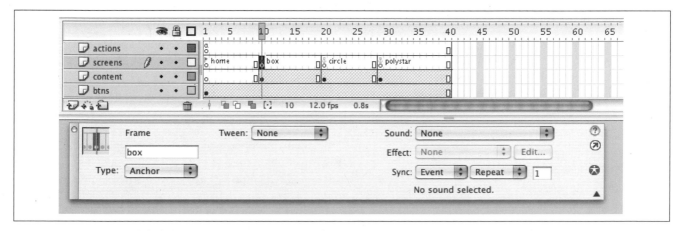

Figure 8-7. Assign the labels box, circle, and polystar to frames 10, 20, and 30 of the screens layer, and set their label types to Anchor.

Let's add the content to each of our screens:

1. Create a new layer named *content* and insert keyframes at frames 10, 20, and 30.

2. At frame 10, drag a *box* instance to the Stage and position it at the center of the Stage (use the Align panel).

3. At frame 20, position a *circle* instance at the center of the Stage. Then, at frame 30, position a *polystar* instance at the center of the Stage. Each labeled frame now contains the shape that corresponds to the label's name.

4. Save and test the movie.

All 40 frames of the movie play without stopping, so each shape flashes by and the buttons don't control any of it. It's time to write some ActionScript to tame the playhead:

1. Select frame 1 of the *actions* layer and open the Actions panel (F9).

2. Enter a *stop( )* command in frame 1 to stop the playhead there: **stop();**.

And now it's time to stop and think for a moment. As you saw earlier, there are two different ways to code the buttons. We can either attach ActionScript directly to the buttons, or we can keep the code separate by putting it in the *actions* layer.

Keeping the code separate from the buttons will make the code easier to access later on (because it will all be in one place—frame 1 of the *actions* layer), whereas attaching the code to the buttons means we'd have to click on each button to access the scripts individually. But to write the code on the *actions* layer, we have to enter it ourselves when we could, instead, use a behavior to write the code for us.

You'd likely rather use the behavior, because it's easier right now, and faster, and you'll probably never use this file again. But, because I'm calling the shots here, I say we write the code ourselves. For one thing, it's good practice. The more familiar you are with ActionScript syntax and commands, the better you'll be at developing Flash

content. Second, in this case, the behavior used to write this code (Movie Clip → GotoAndStop at Frame or Label, accessed via the Behaviors panel) would attach the code directly to the button, and although you think you'll never use this file again, you just might.

You may finish this book, forget how to use a button to jump from one frame to another, and open up this file to see how it was done. You'll click on frame 1 of the *actions* layer, open the Actions panel, and see only a *stop( )* command. Then you'll sit there for a while, scratching your head, wondering where all the code went. In other words, do what I tell you and we'll have no problems.

> **NOTE**
>
> Remember, any code that accesses movie clips, buttons, or text fields via ActionScript won't work unless you assign the item an instance name in the Properties panel, as described in the "What's in a Name" sidebar in Chapter 4. Make sure your instance names are unique so that Flash knows which instance to target when you refer to it from your ActionScript code.

To add the scripts that control the buttons to the *actions* layer:

1. Select each *btn* instance on the *btns* layer, from left to right, one at a time, and assign instance names of box_btn, circle_btn, and polystar_btn to them using the Properties panel.

2. Beneath the *stop( )* command on frame 1 of the *actions* layer, create an event handler that sends the playhead to the box frame label when the user clicks the box_btn button:

   ```
   box_btn.onRelease = function () {
     gotoAndStop("box");
   };
   ```

3. Copy and paste the handler you just wrote into the Actions panel. We need to alter just two words to make it work with the circle_btn clip instance.

4. In the copy of the handler, change box_btn.onRelease to circle_btn.onRelease.

5. Change gotoAndStop("box") to gotoAndStop("circle").

6. Make another copy of the first handler. In the new copy, change box_btn.onRelease to polystar_btn.onRelease and change gotoAndStop("box") to gotoAndStop("polystar").

7. Your code on frame 1 of the Actions panel should look like this:

```
stop();

box_btn.onRelease = function () {
  gotoAndStop("box");
};
circle_btn.onRelease = function () {
  gotoAndStop("circle");
};
polystar_btn.onRelease = function () {
  gotoAndStop("polystar");
};
```

8. Save and test the movie.

Hooray! We have a functioning movie. When you click each button, the playhead jumps to the appropriate frame and displays the content on that frame. Yes—this is how the pros do it, too. Mystery solved. In fact, you can use this technique with movie clips as well as buttons.

Hand-coding versus behaviors

I'm going to give you a chance now to compare scripting methods. Earlier, I had you write the code for the buttons on the *actions* layer despite the belief that using behaviors would take less time. Let's test that theory and see if it's true:

1. Choose File → Save As and save the project as *navigation_using_behaviors.fla* in the *08* folder.

2. Delete everything but the *stop( )* command from frame 1 of the *actions* layer using the Actions panel.

3. Select the box_btn instance and open the Behaviors panel.

4. Click the Add Behavior button in the Behaviors panel and choose Movie Clip → Goto and Stop at Frame or Label to open the dialog box for that behavior.

Above my head right now is one of those little thought balloons you see in comic strips, showing my thoughts as

I configure this behavior. Follow along here and configure the behavior the same way I do, as shown in Figure 8-8.

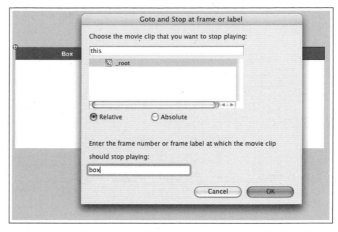

Figure 8-8. The Goto And Stop at Frame or Label dialog box, configured as it should be.

My thoughts:

"Hey, this dialog box is a little confusing. I'm supposed to choose the movie clip I want to stop playing, but there is no movie clip on the Stage. And where did the symbol called _root come from?

"The main timeline is the root timeline of a movie, so that may be what I want. Why Flash thinks it's a movie clip, I have no idea. Now, do I choose Relative or Absolute? Well, if _root is the main timeline, and this button is on the main timeline, I guess Relative is okay. I'll go with that one.

"Now, I'm supposed to enter the frame number or frame label at which the movie clip should stop. Since _root is the (so-called) movie clip, I want it to stop at the box frame label. All righty then—I'll just type **box** into this field and click OK. I'm pretty sure I got it right, but that dialog box is rather cryptic!"

Most beginners are uncomfortable moving forward if they're not sure they're on the right track, especially if a procedure contains multiple steps. If you're not sure if something is right, you can always undo it. Don't be too quick to retreat, however; forging ahead often accomplishes your goal and leads you back to familiar territory.

Keeping your cool is an important part of learning a programming language. After a few deep breaths, let's continue:

1. Review the script that was written by the behavior in the Actions panel. It looks like this:

```
on (release) {
    //Movieclip GotoAndStop Behavior
    this.gotoAndStop("box");
    //End Behavior
}
```

2. The script looks right, so apparently all we have to do for the other buttons is enter the name of a frame label into the behavior's dialog box and we're on our way. Select the circle_btn instance and apply the Goto and Stop at Frame or Label behavior to it. This time, enter circle as the frame label at which you want _root to stop.

3. Repeat Step 2 for the polystar_btn instance and enter polystar as the frame label.

4. Save and test the movie.

Surprise, surprise—the movie still works. The process, however, was not easy, because we had to muddle through the behavior's dialog box and that particular dialog box doesn't make much sense. It'll be easier next time, because now we know how to do it, but the point is this: it wasn't really faster or easier to use the behavior than it was to hand-code the ActionScript. While this is not true all the time, the behaviors built into Flash often either can't help us accomplish what we need to do, or the dialog boxes used to configure them are unclear. That said, if you start creating your own behaviors (by writing the custom XML files required to generate them), you can improve this situation by building a ton of behaviors that in fact are useful for you.

Ultimately, the best way to learn ActionScript is to write it yourself. The most likely use of the built-in behaviors is for people who have little understanding of ActionScript and want to build quickly or perhaps want to study the code generated by behaviors to learn more. Beyond that, behaviors won't really be useful or beneficial unless you create your own to distribute to other developers (a subject well outside the scope of this book).

A final touch for usability

Most web sites have more than one section, each of them made up of several pages. This can make it easier for the user to become lost than to develop a mental map of the site. To remedy this, many web developers use elements within web pages to indicate which page of what section the site visitor is currently viewing. The navigation bar for the site might display the section name in a different color, and a page title might be used to indicate where the visitor is within that section. Amazon.com, for example, uses tabbed navigation, with each tab in the navigation bar representing a different "store." Each tab turns a different color as you enter that online store, and the top of the content area of each page includes a page title.

In the navigation project we just completed, each button sends the playhead to a different frame in the timeline and displays a shape, but there is no indication of what screen we're currently viewing. It's fairly obvious to us, because we know what squares and circles look like, but a real-world web site would be considerably more cryptic to new or sight-impaired users. Regardless, as designers, we should never assume that the user has the same knowledge we do. If this project were being used to teach children about different shapes, they would need to know what shape is currently being shown (though, since most young children can't read, you might use audio cues instead).

Let's add one final touch to the project to tell users which screen they're on:

1. Open *navigation.fla*.

2. Double-click on the *box* symbol in the Library to enter Edit mode for the symbol.

3. Add the word **Box** to the center of the shape and return to Scene 1.

4. Repeat Steps 2 and 3 for the *circle* and *polystar* symbols, adding the words **Circle** and **Polystar** to the center of the shapes.

5. Save and test the movie.

Now, each shape displays its own name. In just a few steps, we made the project much more usable. Small additions like this one are often the difference between projects that confuse and projects that serve the user's needs.

My goal for this book is to teach you how to use Flash to accomplish your goals. Part of your goal with Flash should always be to create content that is easy to use and makes sense (unless mystique is part of the design concept, as with *http://donniedarko.com*).

For some phenomenal advice on how to make your projects more usable, check out the following books:

- *Don't Make Me Think! A Common Sense Approach to Web Usability* (New Riders)

- *The Big Red Fez: How to Make Any Web Site Better* (Fireside)

These books are focused around web usability, but the knowledge gained from them can (and should) be applied to every project you create.

CREATING A QUIZ

We've learned about basic interactivity and how to create button states. We've also seen how to create application states on the main timeline by simply jumping to a labeled frame. Believe it or not, those basic skills are used in a wide variety of business applications. Many companies use Flash to present educational material to inform employees and customers about promotions, procedures, and product information. In fact, companies like Thomson NETg (*http://www.netg.com*) and CyberScholar (*http://www.cyberscholar.com*) offer e-learning course development to clients, and much of the content is built with Flash.

Of course, Macromedia has researched common uses of Flash and tried to provide ready-made solutions to common requirements. Flash includes several templates that can be used to quickly create presentations, slide shows, and quizzes, and the functionality of each is built into the template (Flash Pro even includes templates for mobile devices, such as PDAs and cell phones). In this section, we'll use a quiz template to construct a three-question quiz about what you've learned so far, and in Chapter 11, we'll take a look behind the scenes and learn how to build a simple template ourselves.

Using templates

The first thing we need to do is choose a quiz template:

1. Close *navigation.fla*, if it's still open. Closing all open documents reopens the Start screen if the On Launch Show Start Page option is selected under Edit → Preferences → General.

2. From the Start screen, choose Quiz from the Create from Template menu. (If the Start screen isn't visible, choose File → New to open the New Document dialog box and click the Template tab.) This displays the New from Template dialog box, as shown in Figure 8-9.

3. Choose Quiz_style2 from the Templates category in the dialog box and click OK. The quiz template opens.

4. Save the file as *quiz.fla* in the *08* folder.

The quiz template has five layers: *Actions*, *Title*, *Interactions*, *Controls*, and *Background*. The *Interactions* layer contains eight frames, six of which contain prebuilt learning *interactions*. Each interaction represents a typical style for a quiz question, such as multiple choice. Frame 1 is the welcome screen for the project and frame 8 is the results screen. For this exercise, we'll use the multiple-choice learning interaction on frame 6:

1. Select frame 6 of the *Interactions* layer and choose Edit → Copy.

2. Select frames 2, 3, and 4 on every layer and choose Edit → Timeline → Remove Frames (Shift-F5) to delete those frames. Since we need only three questions, we need to get rid of the extra frames.

3. One at a time, select frames 2 and 4 of the *Interactions* layer, delete the contents of each frame using Edit → Clear (so as not to copy them to the clipboard), and choose Edit → Paste in Place. Now, frames 2–4 contain multiple-choice questions.

Notice the box containing instructions offstage left at each frame. Each box is a *component*, which you'll learn more about in Chapter 11. Right now, all you need to know is that each component is configurable, and each

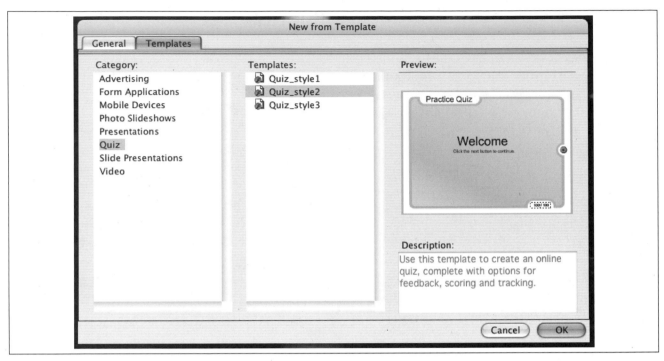

Figure 8-9. The New from Template dialog box.

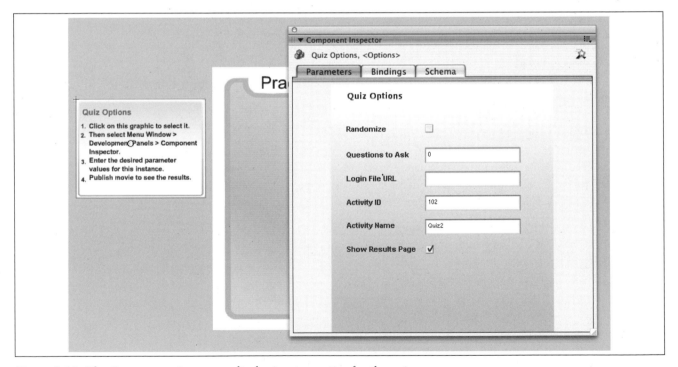

Figure 8-10. The Component Inspector, displaying properties for the quiz.

one controls part of the quiz. Let's configure the quiz itself first, then the learning interactions:

1. At frame 1, select the Quiz Options box, which is located offstage left in the work area and contains instructions for configuring the quiz.

2. In the Properties panel, click the Launch Component Inspector button to open the Component Inspector panel (shown in Figure 8-10), which shows some configurable properties for the quiz. If you need to increase the size of the panel, click and drag from the lower-right corner.

3. In the Questions to Ask field of the Component Inspector, enter **3**.

The Quiz Options component allows us to configure several things, including whether the questions appear in a random order, an activity ID and activity name, and whether we want a results screen. For this project, the number of questions is the only variable we need to change.

Let's move on to the first learning interaction. Let's create a multiple-choice question:

1. Drag the playhead to frame 2 and click on the Multiple Choice Interaction box, which is located offstage left in the work area and contains instructions for using the interaction. This selects the entire contents of the learning interaction, which is a movie clip named *Multiple Choice*.

2. Choose Modify → Break Apart or press Ctrl/Cmd-B once to break apart the clip.

3. Deselect all the assets by clicking somewhere outside them on the Stage.

4. Select the offstage Multiple Choice Interaction box again. The Component Inspector displays default options for the interaction.

Naturally, we need to customize the generic interaction so that it looks like the multiple-choice question we want to ask of the users (as shown in Figure 8-11). We can edit several things in this component: the interaction ID, question, instance name of each checkbox component (the defaults are *CheckBox1* through *CheckBox5*), and

the label of each checkbox. There are also three buttons at the bottom, labeled Start, Options, and Assets.

Let's start building our quiz by configuring the first interaction:

1. In the Interaction ID field in the Component Inspector, change the ID to **Interaction_01**.

2. In the Questions field, replace the placeholder text with **Which of the following is a symbol type in Flash?**

3. Leave the Instance fields, which represent possible answers, for the checkboxes alone—the default names are fine—but change the Label fields for answers 1–3 to **Timeline**, **Button**, and **Jambone**, in that order.

4. The answer to our question is item #2, "Button." In the Correct column, check #2, so that "Button"

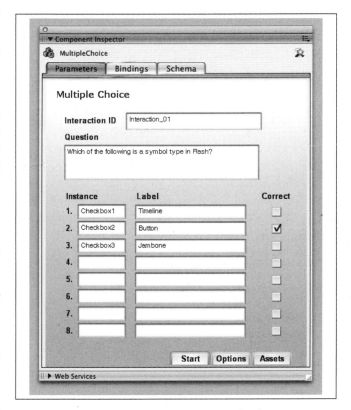

Figure 8-11. The Component Inspector, displaying properties for the learning interaction on frame 2.

is marked as the correct answer to the question. Uncheck the other checkboxes.

5. Click the Options button at the bottom of the Component Inspector and enter **3** into the Tries field of the Options screen. The user will have three chances to guess the right answer to the question (of course, with this many chances, even my dog could guess correctly).

6. Click on the Assets button in the bottom of the Component Inspector to open the Assets screen. Change the Check Answer control button text to **Am I Right?**

7. There are only three possible answers to this question and the template has placeholders for five answers by default, so delete the bottom two checkboxes on the Stage.

8. Save and test the movie.

When the Preview window opens, answer question 1 incorrectly by choosing the answer Timeline and clicking the Am I Right? button. The text next to the button reports that the answer is incorrect and you can try again. After you click the Reset button, choose the correct answer, and the quiz will advance to the next question.

Hopefully, you know that Jambone is not the correct answer. Jambone is a word a friend of mine made up to torment his former coworkers. It can be used in place of any noun, like "whatchamacallit" or "thingy." Don't bother looking it up. And if you happen to work with my friend, don't bother looking for a jambone in the supply room, no matter what he tells you.

To continue with our quiz, let's define question 2:

1. Close the Preview window.

2. To set up the next quiz interaction, move the playhead to frame 3, select the Multiple Choice Interaction box, break apart the interaction assets, deselect everything, and select the box again. The options for this interaction appear in the Component Inspector.

3. In the Questions field, enter **What is the name of the programming language used with Flash?**

4. In the Label column, enter **FlashScript**, **JavaScript**, and **ActionScript** for answers 1–3. Check ActionScript in the Correct column and uncheck the other answers.

5. Click the Options button, and on the Options screen enter **3** in the Tries field.

6. On the Assets screen, enter **Did I Get It?** as the Check Answer control button label.

7. Delete the bottom two checkboxes on the Stage. Again, there are only three possible answers to the question.

We're almost done, so hang in there for just another minute. To create the third and final multiple-choice question:

1. Repeat Steps 1 and 2 from for the interaction on frame 4.

2. In the Questions field, enter **Do you like Flash Out of the Box?**

3. For the first two checkbox labels, enter **Yes!** and **Um... no**. Check **Yes!** as the correct answer (how could you not like *Flash Out of the Box*?) and uncheck the other answer.

4. On the Options screen, leave the Tries field set to 1. I don't think you'll need more than one chance to answer this question.

5. On the Assets screen, enter **I Know This One!** as the Check Answer control button label.

6. Delete the three excess checkboxes on the Stage; there are only two possible answers to the question.

7. Save and test the movie.

And we're done!

Start the quiz and answer either correctly or incorrectly for each of the first two questions—you have three tries to get each of them right. For the third question, go with your instincts. (Yes, you like *Flash Out of the Box*.)

The last screen of the quiz tallies and displays the results. Hopefully, you'll score 100%. Close the Preview window and *quiz.fla* when you're done.

We'll talk more about components later on, using them to create a form in a Flash movie. In the meantime, try using the word *jambone* to confuse a loved one. For example, say, "Honey, I can't find the jambone. Did you move it?"

Ahhhh…good times.

MORE FUN WITH BUTTONS

You know those neat animated buttons that are sometimes used to get around cool web sites like love+rage (*http://loveandrage.net*)? I know, I know—it's shameless to plug my own site like that, but do you want to know how to make animated buttons anyway? Here's one to get you started. Beyond this, your imagination is the only limiting factor.

We'll build an animated button by creating an animation sequence within a movie clip and then adding the movie clip to a button's timeline:

1. Open *animated_buttons.fla*, located in the *08* folder. I've started this file for you, so we can skip some of the setup. On the Stage, there is one line of text, on a layer named *text*, which is locked (indicated by the padlock icon next to the layer name).

2. Create a new layer, name it *btns*, and drag it to the bottom of the layer stack.

3. Press Ctrl-F8 to open the Create New Symbol dialog box. Name the symbol *btn_rollover*, select Movie Clip (not Button!) as the Behavior type, and click OK.

4. In Edit mode for the *btn_rollover* symbol, draw a light gray filled rectangle, and delete the stroke.

5. Position the rectangle at (0, 0) and resize it to 80 × 20.

6. Add a keyframe at frame 5.

7. At frame 1, select the rectangle and enter **1** into the Height field in the Properties panel. Position the rectangle at (0, 10).

8. Apply a shape tween to frames 1–5.

9. Add a new layer to the timeline of the *btn_rollover* symbol and name it *actions*.

10. Insert a keyframe at frame 5 and add a *stop( )* command to the Actions panel: **stop();**.

11. Press Enter to play the animation.

The rectangle begins short and increases in height from its center point. The *stop( )* command stops the animation at frame 5.

Now we will nest the movie clip inside a button:

1. Without returning to Scene 1, press Ctrl-F8 to create another new symbol.

2. Name the symbol *btn* and choose Button (not Movie Clip) as the Behavior type.

3. In Edit mode for the *btn* symbol, select the Over frame and add a keyframe there (by pressing F6).

4. For the Over state, drag the *btn_rollover* movie clip symbol to the Stage and position it at (0, 0). Leave the Up state empty, as shown in Figure 8-12. That's right—empty.

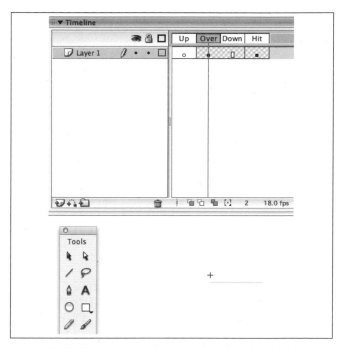

Figure 8-12. The timeline for the btn symbol, with the btn_rollover clip in the Over frame.

5. Return to Scene 1 and drag an instance of the *btn* symbol to the Stage. Size it to 85 × 1 and position it at (0, 12.5). Yes, you can use decimal values for pixel positioning (Flash simulates fractional pixels using antialiasing). We use 12.5 for the Y coordinate because it is the vertical center of the Stage, which is 25 pixels high. We make the button 85 pixels wide to stretch from the edge of the Stage to the first vertical divider line (the one between words in the text). We're stretching the button's width so it takes up the whole space between divider lines in the text.

6. Now that we can see the button in relation to the rest of the Stage, double-click it to edit the *btn* symbol in place.

7. Insert a keyframe in the Hit state of the *btn* symbol.

8. Draw a rectangle, position it at (0, 12.5), and size it to 80 × 25. It now covers the Stage from the left edge to the first vertical divider line in the text. Since there is nothing in the Up state of the *btn* symbol, the hit area will be used to activate it. Rolling over the button will display its Over state, where the movie clip first appears, and the movie clip will begin to play automatically.

9. Return to Scene 1. The button displays as an aqua-colored rectangle, as shown (in black and white) in Figure 8-13. The aqua color's only purpose is to enable you to see the button while working with it in Flash. It does not appear in the published movie.

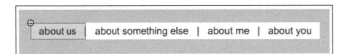

Figure 8-13. The btn instance displays as an aqua-colored rectangle.

10. Save your work and test the movie.

As planned, when you roll over the "about us" text, the corresponding button's hit area is triggered, its Over state displays, and the animated movie clip on that frame begins to play. When you roll outside of the hit area for the button, it is invisible. Why? Because there is nothing on the Up frame of the *btn* symbol, so nothing is shown.

Now, what about that weird aqua-colored rectangle? Since there is nothing in the Up state of the *btn* symbol and a hit area is defined in the Hit state, the hit area is displayed so we can see where to position the button on the Stage.

To finish up, we need a few more buttons:

1. Alt-drag (Windows) or Option-drag (Mac) the *btn* instance on the Stage to create three more instances.

2. Resize each instance so that they span from one vertical line to the next, then align them to the top edge of the Stage.

3. Save and test the movie.

When you get tired of rolling over buttons, close the Preview window and close *animated_buttons.fla* as well.

> **NOTE**
>
> If you ever need a button no one can see, leave the Up, Over, and Down states of a button symbol empty, then draw a shape at the Hit frame to define a hit area.

Invisible buttons are great when you want to plant "Easter eggs" in your site (hidden treasures that users might accidentally stumble upon). An object in your movie might appear to be a static graphic but in fact serve as the gateway to a hidden section of your web site. WB's *Smallville* web site uses this technique to allow access to the hidden "Luther Corp intranet" microsite, but you'll have to buy the *Smallville* Season 1 DVD to learn about the hidden button and get the password for entry.

One invisible button can be used to create any number of clickable areas (a.k.a. hotspots). If you want clickable areas but you don't need buttons with multiple states, you can use multiple instances of a single invisible button positioned in front of other movie assets. This avoids having to create separate button symbols for each clickable area. Using one button symbol cuts down on file size (even if you use many instances of the button), and it's often easier to create one button than it is to create several.

Finally, our Flash movies are starting to include some interactivity. From here on, we'll build more and more functionality into our movies, and this chapter should better prepare you for what's coming. So far we've seen how to:

- Assign a function to a button in order to make it respond to mouseclicks.

- Use ActionScript to launch a web page from a button using the *getURL( )* command.

- Jump from frame to frame within a Flash movie using frame labels and *gotoAndPlay( )* or *gotoAndStop( )*. By the way, we could have jumped to a frame by specifying the frame number instead of the frame label name. Using frame label names, however, makes our code easier to understand and avoids breaking the code if frames are inserted or deleted (which often changes existing frame numbers).

- Use Flash's built-in templates to quickly construct a quiz.

- Animate buttons by embedding movie clips within them.

To get some practice adding ActionScript to buttons, try coding the buttons in the *animated_buttons.fla* file to go to various web sites. If you want complete freedom for your buttons, you can mimic button behavior using movie clips, as described in Hack #63—"Button Movie Clips"—of *Flash Hacks* (O'Reilly).

Also, visit some of your favorite Flash sites to see how other developers design their buttons. Does animation in a button contribute to the overall look of the site or does it distract you? How do animated buttons integrate with the site's design to blend in with it? Does the button's design contribute to the user experience?

Studying the work of other Flash designers is a wonderful way to get ideas. Learn what you can about how elements in site designs work together to create a cohesive look.

Specifically, study when Flash is used and, even more so, when Flash is not used. Many sites benefit from integrating Flash with other HTML content rather than being a Flash-only site.

One of the major drawbacks to using navigation built with Flash is that search engines like Google can't use their automated search bots to spider their way through your site. Flash content cannot always be read by the search bots, and therefore they can't follow the links in your navigation to index every page in the site. For this reason, it's important to include links to other pages within your site using plain HTML. Often, this is done by adding a small section of text links at the bottom of each page that go to the same pages as the Flash navigation. (You can see an example of this text-link section on ebay.com at the bottom of each page.) Arguably, the best solution to date is the Flash Search Engine SDK (free from Macromedia), which is designed to convert Flash text and links into HTML for search engine indexing. For additional information and details on workarounds, see *http://www.netmechanic.com/news/vol6/promo_no12.htm*.

Regardless, Flash navigation is often a good way to spice up the look and functionality of a site. As long as you are aware of the drawbacks and take steps to remedy them, Flash navigation can go a long way in helping you convey your design concept for any project. Also, as you glimpsed earlier, a Flash-based quiz or presentation can provide a smoother user experience; it requires fewer page refreshes and can contain functionality—such as audio and animation—that is difficult to create using traditional web development tools. Flash-based content is generally more consistent across multiple browser versions and platforms—provided the user has the necessary version of the Flash Player installed—allowing training and support to be uniform across a spectrum of users.

In the next chapter, we'll expand our horizons in regard to both interactivity and media by creating a television set and streaming video into it via the use of controller buttons.

NINE

SOUND, TRANSITIONS, AND STREAMING VIDEO

You already have a lot of skills under your belt, allowing you to accomplish some pretty exciting stuff. This chapter builds on that experience to create a television set complete with streaming video and visual transitions. Along the way, you'll expand your repertoire to include masking and sound editing.

In Chapter 5, we imported a video into Flash and ended up with an 80 KB .swf file that streamed a 2 MB .flv file. In this chapter, we'll turn a box into a television set, add some buttons to it, and stream three separate videos into a .swf file that is less than 1 KB. To do this, we'll manipulate line art, use a *mask* to define the area in which video is displayed, add a video object to the Flash document, and use ActionScript to open a streaming connection for the video.

Using ActionScript to stream video is just one of several ways to load external files into the Flash Player and display them. In later chapters, we'll load external images into a Flash movie. We'll also load other movies, text, and even a Cascading Style Sheet (CSS) file to format the text. Using external files helps cut down the time it takes to load and start Flash content, either online or on CD-ROM, improving the experience for the user.

True, you still have to load the external assets, but at least this way, you can show something to the user while that's happening. Also, if an asset is set up to be loaded only upon user request, such as via a button click, and the user never takes the action (clicks the button), the asset never needs to load, saving the user bandwidth and load time.

MANIPULATING ARTWORK

So far, we've created squares and other primitive shapes, but often you'll need to create a complicated shape using multiple built-in tools. In this section, we'll see how the drawing tools in Flash can be used to create a television set.

Combining graphic elements to create one image

The first thing we need is...yup...a box. But this time, we'll reshape and add to it to make it look like the cabinet of a television set:

1. Create a new Flash document with Stage dimensions of 280 × 400 and save it as *tv_set.fla* in the *09* folder.

2. Draw a 200 × 250 pixel rectangle on the Stage with a black stroke. For the fill color, choose the No Fill swatch in the color chooser (the one with a red line through it, as indicated in Figure 9-1). This means no fill will be applied to the rectangle when we draw it.

3. Drag two horizontal guides from the horizontal ruler onto the Stage, and position them approximately 10 pixels above and below the rectangle. (Use View → Rulers to display the rulers if necessary.)

4. Drag two vertical guides from the vertical ruler onto the Stage, and position them 10 pixels to the left and right of the rectangle.

Old-style TV sets often have a rounded appearance, so let's turn the straight lines into curved lines:

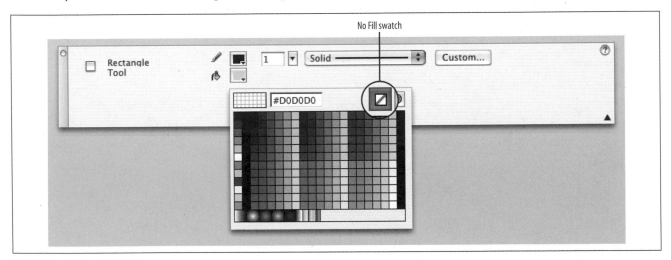

Figure 9-1. Choose the No Fill swatch to draw without a fill color.

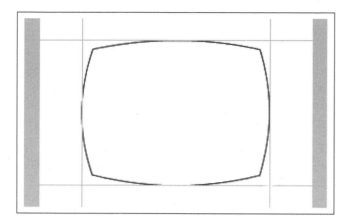

Figure 9-2. Click and drag to bend lines.

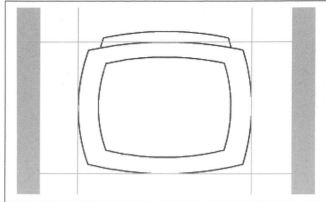

Figure 9-3. Copy and paste a portion of the rectangle to create a back for the television.

1. Using the Selection tool, move the cursor over one of the strokes for the rectangle. A small, curved line appears next to the cursor. Click on the stroke and drag it to the horizontal green guide above the box, then release the mouse button.

2. Repeat Step 1 for the three remaining strokes until all the lines are curved, as shown in Figure 9-2.

Next, we need to create an area for the television screen. We'll do that by copying the round-edged rectangle we just completed:

1. Select the entire stroke for the round-edged rectangle (by double-clicking it with the Selection tool) and choose Edit → Copy.

2. Choose Edit → Paste to make a duplicate copy of the round-edged rectangle on the Stage.

3. Before deselecting the duplicate, decrease its size about 15% (using the Free Transform tool while holding down the Shift key), then move it to the center of the first rectangle.

4. To give the image depth, we'll add on a curve to act as the back of the television, as shown in Figure 9-3:

   a) Click and drag to select the top 1/4 inch of the large rectangle (including the top line and a small bit of the vertical lines adjacent to it).

   b) Copy and paste the selection above the original top line.

   c) Scale the selection down about 15% smaller than the original.

   d) Position the selection above the large rectangle, as shown in Figure 9-3.

We'll color in the television set in a minute, so the depth will become more apparent.

Now, let's give the television set legs and an antenna:

1. Drag the guides on the Stage back to the rulers in the work area. Release each guide when it is over a ruler. This removes each guide from the Stage.

2. Activate the Line tool and draw a leg composed of three lines under the right corner of the television. Group the lines and position the leg as shown in Figure 9-4.

3. Copy and paste the leg to duplicate it, then choose Modify → Transform → Flip Horizontal to reverse the graphic.

4. Position the second leg on the other side of the television set.

5. Still using the Line tool, draw two diagonal lines to serve as the antenna, extending upward from the top of the television set.

Finally, we'll color in the various parts of the set, as shown in Figure 9-5. We'll use the Paint Bucket tool to complete the image:

Figure 9-4. Add legs and an antenna to the television set.

Figure 9-5. The completed television set.

1. Activate the Paint Bucket tool and choose light gray as the fill color.

2. Click between the large and small rectangles to apply a fill to the body of the television set.

3. Choose dark gray as the fill color and apply it to the top section (back) of the set. Apply a dark gray fill to the legs as well.

4. Choose Radial from the Fill Style drop-down list in the Color Mixer. Make one of the gradient colors medium gray and the other a slightly darker gray.

5. Click inside the screen area of the television set to give it its bubble look. Your completed television set should look similar to Figure 9-5.

The image is almost complete. We need to add three buttons, each of which will load a video. We'll economize, though, by using one button symbol:

1. Create a new layer named *btns* above *Layer 1*.

2. Activate the Oval tool, select black as the fill color, then choose the No Fill stroke swatch so that no stroke will be applied to the next drawing.

3. On the *btns* layer, draw a very small circle on the Stage and convert it to a button symbol named *btn*.

Remember, you can use the Free Transform tool to resize the circle after you've drawn it.

4. Make two more copies of the *btn* instance and position the three instances in a vertical row on the right side of the television set, as shown in Figure 9-6.

Adding a video object

To stream video into our television set, we first need to create a video object. A video object is, essentially, a scalable container into which a video can be loaded. Soon, we'll write ActionScript to load the video dynamically and display it inside the video object. To create the video object:

1. Lock *Layer 1* (by clicking the small black dot next to the layer name, in the padlock column). We don't want to accidentally edit something on that layer.

2. Open the Options menu in the Library and choose New Video. This adds a symbol named *Embedded Video 1* to the Library.

3. Create a layer named *video_obj* and drag an instance of *Embedded Video 1* to the Stage. Resize it so that it's only slightly larger than the screen area of the

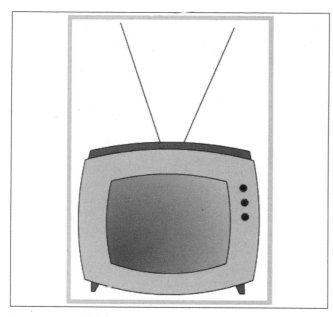

Figure 9-6. Add three instances of the btn symbol to the television set.

television set and position it in the center, as shown in Figure 9-7.

4. Assign the video object an instance name of my_video and lock the *video_obj* layer.

In a few minutes, we'll reference my_video in the Action-Script for the project. First, we need to finish the television set by creating a mask for the screen area.

Using a mask to trim the video's border

We want to play videos within our television screen. The videos are rectangular, but the screen is a round-edged rectangle. We'll use a mask to hide the edges of the videos so they match the screen area of the television set. See the "Masks" sidebar on the next page for an introduction to masks. See Figure 9-8 for a conceptual illustration of the process of masking a layer.

We'll use multiple layers to achieve the desired effect. We'll create a screen that displays when no video is

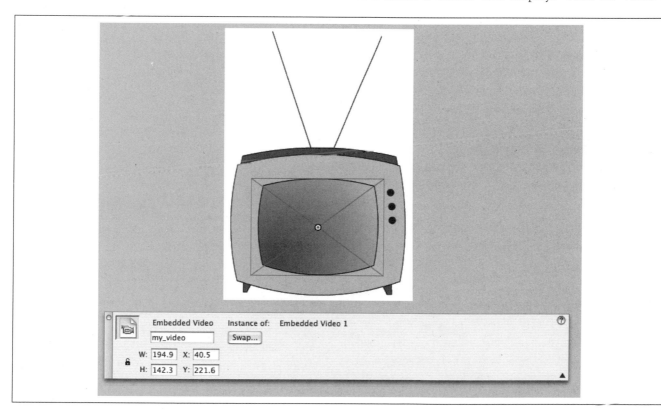

Figure 9-7. Add a video object to the Stage.

loaded (on *Layer 1*), a second screen for use as a mask (on the *mask* layer), and a copy of the screen's border (on the *screen_border* layer) so that the border appears in front of the video when it is playing on the screen. The contents of the *mask* layer do not appear in the final movie. The mask simply defines an area of the layer beneath it to display. Also, nothing contained in the masked layer that falls outside of the mask area appears in the movie. The mask itself represents the visible area of the masked layer, as depicted in Figure 9-8.

Let's add our video, including a masking layer to round off the edges:

1. Create two new layers above the existing *Layer 1* and *video_obj* layers; name the new layers *mask* and *screen_border*.

2. Unlock *Layer 1* and select the fill for the screen area of the television set, then copy it to the clipboard (Ctrl-C or Cmd-C).

3. Select the *mask* layer, right-click (Windows) or Cmd-click (Mac) on the Stage, and choose Paste in Place from the contextual menu to add a duplicate of the screen graphic to the *mask* layer.

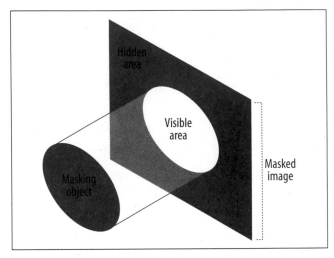

Figure 9-8. *The masking layer controls what portions of the masked layer are visible.*

4. Lock the *mask* layer. We need to copy and paste another element from *Layer 1*.

5. Select the stroke for the screen on *Layer 1* and copy it.

6. Paste the stroke in place (using the Paste in Place technique from Step 3) on the *screen_border* layer, then lock that layer as well.

MASKS

We've seen that Flash animations are created by superimposing one or more layers in an animation (similar to layers you'd find in Photoshop and other graphics programs). We've also seen how both the main timeline and movie clip timelines organize the layers and display their contents over time. *Masks* are often used to create traditional visual effects in Flash, such as a spotlight effect, in which one layer is viewed through the "hole" created by the masking layer. That is, the *masking layer* defines the area of the underlying *masked layer* that remains visible (the remainder is "masked off" and therefore invisible). The masking layer masks only the content of a masked layer; it does not affect content on other layers.

Think of masks as "viewing windows." The graphical shape you place on a masking layer acts as a window, allowing a partial view of the layer beneath it. This is similar to how you can look through a window in your house to see the front yard, but you can't see through the walls, which mask the view of the neighbor's house.

To create a masking layer (or simply "mask layer"), insert a new layer in the timeline above the layer you want masked. On the masking layer, create a shape to be used as the mask. Typically, masks are black, but any color will do. Wherever the mask layer contains pixels, the masked layer will be visible (as depicted in Figure 9-8). That is, if the masking layer has no content, it hides the masked layer entirely.

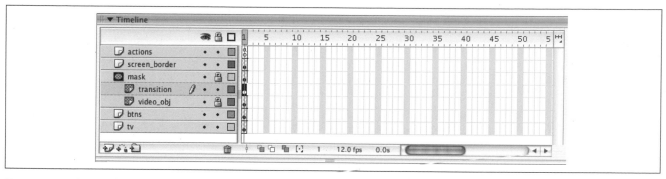

Figure 9-9. The masked layer appears indented beneath the masking layer in the timeline.

7. Lock *Layer 1*. We're all done with *Layer 1*. We need to do just one more thing to create the mask.

8. Right-click (Windows) or Cmd-click (Mac) on the *mask* layer's name and choose Mask from the contextual menu. This is the same as setting the layer's type to Mask in the Layer Properties dialog box accessible by double-clicking the layer name or via Modify → Timeline → Layer Properties.

The *mask* layer's icon changes to a mask icon and the *video_obj* layer appears indented underneath it in the timeline, as shown in Figure 9-9. Both layers are locked (this happens whenever you apply a mask layer, even when you don't lock them manually). Also, the video object appears as a yellow X in the screen area, and the edges of the object are cut off.

As outlined earlier, we've successfully used multiple layers to achieve the desired effect of a video playing within the rounded rectangle shape of the television screen.

Once you've created a shape for your mask, set the mask layer's Type to Mask in the Layer Properties dialog box, accessible under Modify → Timeline → Layer Properties. (You can also right-click (or Cmd-click) on the masking layer and choose Mask. Either method results in the layer below it in the layer stack becoming masked.)

Converting a layer to a Mask layer type automatically locks both it and the layer beneath it (the one being masked) in the layer stack. To edit either layer, simply unlock the layer using the padlock column in the timeline. If you wish to mask more than one layer with the same masking layer, simply drag the additional layers on top of the mask layer and drop them. Each masked layer appears indented underneath the masking layer as shown in Figure 9-9 (similar to what we've seen with respect to guide layers and layer folders).

Flash MX added the ability to create scripted masks in which a mask defined by one movie clip is used to mask another movie clip's contents. A scripted mask, as the name implies, is a mask applied dynamically at runtime with Action-Script via the *MovieClip.setMask( )* method. Applying a runtime mask is akin to creating a mask layer during authoring time, except that it affords much more flexibility. The mask used over a given clip can be changed at runtime, and new masks can be created at runtime. Again, although you can animate via the timeline in the authoring tool, you can create more sophisticated animations via ActionScript. For more information on masks, see the online Help topic How Do I → Basic Flash → Work with Layers → Add a Mask Layer.

STREAMING VIDEO WITH ACTIONSCRIPT

If you're not using Flash Pro or don't want to weigh down your Flash movie by using Media components—the components included with Flash MX 2004 and Flash Pro add substantial weight to the file size of a movie—ActionScript is the way to go when you need to stream video into Flash. A few lines of code accomplish the same thing the Media-Display component could, with a smaller file size.

Opening a streaming connection to the server

The verb *stream* means to begin playing external content before it is downloaded in its entirety. Macromedia also uses the term *stream* (or *data stream*) as a noun to describe any audio or video data being provided on the fly from the server or disk. In Chapter 5, we streamed an external video using prebuilt components. To stream video into our movie manually, we need three things: a connection from Flash to the server, a data stream that runs through that connection, and a video clip. Don't confuse a video clip with a Flash movie clip. A video clip is just the name typically used for a short video segment.

The CD-ROM provided with this book includes the videos (located in the *09* folder). We'll get to those details in a moment. First, let's create the connection and video stream using ActionScript. Essentially, we'll tell Flash, "I'd like to open a connection to the server, start a stream through that connection, and attach whatever video that loads through the stream to the video object on the Stage." See Figure 9-10 for a schematic reference.

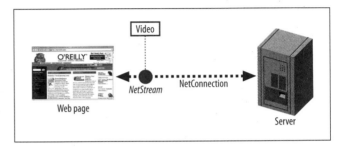

Figure 9-10. The video-streaming process.

VARIABLES

Variables are containers for data. To store data in Flash, we must define a variable and assign it a value. The variable's value can be anything from a new ActionScript object (such as with the `my_conn` variable used in this exercise, whose value is a *NetConnection* object) to something as simple as a number. Variables can have any datatype within a Flash movie (including *Number*, *Boolean*, and *String*, just to name a few).

ActionScript 2.0 syntax can be used to specify the datatype for the variable so Flash always knows what type of data is contained by it. For example, if we wanted to store the number 5 so we could reference it later in the movie, we would write the following:

```
var myNumber:Number = 5;
```

First, we use the keyword `var` to tell Flash we're declaring a variable. Next, we specify the variable name (`myNumber`) and assign it a datatype following a colon (`:Number`). Then, we optionally assign it a value (in this case, `= 5`) and finally use a semicolon to terminate the variable declaration.

To test this out, create a new Flash document and enter the preceding code into the Actions panel on frame 1, followed by:

```
trace (myNumber);
```

The *trace( )* command simply tells Flash to display something in the Output panel (which appears only when working in Preview mode of the Flash authoring environment, not when running a *.swf* in a browser). In this case, we tell it to display the value of the `myNumber` variable. Testing the movie produces the following in the Output panel:

5

Here's how to stream the video:

1. First, we'll create an instance of the *NetConnection* class and give it the name my_conn (a *class* is simply the set of instructions for how an ActionScript object operates; see the "Methods" sidebar in Chapter 10 for more information). To do this, create a new layer named *actions*, and add the following code to the Actions panel on frame 1 of the *actions* layer:

   ```
   var my_conn:NetConnection = new NetConnection ();
   ```

2. Next, we need to establish a connection to the server, which, in this case, is just your hard drive. To do this, we'll use the *connect( )* method of the *NetConnection* class. (The my_conn variable returned in Step 1 is an instance of the *NetConnection* class, so we can invoke the *connect( )* method on it.) The placeholder null must be passed into the *connect( )* method as the initial argument for the connection when creating a local connection (this is Macromedia's rule, not mine).

   ```
   my_conn.connect(null);
   ```

3. To start a stream, we need an instance of the *NetStream* class. We'll give this instance a name as well. Let's name it my_stream (breathtakingly original, aren't I?):

   ```
   var my_stream:NetStream = new NetStream (my_conn);
   ```

4. Next, we'll attach the external video clip that is loaded through my_stream to the my_video instance (the video object we created earlier on stage):

   ```
   my_video.attachVideo (my_stream);
   ```

5. Finally, we'll set a small buffer time—five seconds for our purposes—so the Flash Player loads part of the external video before playing it, ensuring smooth playback:

   ```
   my_stream.setBufferTime (5);
   ```

This part of the script is done. Your completed script should match Figure 9-11.

All we need to do now is load the video clips. We'll use the three buttons we created earlier to load and play the three different videos.

Loading video clips

Drawing upon our experience with buttons from previous chapters, we'll use the *btn* symbol to create the television controls that load various videos. We've already set up the connection and stream—we just need to load the

To experiment a bit further, test a movie containing the following script:

```
var myTitle:String = "geek.";
var myMessage:String = "Hello! I am a big ";
trace (myMessage + myTitle);
```

See for yourself what this produces. (Hint: when dealing with strings, the + operator appends the second variable to the first, known as *concatenation*.)

Variables have many uses. For example, a quiz built in Flash might require tracking the user's score. To do this, we might create a variable named theScore and give it an initial value of 0. Then, when the user chooses a correct answer, we could increment the variable's value, adding 1 for each right answer. Something like this, perhaps:

```
// Declare a variable and assign it a datatype and an
// initial value. In this case, reset the score to zero.
var theScore:Number = 0;
// Write a condition to check the answer
if (answer == "True") {
  // Increment the score by 1
  theScore ++;
  // Go to the next question
  gotoAndStop("question_two");
}
```

Over the next several chapters, we'll use variables for a variety of purposes, so you'll have plenty of chances to see how they are used and what benefits they offer.

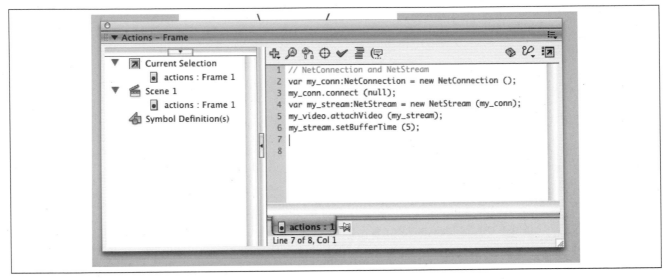

```
// NetConnection and NetStream
var my_conn:NetConnection = new NetConnection ();
my_conn.connect (null);
var my_stream:NetStream = new NetStream (my_conn);
my_video.attachVideo (my_stream);
my_stream.setBufferTime (5);
```

Figure 9-11. The completed script for streaming video into Flash.

videos. To do this, we'll write button event handlers that use the *play( )* method of the *NetStream* class to play the streaming video:

1. Select each *btn* instance on the Stage, one at a time, and give them instance names of scrappy1_btn, scrappy2_btn, and scrappy3_btn. The three video clips we're using here were created from Chapter 5's *SniffingForCats.mov* file starring Scrappy the dog.

2. Add the following event handler script to the *actions* layer on frame 1, below the code you've already written:

   ```
   scrappy1_btn.onRelease = function () {
       my_stream.play ("scrappy_1.flv");
   }
   ```

3. Copy and paste the event handler script twice more. In the two new versions, change scrappy1_btn to scrappy2_btn and scrappy3_btn. Also change the names of the *.flv* files being called from *scrappy_1.flv* to *scrappy_2.flv* and *scrappy_3.flv*. (To remind yourself about *.flv* files, see Chapter 5.)

4. Your script should look like this:

   ```
   scrappy1_btn.onRelease = function () {
       my_stream.play ("scrappy_1.flv");
   }
   scrappy2_btn.onRelease = function () {
       my_stream.play ("scrappy_2.flv");
   }
   scrappy3_btn.onRelease = function () {
       my_stream.play ("scrappy_3.flv");
   }
   ```

5. Save and test the movie.

When you click a button on the television set, a video clip loads into the video object on the Stage and plays. The clip is masked by the screen-shaped graphic on the mask layer, so the video appears only inside the television's screen area.

Also, notice that the file size for the movie is less than 1 KB. That's pretty impressive for a movie that's streaming three different video clips, huh?

> **NOTE**
>
> The server from which the video streams is nothing more than whatever computer is storing the video files. In this case, it's your own computer. To move this whole operation to the Web, simply post the *.swf* and *.flv* files to your web server. This type of streaming video does not require Flash Communication Server MX (FlashCom). If you have many videos, you might consider placing them in a subfolder named *Videos* during development and simply posting them in the same relative position on your server (in a folder named *Videos* below the folder where the *.swf* file is uploaded).

TRANSITIONS AND SOUND

No old-style television would be complete without static fuzz between channels, and no static fuzz would be complete without that classic static fuzz sound. In this section, we'll create a transition that plays when switching between channels on the television set. To do this, we'll create a movie clip that contains a bitmap and sound clip, and we'll use ActionScript to trigger the transition between channels. For this project, we'll import sound directly into Flash. In Chapter 10, we'll stream external sound clips into a Flash movie in much the same way we streamed video in this chapter.

A transition with sound

As is often the case, we want to create a transition with an accompanying sound. First, we'll set up the movie clip to hold both the audio and graphics for the transition: a snowy, static screen:

1. Press Ctrl/Cmd-F8 to open the Create New Symbol dialog box. Create a movie clip symbol and name it **trans_mc**.

2. In Edit mode for *trans_mc*, add two layers, so there are three total, and name the layers *actions*, *screen*, and *audio*, from top to bottom.

Now we're ready to import the audio and bitmap image:

1. Select frame 2 on the *audio* layer and convert it to a keyframe (by pressing F6).

2. Press Ctrl/Cmd-R to import an asset. Of course, you can also use File → Import → Import to Library or Import to Stage. Locate *static.mp3*, which is in the *09* folder, and choose it. The sound clip imports into the Library. (Bitmaps and other visual assets would import to the Stage, but audio imports only to the Library. Here we use the term "sound clip" in the colloquial sense. A sound is a type of asset, but it is not a movie clip. That said, a movie clip can contain sound, just as it can contain other assets such as bitmaps.)

3. Drag *static.mp3* to the Stage. Audio is audible but not visible in the published movie, so place it anywhere you want. Notice that frame 2 of the *audio* layer now displays a small, squiggly line. The squiggles are a visual representation of the sound waves that compose the sound clip.

4. Select frame 6 of the *audio* layer and press F5 to add frames so the *audio* layer extends to frame 6. The entire sound clip is now visible as a sound wave in the timeline.

5. Press Enter or Return to play the sound.

The sound definitely sounds like static, but there is a slight pause before the sound starts. Let's edit the sound to see if we can remove the pause.

Without sound editing software, we would often be stuck with imperfect sound files. Sometimes sounds that are meant to loop don't loop seamlessly, and sometimes, as in this case, a sound starts a split second later than it should. Fortunately, Flash has rudimentary sound editing functionality built into it. It is technically a sound effect/filter feature, not a sound editor per se. The original sound remains unchanged—only the instance is modified (just like changing the properties of a symbol instance). It's limited but useful nonetheless. Let's use it to edit our static sound:

1. Select frame 2 of the *audio* layer, where the sound clip is placed.

2. In the Properties panel, click the Edit button next to the Effect drop-down list. The Edit Envelope dialog box, as shown in Figure 9-12, opens. The two graphs display the sound waves in the right and left stereo channels for the sound clip. The horizontal bar in the center of the panel displays the time of the sound clip in seconds. Click the magnifying glass to zoom in.

3. Click on the Play button in the dialog box. Notice that there is a slight pause between releasing the mouse button and the beginning of the sound. You can see this in the sound wave graphs as well. The flat part of the line represents an area of the sound clip where there is no sound.

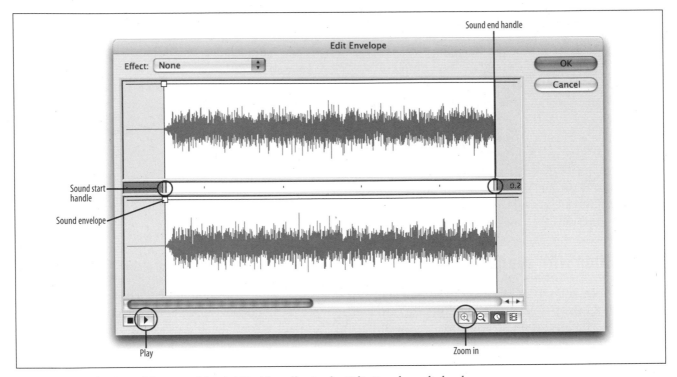

Figure 9-12. The Sound Start and Sound End handles in the Edit Envelope dialog box.

4. Drag the Sound Start handle, on the left side of the time bar, to the right, past the flat part of the sound wave, as shown in Figure 9-12, and release it. The section between the left edge of the panel and the handle is now grayed out. This means the beginning part of the sound, where no audio is present, will be ignored.

5. Drag the Sound End handle, which by default is at the end of the sound, to its left to cut off the end of the clip, where no audio is present, as also shown in Figure 9-12.

6. Click the Play button again to hear the modified version of the sound to make sure you are satisfied with the changes.

7. Click OK to close the dialog box.

By cutting off the beginning of the sound clip, we're ensuring that the sound will start immediately. We'll complete the visual portion of the transition before testing this in the published movie. Again, the original sound is not altered, only the instance is.

> **NOTE**
>
> You can modify instances of a sound clip in Flash all you want— cropping the beginning, fading out the end, etc.—but the entire sound clip still lives in the Library and is exported as part of the published movie, which consequently adds to the file size of your *.swf*.

If you do not need the entire sound clip, it is best to use an external sound editor to shorten and otherwise edit the sound before importing it into Flash. Popular sound editing programs include:

Macromedia's SoundEdit
   http://www.macromedia.com/software/sound

Sony SoundForge (formerly from Sonic Foundry)
   http://mediasoftware.sonypictures.com/products/
   soundforgefamily.asp

Adobe Audition
  http://www.adobe.com

Audacity (open source)
  http://sourceforge.net/projects/audacity

Publishing a movie with a larger sound clip than you need is one of the most common causes of unnecessarily excessive file size. In other words, don't do it. If I catch you doing it, I'm coming after you, and we're gonna have another little chat about respecting your audience.

Creating a transition

To finish our transition, we need to create the visual static fuzz effect. To do this we'll start with a static bitmap and create variation by flipping it a few times:

1. Select frame 1 of the *screen* layer and import *static.png* from the *09* folder as a single flattened bitmap.

2. Convert *static.png* to a graphic symbol named *static* and position it at (0, 0).

3. Add a keyframe to frame 2 of the *screen* layer and flip the image horizontally by choosing Modify → Transform → Flip Horizontal.

4. Add a keyframe to frame 3 and flip the image vertically using Modify → Transform → Flip Vertical.

5. Add another keyframe to frame 4 and flip the image horizontally (yes, again). Each frame now displays the static image differently. Alternating between only two images over two frames makes it too easy for the users to detect a pattern. Flipping it multiple times over several frames improves the illusion that it's really random, static fuzz. Confuse and disorient... that's what I always say (heck, it's how I got my wife to marry me).

6. On frame 1 of the *actions* layer, add a *stop( )* command. This way, the movie clip is stopped to begin with, and we can use ActionScript to tell the movie clip when to play. We'll do this in a minute.

7. Press Enter or Return to see the animation.

The fuzz animation is short, but it's as long as it needs to be. The animation will provide the illusion that the television shows static when switching channels. Let's finish

the movie clip that contains the audio, video, and static transition:

1. Return to Scene 1.

2. Add a layer named *transition* to the timeline, between the *video_obj* and *mask* layers. The *transition* layer is now one of the layers that will be masked, as indicated by the fact that it is indented along with the *video_obj* layer under the *mask* layer. A single mask layer can mask multiple layers.

3. Drag the *trans_mc* symbol from the Library to the Stage (onto the *transition* layer) and position it so it covers the screen area of the television set, as shown in Figure 9-13.

4. Assign the movie clip the instance name trans_mc, then lock the *transition* layer so the *mask* layer masks the movie clip. Mask layers do not mask anything while working in Flash unless the masking layer and all masked layers are locked.

Figure 9-13. trans_mc is one of the objects that will be masked, and covers the screen area of the television set.

5. Select frame 1 of the *actions* layer and open the Actions panel. Update each event handler to tell the transition movie clip to play when the button is clicked (changes shown in color):

```
scrappy1_btn.onRelease = function () {
  trans_mc.play();
  my_stream.play ("scrappy_1.flv");
}
scrappy2_btn.onRelease = function () {
  trans_mc.play();
  my_stream.play ("scrappy_2.flv");
}
scrappy3_btn.onRelease = function () {
  trans_mc.play();
  my_stream.play ("scrappy_3.flv");
}
```

6. Save and test the movie.

This is almost the effect we want, but the static appears even after you click the buttons on the television set. Let's fix the trans_mc clip so it does not appear unless we want it to:

1. Close the Preview window.

2. Double-click the *trans_mc* symbol in the Library to enter Edit mode for the symbol.

3. Select frame 1 of the *screen* layer and delete the bitmap on that frame.

4. Return to Scene 1. Notice that the trans_mc instance has disappeared. If you unlock the *trans_mc* layer and select frame 1, only the small circle at (0, 0) that represents the trans_mc instance's position is visible on the Stage. In other words, the instance is present, but there is no bitmap or graphic in the first frame of its timeline, so it displays as an empty clip on the main timeline.

5. Save and test the movie.

Now the movie functions correctly. When you click a button to change the channel, trans_mc begins to play, so the static appears and sound plays. When the transition is done, it returns to frame 1 of its own timeline and stops (because of the *stop( )* command on frame 1 of trans_mc). The empty frame prevents the static fuzz image from displaying when the transition is not playing.

Organizing the library

This project's Library has gotten a little messy since we started it. The Library contains one each of several types of assets: button symbol, video object, graphic symbol, sound, bitmap, and movie clip symbol. If this project got any larger, it could be difficult to locate symbols and assets within the Library easily. To remedy the situation, let's organize our Library:

1. Click the New Folder button in the Library panel twice to create two new folders. Name them *assets* and *external_media*. Just like symbol names, you can double-click on the name of a library folder to edit the name.

2. Drag *static.mp3* and *static.png* into the *external_media* folder.

3. Drag the remaining assets (symbols) into the *assets* folder.

4. Double-click the folder icons to expand them and display their contents, as shown in Figure 9-14.

5. Save your work.

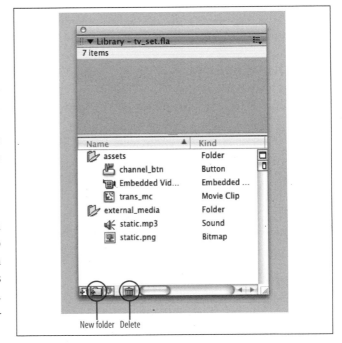

Figure 9-14. One well-organized Library.

There are many ways to organize a library. Some developers like to use folders for each type of asset, while others organize assets according to their function. For example, in a Flash file for a cartoon, the Library might be organized so that each character's assets are in one place, organized in subfolders to keep animated and inanimate symbols separate. A movie clip for a walking sequence could be in a folder with blinking eyes, while the hair and nose might be in another folder. You can add as many folders as you want, and you can nest other folders inside them. How you organize the Library does not affect the movie at all. The important thing is just to stay organized so assets are always easy to find. Large projects can contain hundreds of assets, and keeping organized is key to maintaining a good workflow.

NOTE

If your project has too many Library assets to find easily, or if you're just too messy of a person to bother getting organized, you'll be happy to know the contents of the Library panel can be sorted (by name, kind, use count, linkage, and date modified) and are also searchable via the Movie Explorer (Window → Other Panels → Movie Explorer).

To delete folders in the Library, use the Delete button (the trash can icon) just as you would to delete symbols. Be aware that deleting a folder also deletes all of its contents. If you want to keep certain assets from a folder you plan to delete or want to reorganize your Library, simply drag assets from one folder to another. Although deletes can be undone, it is a good idea to make a backup copy of your *.fla* before doing anything major.

Our multimedia television set proves that you now have a handle on how to work with many different asset types, including bitmaps, sound, symbols, and video. You've come a long way since the humble rectangular boxes at the beginning of this book!

In this chapter, you learned how:

- Our hero, the box, is a great starting point for a much more complex graphic, such as a television set

- Video can be streamed into Flash via a few lines of ActionScript

- Mask layers enable you to hide parts of graphics and animations

- Movie clips can be used to create a visual transition between parts of a movie

- Sound can be imported into Flash and edited on a primitive level

- The Library can be organized to help you maintain a good workflow

There is no real limit to what you can accomplish with transitions and masking. *Flash Hacks* (O'Reilly) includes numerous stunning effects you can create using the same basic techniques learned here, including color video transitions, pixel wipes, and animated masks.

This chapter has given you a firm foundation from which you can experiment. To expand your horizons further, we'll do some more complex things in the next few chapters, such as construct a preloader for a large movie, build a presentation, and create a movie for use on a handheld. We're getting to the really cool stuff now!

10

LOADING ASSETS ON THE FLY

In this chapter you'll really begin to flex your Flash muscles. You'll load external JPEGs on the fly, use ActionScript to create a preloader, optimize images in Fireworks, use built-in components, and even create your own custom component. So hang on tight!

This chapter focuses almost entirely on solving one problem: finding the best way to load external assets into a Flash movie while it's running. This goal can be accomplished in several ways, and each approach has its merits. We'll work with each method and learn which is best in any given situation.

"So," you wonder, "why do I want to load assets into a Flash movie dynamically when I can just import them at authoring time?" And that is a good question, for which there are several answers.

First, as good as Flash's built-in compression engine is, it's not good enough in all situations. You can't import a bitmap image weighing 100 KB into a Flash document and expect to produce a *.swf* file that is small enough to load quickly over a dial-up connection.

Second, Flash projects are often more complex than what we've created so far in this book. Web sites, photo galleries, presentations, printable advertisements, and many other things can all be created with Flash, and it is rarely an economical use of file size to cram all the necessary assets into one Flash document. Adding one bitmap image to a Flash project may not affect the file size much, but try adding 10, each of which is used in a different screen of a presentation. Try adding 30 bitmaps as part of a photo gallery. The size of your Flash movie balloons and becomes a bandwidth hog. Since web users tend to live by "the 10-second rule," which dictates that anything that takes longer than 10 seconds to load is not worth waiting for, it's almost always a good idea to modularize Flash content. (Content that takes longer than 10 seconds to load also makes the user think either she has done something wrong or the page may never load due to some other failure, such as a broken link.) Splitting projects into multiple pieces and loading each module only as required is key to creating Flash content that runs smoothly and loads quickly. You may be wondering if using external assets simply shifts the download burden to a later time. And the answer is yes, it does, but the point is that the external content may never be needed (when was the last time you needed to see all the content of a web site in one visit?). By keeping it external and loading it on demand, the user only has to wait for content that is actually needed.

Third, complex Flash documents can be hard to maintain or update after you've created them. Once you've completed a project and left it alone for several months, it can be downright difficult to refamiliarize yourself with the inner workings of the project to perform a revision. You have to weed through the ActionScript, decipher which movie clips are located where (and whether they are nested inside other clips), and determine how everything is laid out in various timelines. Splitting up sections of the project makes each project element smaller and easier to revise. Also, a modular structure can speed up the development significantly, especially if more than one person is working on the same Flash project. Joe can work on the "Contact Us" section of a Flash site while Franz works on the "Products" section. Amy can work on the graphics for the project while you write ActionScript for the shopping cart (you're ready for that, right?).

USING ACTIONSCRIPT TO MODULARIZE CONTENT

One way to modularize a Flash project is to create separate movies for each part, or module, of your project and load each one as it's needed. Another way is to keep bitmaps external to your Flash document, loading them dynamically while the published movie is running. For now, we'll focus on the latter.

Loading bitmaps on the fly

Let's start our problem-solving journey by working with ActionScript's *loadMovie( )* command, which despite its name can also be used to load external bitmaps (provided they're in non-progressive JPEG format). This command

> **NOTE**
>
> Macromedia's Flash Player census shows that Flash Player 5 or higher is installed on 98% of Internet-connected computers, so it is not usually necessary to publish *.swf* files for Flash Players older than version 5. Flash Players 5 and 6, in fact, are often installed on mobile devices, such as handhelds, PDAs, and even cell phones.

works all the way back to Flash Player 3, so it can be relied upon when creating content for users with older versions of the Flash Player.

Before we can load a JPEG file, we have to set up the Flash document:

1. Create a new Flash document and save it as *loadMovie.fla* in the *10* folder.

2. Change the Stage dimensions to 500 × 375.

3. Draw a box on the Stage (the fill and stroke colors don't matter, nor does the size). This time we'll use the box as a so-called *container*, a shell into which other content is loaded. In a moment, we'll use ActionScript to load a bitmap into this movie clip (the box itself will be replaced by the loaded image).

4. Select the fill and stroke of the box and press F8 to convert it to a movie clip symbol. Name the symbol *container_mc*.

5. Position the movie clip instance at (0, 0).

6. Assign the *container_mc* instance the instance name container_mc (consistency is so predictable). Your document should match Figure 10-1.

Next, we'll use ActionScript's *loadMovie( )* command to load a bitmap image into the container_mc instance:

1. Create a new layer named *actions*, select frame 1 of that layer, and open the Actions panel.

2. In the Actions panel, start writing the command:
   ```
   loadMovie(
   ```

3. The opening parenthesis of the command prompts a code hint that tells us we need to also enter a URL, target, and access method for the command. The access method parameter (either "GET" or "POST") is optional, and the default ("GET") is appropriate for this script, so specify the URL and target only. Your finished code looks like this (the URL is typically a filename in quotes, and the target movie clip's name should also be in quotes):
   ```
   loadMovie("water.jpg", "container_mc");
   ```

4. Save and test the movie.

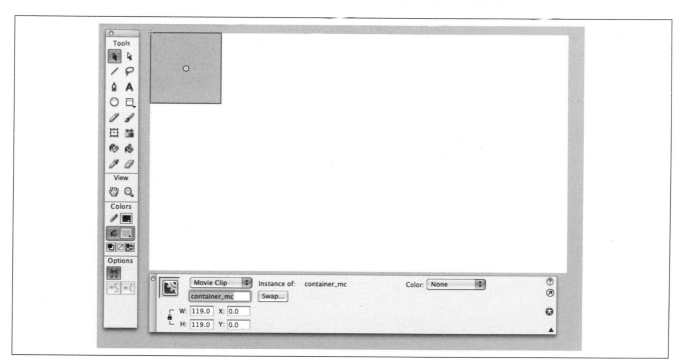

Figure 10-1. The container_mc clip positioned at (0, 0).

Well, the JPEG image loaded into the movie, but it's not aligned to the top-right corner of the Stage as it should be. Let's fix that:

1. Close the Preview window.

2. Double-click *container_mc* to edit it in place.

3. Move the box graphic inside of *container_mc's* timeline to (0, 0).

4. Return to Scene 1 and realign the container_mc instance to (0, 0). The readjustment is necessary because moving the box on the symbol's timeline (in Step 3) also moved the timeline instance relative to the Stage.

5. Save and test the movie again.

Now the image loads into the top-left corner of the Stage and looks great.

The *water.jpg* bitmap image in the *10* folder is 196 KB, but the *.swf* file is only 148 bytes—less than 1 KB. Pretty cool, huh? Since we're loading the bitmap image dynamically, we could, at any time, replace *water.jpg* with a new or updated image of the same name, and *loadMovie.swf* would still load it. There is no need to reopen the *.fla* file to make a revision and no need to republish the *.swf*. And we did it all with one line of code. So many benefits, so little time.

That works fine when loading files from your local computer, but how do you get it to work when you upload it to a web server?

NOTE

The ActionScript will work as is when you upload the *.swf* and *.jpg* files to a web server. Simply make sure the server's directory structure mirrors that used during local development. Because we used relative paths, the *.swf* will find the *.jpg* when you post it to a server, provided they're in the same directory. Of course, you can load an image from any location by passing an absolute URL, such as "http://www.flashoutofthebox.com/water.jpg", when invoking *loadMovie( )*.

Want to see how to make it even easier? Let's try the *loadMovieNum( )* command, which is similar to *loadMovie( )* but doesn't require the container clip:

1. Close the Preview window.

2. Choose File → Save As and save the file as *loadMovieNum.fla* in the *10* folder.

3. Delete the container_mc instance from the Stage. We don't need it to use the *loadMovieNum( )* command. Also, delete the *container_mc* symbol from the Library (using the trash can icon in the Library panel) and the *container_mc* layer from the timeline (using the trash can icon in the Timeline panel).

4. In the script on frame 1 of the *actions* layer, change loadMovie to loadMovieNum, then change "container_mc" to 1, so the script looks like this:

```
loadMovieNum("water.jpg", 1);
```

5. Save and test the movie.

Wow—this method for loading assets doesn't require anything but one line of code. How cool is that?

As an alternative to loading assets into movie clips with *loadMovie( )*, you can use *loadMovieNum( )* to load assets into a specific *level*. The 1 in the ActionScript we just wrote is a level number. The main timeline is level 0, or the *root* level, and you can load assets into any level from level 0 to (really odd and obscure fact coming...) level 2,130,706,429. (I'm sure there's a reason it doesn't work at level 2,130,706,430, but I don't know what it is, and no one at Macromedia seems to either. I guess we'll just have to accept it and move on.)

Zen and the art of preloading

There is one big problem with our project that we haven't talked about yet. If we post this file online and a user on a dial-up Internet connection tries to load it, it will likely take longer than 10 seconds, and that's a bad thing. Even though our *.swf* file is less than 1 KB, the bitmap it's loading is almost 200 KB. The *.swf* will load just fine, but the *water.jpg* image might not show up for another minute or two. To solve this problem, we'll create a *preloader* for the file.

WARNING

Loading an image (or for that matter, another *.swf*) into level 0 using *loadMovieNum( )* replaces the main movie. And if you use *loadMovie( )* but specify a nonexistent clip as the target, again, Flash replaces the main movie with whatever you are loading. So be sure to specify an unoccupied level or appropriate clip when using *loadMovieNum( )* and *loadMovie( )*. The *loadMovieNum( )* method uses an integer such as 1, 2, or 3 to specify the level into which to load the content. However, when using *loadMovie( )* or other methods that expect strings for the target destination, use strings such as "_level1" or "_level2" to specify level numbers. If you specify _level1 without the quotes and level 1 does not yet exist, Flash will load the new content into the current level instead (which will unceremoniously displace the currently running movie).

A preloader is a chunk of functionality we create mostly with ActionScript that checks the status of the load process and displays it visually so the user always knows when something is loading. It's up to us to make sure the load doesn't take a long time, but it's ultimately up to the user to decide if he wants to wait for it to complete. Beyond the basic status offered by standard preloaders, some Flashers design the preloader animation to be entertaining, or ease the wait with other distractions. More ambitious designers integrate preloaders tightly into the design, so the experience appears seamless. A great example of this is Mini USA (*http://www.miniusa.com*), where preloaders run almost unnoticeably while you're busy reading a quote about Mini Coopers. By the time you're done reading the quote, the content has loaded and you're launched automatically into whatever site section you requested.

Our preloader will use text to display the percentage of bytes loaded. Every time 1% of an asset is loaded into our Flash movie, the number in the text field will increment by 1. When the percentage reaches 100%, the asset is fully loaded and displays in the movie. While this isn't the most visually exciting preloader in the world, it does

serve the purpose of keeping the user informed and is a good starting point for exploring the visual possibilities of preloaders in your own work.

First, we'll set up the file similarly to how we did in the preceding section:

1. Create a new Flash document and save it as *preloader. fla* in the *10* folder, then change the Stage dimensions to 500 × 375.

2. Draw a box, convert it to a movie clip symbol named *container_mc* (remember to set the top-left corner as the registration point in the Convert to Symbol dialog box), position it at (0, 0), and assign it the instance name container_mc.

3. Rename *Layer 1* to *container_mc*.

We need one more element for our preloader: a text field to display the percentage counter. Since this number changes, we can't use static text and must use a dynamic text field. The data displayed in the text field is generated by the preloader script. We'll add the field now and reference it in the script:

1. Create a new layer named *text*.

2. Activate the Text tool and choose Dynamic from the Text Type drop-down list in the Properties panel.

3. Set the font for the text field to Arial or Verdana with a point size of 14. Set the font color to medium gray.

4. Click once on the Stage to create a dynamic text field. Before deselecting it, drag the handle in the bottom-right corner of the field to the right to expand the size of the field. Make it about 430 pixels wide, as shown in Figure 10-2.

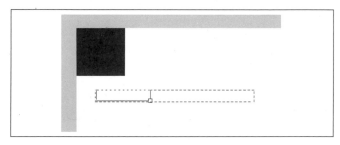

Figure 10-2. Stretch the dynamic text field to about 430 pixels (five or six inches).

5. To deselect the text field, click outside of it, then press V to activate the Selection tool. (If you leave the Text tool active, you'll create another text field the next time you click on the Stage, but we need only one.)

6. In the Properties panel, assign the text field the instance name info_txt. The _txt suffix, like the _mc suffix in the instance names of movie clips, prompts code hints in the Actions panel.

7. Click the Align Left option in the Properties panel.

8. Save your work.

Now we can start scripting our preloader.

Scripting the preloader

In this section, we'll use ActionScript to create the functionality of the preloader. This will give users a visual indication that something is being loaded into the Flash movie. Without it, users may never realize our 196 KB image is downloading and will eventually appear.

To create the preloader:

1. Create a new layer named *actions*.

2. Select frame 1 of the *actions* layer and add the following to the Actions panel:

```
var my_mcl:MovieClipLoader = new
        MovieClipLoader();
```

This creates an instance of the *MovieClipLoader* class and stores it in a variable named my_mcl. Moreover, it declares that my_mcl has a datatype of *MovieClipLoader* (new MovieClipLoader( ) returns an instance of the *MovieClipLoader* class). This means that the ActionScript 2.0 compiler will complain if we try to store any other type of data in my_mcl. For more information on datatypes, see the "Datatypes" sidebar.

NOTE

Don't confuse movie clip instances with other types of ActionScript objects. Placing a movie clip symbol on the Stage creates a movie clip instance, whereas creating an instance of an ActionScript class with the *new* operator creates an ActionScript object. Movie clip instances are typically derived from symbols stored in the Library and usually contain at least one graphic. Pure ActionScript objects (as opposed to movie clip instances, which are technically also objects) often have no visual representation. For a thorough explanation of creating objects and classes in ActionScript, see *ActionScript for Flash MX: The Definitive Guide* and *Essential ActionScript 2.0* (both from O'Reilly).

DATATYPES

Datatypes are exactly what the name implies: types of data. Flash recognizes many datatypes, including *Number* (a numeric value), *String* (zero or more characters, wrapped in quotes), *Boolean* (a true or false value), and *MovieClip* (at last, something you recognize). Each class, including *MovieClipLoader* or any other custom class created by a developer, effectively defines a custom datatype of the same name.

ActionScript 2.0, first introduced in Flash MX 2004 and Flash Pro, makes use of *strict typing*, which is common in other programming languages, although it wasn't supported in ActionScript 1.0. Specifying the datatype of a variable after a colon (i.e., using so-called *post-colon syntax*) tells Flash what kind of data the variable is allowed to contain. The ActionScript 2.0 compiler displays warnings (type mismatch errors) in the Output panel at compile time if the code attempts to store the wrong kind of data in a variable. The compiler also generates an error if you try to invoke an unsupported method, such as trying to invoke a method of the *MovieClip* class on an instance of the *Date* class. (*Methods* are functions supported by a given class as

When you're ready, let's continue. I'll talk soon about the concepts behind each element of this script, but for now, just follow along:

1. Next, we'll create a *listener* object (a generic ActionScript object whose only job is to listen for events and run code in reaction to them) to monitor load progress. See the "Event Listeners" sidebar on the next page for more information.)

   ```
   var my_listener:Object = new Object();
   ```

2. First, we want to detect the *onLoadError* event, which is generated by the *MovieClipLoader* instance if the image does not load. We'll use the listener object we created in Step 1 to report an error to the user:

   ```
   my_listener.onLoadError = function (mc) {
     info_txt.text =
   "Error: A file did not load. Sorry about
   that.";
   };
   ```

The next thing we need to do is monitor the *onLoadProgress* events that are broadcast by the *MovieClipLoader* instance. Again we'll use the listener object to monitor these events and display the percentage loaded as the download progresses.

The *onLoadProgress( )* event handler defined for our listener will display changing percentage numbers in the text field. To do this, we'll have to use a little basic math (yep, it turns out that junior high school actually served a purpose beyond acclimating you to embarassing social situations).

To create the *onLoadProgress( )* event handler, we define a function and assign it to the listener's onLoadProgress property:

```
my_listener.onLoadProgress = function (mc,
loadedBytes, totalBytes) {
  info_txt.text = Math.floor(loadedBytes/totalBytes
* 100) + "%";
};
```

When we set up our listener to monitor the *MovieClipLoader* instance, as we'll do momentarily using the *MovieClipLoader* instance's *addListener( )* method, the listener's *onLoadProgress( )* event handler is invoked automatically as the content downloads.

In this case, the function uses the loadedBytes and totalBytes parameters to calculate the percentage of the content that has downloaded. I know it looks complicated, but *Math.floor( )* simply rounds the floating-point number down to the nearest whole number. The rest of the code displays the results in the info_txt dynamic text field with some nice formatting.

The equation we use to calculate the percentage is loadedBytes/totalBytes * 100. The / operator indicates division, and the * operator indicates multiplication. So we're telling Flash to determine the number of bytes currently loaded (loadedBytes), divide it by the total number of bytes for the asset (totalBytes), and multiply that number by 100. This equation results in the percentage we need to display in the text field. The + operator is not for addition in this context. Instead, it *concatenates* (joins) text together to form a single string. We use it to append the percent sign (%) to the number resulting from

described in the "Methods" sidebar later in this chapter.) Likewise, it complains if you attempt to access an unsupported property for a given class. This helps to catch errors in which an item is used improperly, which helps you make your code more reliable.

We use strict typing in this chapter, in which each variable is manually assigned a datatype. In addition to helping catch errors, *typing* a variable (i.e., declaring its datatype) allows Flash to provide code hints in the Actions panel. For example, declaring my_mcl to be of type *MovieClipLoader*

activates the code hint drop-down list whenever we write my_mcl followed by a dot in the Actions panel. In this case, the code hint drop-down list displays methods and properties specific to *MovieClipLoader* objects, which helps us write code faster.

If you don't specify a datatype (i.e., you omit the colon and datatype when declaring a variable), the compiler can't perform type checking. This allows the ActionScript 2.0 compiler to compile legacy ActionScript 1.0 code without error.

the equation so that the displayed text includes a percent symbol at the end (e.g., 69%).

As you can see, it takes more time to explain and understand the line of code than it does to write it. But don't fret. We're learning to talk to Flash in its own language, and learning a new language can take time. On a positive note, mastering this new language means you'll be able to talk to your computer. The downside is that you'll be talking to a computer. You're about an inch away from being a geek.

Although we've defined our event handlers for the listener object, it won't receive any events until we add it as a listener for the *MovieClipLoader* instance. Once we do that, we need only one line of code to load an external JPEG or SWF file into the container_mc instance.

So let's add the listener object as a listener using *addListener( )* and load the JPEG instance using *loadClip( )*:

1. Beneath the code you've written so far in the Actions panel, enter the following command. This makes the my_listener object a listener of the my_mcl *MovieClipLoader* instance (translation: my_listener gets notified whenever my_mcl.loadClip() is used to load something):

   ```
   my_mcl.addListener (my_listener);
   ```

2. Finally, use the *MovieClipLoader.loadClip( )* method to load our JPEG image. As discussed in the later "Methods" sidebar, we invoke *loadClip( )* on an instance, in this case my_mcl:

   ```
   my_mcl.loadClip ("water.jpg", "container_mc");
   ```

3. Save and test the movie.

Um...yeah. The image loads like it's supposed to, but we just wrote this whole script to create a percentage counter on the Stage, and the darn thing doesn't work. It's time to quit using the *MovieClipLoader* class and go back to using *loadMovie( )*, right?

No, no, no. Hold on a second. In reality, the *MovieClipLoader* script does work (and very well, thank you), but the *onLoadProgress( )* method, which is used to create and display the percentage of bytes loaded in the text field, does not run when you are loading a file from your local hard drive.

To get around this little caveat, I've put a copy of *water.jpg* on the support web site for this book. Let's modify the code and see if we can get the preloader to work:

1. In the last line of the preloader script, replace "water.jpg" with "http://www.flashoutofthebox.com/water.jpg".

2. Save and test the movie.

Aha! That's much better. We should fix one small thing before moving on, though. When the load is complete, the text field continues displaying 100%, which is no longer needed and sort of ugly. So let's clear the percentage from the text field once the loading completes:

1. Between the *onLoadProgress( )* function and the *addListener( )* statement, add the following code to clear the text from the info_txt instance once the load is complete:

EVENT LISTENERS

Because Flash content is often delivered over the Internet, there is a delay between the time assets are requested and when they become available (the download is said to be *asynchronous* because the results are not available immediately). Instead of forcing Flash to pause while waiting for something to download, we can set up a *listener*. A listener is simply an ActionScript object whose job is to listen for events and run code in reaction to them. The events are generated automatically when something of interest happens. The listener object is often separate from the entity that *broadcasts* (generates) the events. A properly configured listener object can listen for events (each event has a specific name) and perform some action in response to them. By way of analogy, you might be cooking dinner while listening for the doorbell to ring. When the doorbell rings (the event), you would perform an appropriate action such as opening the door and greeting your guests.

Many ActionScript classes generate events. For example, the *Key* class broadcasts an *onKeyDown* event whenever

```
my_listener.onLoadComplete = function (mc) {
  info_txt.text = "";
};
```

2. Your completed script should look like this:

```
var my_mcl:MovieClipLoader = new
MovieClipLoader();
var my_listener:Object = new Object();
my_listener.onLoadError = function (mc) {
  info_txt.text =
"Error: A file did not load. Sorry about
that.";
};
my_listener.onLoadProgress = function (mc,
loadedBytes, totalBytes) {
  info_txt.text = Math.floor(loadedBytes/
totalBytes * 100) + "%";
};
my_mcl.addListener (my_listener);
my_mcl.loadClip (
"http://www.flashoutofthebox.com/water.jpg",
"container_mc");
my_listener.onLoadComplete = function (mc) {
  info_txt.text = "";
};
```

3. Save and test the movie.

Now, when the load is complete, the text disappears. The *onLoadComplete( )* function tells Flash to change the info_txt instance to say nothing (indicated by the empty quotes) when the load is complete.

The functions in a script can be written in any order you like, but I find it easier to read ActionScript if I organize the elements of a script into logical pieces. For example, I put all the lines of code for the listener object in succession to keep them together.

We started this chapter with the intent to find the best way to load an external asset into a movie while it's running, and this works just great. The *onLoadProgress( )* method runs as it should, so the percentage counter is working perfectly (that is, if you've followed along and written the script correctly). The *.swf* file is less than 1 KB, and we've successfully provided a way for the user to see when something is loading. Nice work! (Pats self on back.)

I know you're probably frustrated with writing code now. It can be difficult to take in so much information at once, so it's time for some good news. We don't need this script! (Ducks and runs out the door.)

A PRELOADER COMPONENT

I hope that last statement about not needing the code we just wrote didn't upset you too much. The thing is, Flash comes with a set of components, which are pre-built "widgets" meant to standardize the look, feel, and functionality of common Flash elements. One of the included components is the ProgressBar component, which is a preloader. It's used to preload assets into the Loader component.

Using the ProgressBar component

Let's see if the ProgressBar component works better than the script we wrote. There's a possibility it won't, so don't hire a hit man just yet.

a key is pressed and an *onKeyUp* event whenever a key is released; the *Stage* class broadcasts an *onResize* event whenever the Stage is resized. Likewise, the *MovieClip-Loader* class broadcasts events when content is being downloaded, when it completes, and when there is an error. Our listener can detect these events from the *MovieClip-Loader* class by adding itself as a listener (using the *add-Listener( )* method) and defining so-called *event handlers* that match the names of the events (in this case, *onLoad-Progress*, *onLoadComplete*, and *onLoadError*).

It is good practice to remove a listener using *removeListen-er( )* when it is no longer needed. For clarity, we didn't clutter up the code examples in this book, but you can remove my_listener as a listener (which prevents it from receiving further events from my_mcl) as follows:

```
my_mcl.removeListener(my_listener);
```

For many more details on listeners, broadcasters, and the design justification for them, see *ActionScript for Flash MX: The Definitive Guide* and *Essential ActionScript 2.0* (both from O'Reilly).

To implement a preloader using the ProgressBar component:

1. Close the Preview window and close *preloader.fla*.

2. Create a new Flash document and save it as *progressBarComponent.fla* in the *10* folder. Change the Stage dimensions to 500 × 375.

3. Create one new layer for a total of two, and rename the two layers *actions* and *components*.

4. Choose Window → Development Panels → Components to open the Components panel, shown in Figure 10-3.

5. Select the *components* layer, expand the UI Components menu in the Components panel (by clicking on the small arrow), and drag the Loader component to the Stage. This creates an instance of the Loader component on stage and adds the Loader component to the Library.

6. Resize the Loader component instance to 500 × 375, position it at (0, 0), and assign it an instance name of my_loader.

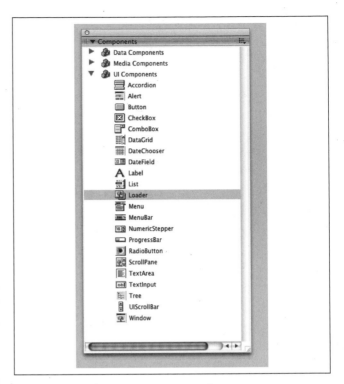

Figure 10-3. The Components panel.

METHODS

The word *method* is often a source of confusion due to its multiple meanings. It is used informally as a synonym for "approach" or "technique." The term is also used to refer to the access method parameter (whose value is either "GET" or "POST") in commands such as *loadMovie( )*. But in formal programming terminology, *methods* are commands that can be executed by an ActionScript class or its instances. For example, the *MovieClip* class supports methods we've used already, such as *play( )* to play the movie clip, *stop( )* to pause the movie clip, and *gotoAndStop( )* to jump to another frame. Methods are just functions associated with a particular class or instances of the class and, as such, define its capabilities.

However, not all functions are methods. So-called *global functions*—such as *setInterval( )*, *getVersion( )*, and *parseFloat( )*—are not methods because they are not associated with a class. They can be accessed from any script by simply using the function name, such as:

```
var currentVersion:String = getVersion();
```

However, methods must be accessed through a class or an instance of the class. The *floor( )* method is part of the *Math* class, which is why we must write `Math.floor()` instead of simply `floor()` to run it. Because it is literally accessed using the name of the class (in this case, *Math*), it is called a *class method* (also known as a *static method*).

However, so-called *instance methods* are invoked on instances of a class rather than the class itself. Instance methods are used when the operation is unique for each instance of the class. For example, each clip can have its own depth, so the *MovieClip.getDepth( )* method is an instance method that returns the depth of the specified movie clip. Although we may write it as *MovieClip.getDepth( )* for

7. Also on the *components* layer, drag the ProgressBar component to the Stage and position the instance in the horizontal and vertical center of the Stage. Assign it an instance name of my_pb.

The Loader component is a bit like the container_mc clip we created earlier, in the sense that *water.jpg* will load into it. It won't do anything here but scale the loaded asset to fit within the component's own bounding box. The ProgressBar component, on the other hand, does quite a lot. It does everything our preloader script is written to do, plus it comes with a nice progress bar to indicate the load progress.

We have to set up the ProgressBar component to monitor the Loader component's progress, and then we have to tell the Loader component what to load. Let's see how it works:

1. Select frame 1 of the *actions* layer and enter the following script into the Actions panel to tell the my_loader instance what to load:

```
my_loader.autoLoad = false;
my_loader.contentPath =
"http://www.flashoutofthebox.com/water.jpg";
my_pb.source = my_loader;
my_loader.load();
```

2. The line my_pb.source = my_loader; from Step 1 tells the my_pb ProgressBar instance to monitor the load progress of the my_loader Loader instance. The same thing can be achieved by selecting the my_pb instance and entering **my_loader** in the Source field of the Parameters tab of the Properties panel.

3. Save and test the movie.

Okay—the image loads again, and the progress bar displays the load progress nicely. But we still had to write four lines of code, and the progress bar doesn't disappear after the image loads.

Fortunately, we can fix the visibility issue by hiding the progress bar behind the newly downloaded image:

1. Select the my_pb instance and choose Modify → Arrange → Send to Back. It doesn't appear that anything happens, but the progress bar is now behind the Loader instance.

2. Save and test the movie.

Everything is perfect now. The progress bar runs, the image loads (which obscures the progress bar now that the load is complete), and life is grand.

---

convenience when discussing it in prose, we would not use this code:

```
// This is wrong
var currentDepth:Number = MovieClip.getDepth();
```

Because it is a movie clip instance method, *getDepth( )* must be accessed using a movie clip instance name:

```
// This assumes someClip is a movie clip instance
var currentDepth:Number = someClip.getDepth();
```

How do you know whether something is a global function, a class method, or an instance method? Until you develop an intuitive sense, refer to documentation for an explanation of how to use each function or method, or just try it and see what works. If you invoke a function incorrectly, Flash may display a compile-time error message in the Output panel when you attempt to test it in the authoring tool. In other cases, the code will compile but will fail silently at runtime, in which case it simply won't achieve the desired result. For full details on why and when Flash detects and displays (or fails to display) compile-time error messages, see *Essential ActionScript 2.0*.

In addition to methods, classes may define event handlers (which handle certain events, such as mouseclicks) and properties (which define the current state of the object, such as its position, size, and color). We've used event handlers, such as *onRelease( )*, throughout the book, and we've used properties such as _rotation and _x. Some classes also broadcast events intended to be handled by separate listeners, as described in the earlier "Event Listeners" sidebar.

Don't get too caught up in the terminology or the theory. By using this book and performing the exercises, you'll develop an intuitive feel for how to write ActionScript. If you want a formal introduction to ActionScript programming, see the resources cited in Chapter 13. For a list of the methods and properties supported by each class, refer to the ActionScript Dictionary in Flash's online Help.

(Pause for reflection.)

You should know me better than that by now. I'm not going to be happy until I'm sure we've used the best possible method to load the image into our movie. And I'm not convinced. Why? Look at the size of the file in the Preview window. It's 30 KB. And we have yet to load the 196 KB bitmap image. Our previous movie was less than 1 KB.

In short, 196 KB + 30 KB = 226 KB, and 226 KB = not good.

Constructing this component-based solution is easier than hand-coding a preloader script, but it's really better only for the developer, not the end user. We may have saved development time, but if we post this file online, every user that accesses it will have to wait for 226 KB worth of files to download, whereas we could get away for less than 200 KB. Furthermore, the user will have to wait for the preloader to load (of all things) before the movie loads the image. Over a dial-up connection, 30 KB takes several seconds to load. We almost need a preloader for the preloader. It's madness. Madness I tell you!

Always—I repeat always—put the user's interests ahead of your own. If necessary, emphasize to your boss or client that the extra development time will be rewarded with higher user satisfaction.

Macromedia developed these components for Flash MX 2004, and many developers have complained about the size of them. The addition of one component to your movie adds substantial file size. This is due to the large amount of shared ActionScript classes used to create them. They do make projects easier to build, but a project's success depends just as much on how well the user can use it as anything else. If it takes two minutes for a user on a dial-up connection to load the project, odds are, she won't stick around to see what it does.

Let's fix this disaster.

NOTE

The bright side to using Macromedia's components is that they share a lot of the ActionScript used to make each one operate. So while adding a single component adds a lot of file size, adding several components increases the file size only marginally beyond that. If you're willing to take the initial hit on file size and expect to use more than five or six components, they can be a great way to build a project quickly. Components are also useful for quickly developing prototypes for client approval. Later, you can optimize download times as appropriate. See "Using Components" in Chapter 11 for alternatives.

Optimizing graphic file size in Fireworks

We know that it's too much to ask the user to load 226 KB just to see one image, but sometimes we can't lower the file size of the image itself without degrading the quality. In this case, though, I think we can.

We'll optimize the image in Fireworks before loading it into Flash.

1. Launch Macromedia Fireworks (if you don't have Fireworks, the CD-ROM includes the installer for the trial version).

2. Open *water.jpg*, located in the *10* folder, by choosing File → Open.

3. Choose File → Export Preview to open Fireworks' Export Preview dialog box, shown in Figure 10-4.

4. If the Quality slider in the dialog box is set to 100%, the image is 196 KB (this may vary depending on your operating system), and that's too big. Drag the slider to 90% and make sure the Remove Unused Colors option is selected. Now, the image is 63 KB, and the quality degradation is barely noticeable.

5. Click Export and save the file as *water_2.jpg* in the *10* folder.

6. Close *water.jpg* without saving it and quit Fireworks.

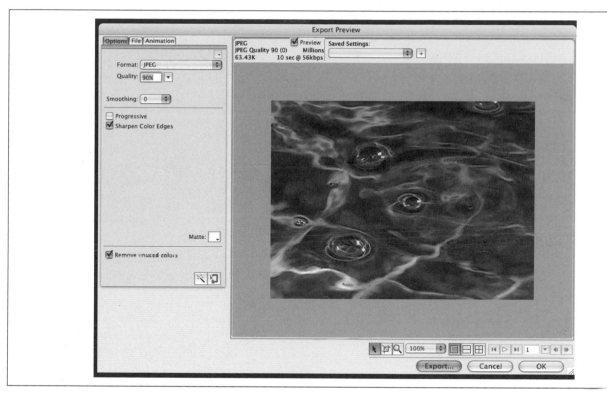

Figure 10-4. The Export Preview dialog box in Fireworks.

With one small adjustment we shaved 133 KB (about 66%) off the file size. We could reduce the file size more and still maintain a high-quality image, but for the purposes of this chapter, we need it large enough to trigger the preloader. Please, don't do this on your own projects. Always lower the file size as much as you can without degrading the quality unacceptably.

The new image will load much faster, so we've solved that problem. But we still have a preloader that weighs 30 KB, and that's not economical. Let's see how we can use our preloader script from earlier to help us out.

Build your own component

Flash is a very extensible program. If you know what you're doing, you can create custom behaviors, commands, tools, and even dialog boxes (but we won't get into that in this book). You can also create your own components.

The preloader script we wrote earlier resulted in a *.swf* file that is less than 1 KB (488 bytes), which is a great solution for this project. Posting *preloader.swf* online and using it to load *water_2.jpg* means the user has to download only 63 KB (instead of 226 KB). The downside to the solution is that we had to write all that code. Don't get me wrong here; I'm a geek, but I don't want to write code over and over again if I don't have to. I'd much rather package up this script and its text field and keep it around to use in other projects.

Once again, Flash makes it easy to reuse code. Components to the rescue!

Let's turn our earlier preloader script into a component. Once we do that, we can simply drag and drop the component into any project and use it to load whatever we want. When we're done, all we'll need to do to configure our custom component is enter the name of the file to load and where to load it.

The first step in creating a component is to package the assets and ActionScript necessary for the component as a self-contained unit. So we'll start by turning our preloader script and its associated text field into a movie clip:

1. Open *preloader.fla*, located in the *10* folder. This file contains the preloader script we created earlier. Save it as *FP7_Loader.fla* in the *10* folder (using File → Save As).

2. Select frame 1 of the *actions* and *text* layers, then right-click (Windows) or Cmd-click (Mac) and choose Copy Frames from the contextual menu.

3. Press Ctrl/Cmd-F8 to open the Create New Symbol dialog box. Create a movie clip symbol named *FP7_Loader* (the name we use for this movie clip becomes the name of the component that appears in the Components panel later on).

4. In Edit mode for *FP7_Loader*, right-click (Windows) or Cmd-click (Mac) on frame 1 of *Layer 1* and choose Paste Frames from the contextual menu. The frame contents and layer names that we copied earlier are pasted into the timeline.

5. Position the text field at (0, 0) so the clip's registration point can be used to align instances of the component on stage (the registration point is the only thing you'll see when you drag this component on stage, so you'd align the component by its registration point, knowing it is in the same spot as the upper-left corner of the contained text field).

Our preloader script was originally written to load a specific image (*water.jpg*) into a specific place (the container_mc clip), but to use it as a component, the script has to work in any situation. To pull this off, we need to generalize the code by making the file to load and the place to load it configurable options:

1. Select frame 1 of the *actions* layer in Edit mode for *FP7_Loader* and open the Actions panel.

2. Modify the *loadClip( )* statement in the preloader script as follows (changes shown in color):

```
var my_mcl:MovieClipLoader = new
MovieClipLoader();
var my_listener:Object = new Object();
my_listener.onLoadError = function (mc) {
  info_txt.text =
"Error: A file did not load. Sorry about
that.";
```

```
};
my_listener.onLoadProgress = function (mc,
loadedBytes, totalBytes) {
  info_txt.text = Math.floor(loadedBytes/
totalBytes * 100) + "%";
};
my_mcl.addListener (my_listener);
my_mcl.loadClip (fileToLoad, whereToLoadIt);
my_listener.onLoadComplete = function (mc) {
  info_txt.text = "";
};
```

The two terms we just added—fileToLoad and whereToLoadIt—are variables. Instead of passing a fixed URL to the *loadClip( )* method and hardcoding the clip or level into which to load the asset, we're telling it to use the values of the variables fileToLoad and whereToLoadIt. These variables act as placeholders; their values will be specified each time we use an instance of the component in a project. You'll see how this works in a minute.

Next, we'll get rid of all the unused assets in the Flash document. Since you'll be keeping this file as the source for your *FP7_Loader* component, it's a good idea to clean it up:

1. Return to Scene 1 and delete everything from the Stage.

2. Delete the *actions* and *text* layers. Rename the *container_mc* layer to *Layer 1*. Since we'll never use the layer again, it's better to give it a generic name so you don't think it's important later on (if you ever reopen this file).

3. Open the Library and delete the *container_mc* symbol.

All that's left in the movie now is the *FP7_Loader* symbol in the Library. Our proverbial house is clean. Next, let's turn the symbol into a component:

1. Right-click (Windows) or Cmd-click (Mac) on the *FP7_Loader* symbol in the Library and choose Component Definition from the contextual menu. The Component Definition dialog box, shown in Figure 10-5, opens.

2. In the Parameters section of the dialog box, we need to create two parameters. Click the Add Parameter button (the button with the + sign) to create a new parameter.

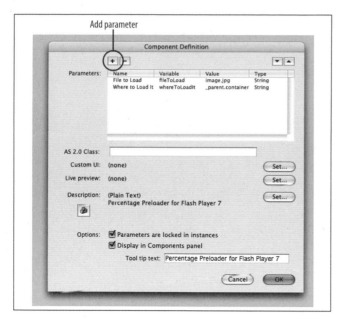

Figure 10-5. *The Component Definition dialog box.*

3. In the Name field for the parameter, enter **File to Load** (with spaces) and press Enter or Return.

4. In the Variable field, enter **fileToLoad** (without spaces, case-sensitive). This is the name of the variable we passed to the *loadClip( )* method in the preceding code example.

5. From the Type drop-down list (which is used to specify the datatype for the variable), choose String.

6. Finally, enter **image.jpg** into the Value field. The name in the Value field is replaceable—we're just using it as placeholder text to prompt the user of this component (you) to enter in the full filename.

We have one parameter—the file to load—ready to go. Before creating the second parameter (whereToLoadIt), let me explain how the component will work. When we drag the completed component into a project, we'll use the Properties panel to enter the URL or path of a file to load. This filename becomes the value of the fileToLoad variable in the component's script. When the *loadClip ( )* command is run, Flash will load the asset located at the URL or path specified by the variable.

For example, if we drag the component into a new project and enter **http://www.flashoutofthebox.com/water_2.jpg** into the File to Load field in the Properties panel, the component's *loadClip ( )* command will find and load the asset at that URL.

In addition to the URL (or file path) of the loaded asset, we need to specify the target destination—either a movie clip or a level. So let's create our component to accept a value for the whereToLoadIt variable, which will later be passed to the *loadClip ( )* command:

1. Create another new parameter using the Add Parameter (+) button in the dialog box.

2. Set its Name field to **Where to Load It**.

3. Set its Variable field to **whereToLoadIt**.

4. Set its Type to String.

5. Enter **_parent.container_mc** into the Value field.

The expression _parent.container_mc refers to the container_mc movie clip attached to the timeline of the clip containing the component. In other words, the component and container_mc should be attached to the same timeline (e.g., both placed on the main timeline or both nested within the same movie clip).

The _parent property simply identifies the timeline that contains the current clip. When used from within an instance attached to the main timeline, _parent refers to the _root timeline. Don't use _parent from the main timeline itself because it won't work (the _root timeline has no parent because it is at the top of the hierarchy).

Only a few steps left—hang in there. Once we're done, you'll never have to create this particular preloader again, and you'll know how to make your own component. Later in your life, you can build other, fancier preloaders and turn those into components too. Or maybe you'll just recoil in horror the next time someone asks you to write a component. Who can say?

Let's set up a text description for our custom component:

1. In the Component Definition dialog box, click the Set button across from the Description label (as seen

in Figure 10-5) to open the Component Description dialog box, shown in Figure 10-6.

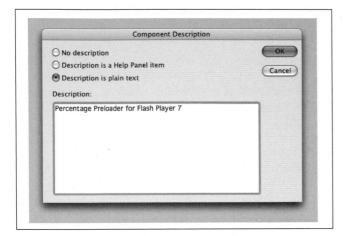

Figure 10-6. The Component Description dialog box.

2. Select the Description is Plain Text radio button. This displays a text field in which you can write a description. Enter **Percentage Preloader for Flash Player 7** into the field and click OK to close the dialog box.

3. Back in the Component Definition dialog box, under Options, check the Display in Components Panel option and enter **Percentage Preloader for Flash Player 7** into the Tool Tip Text field.

4. Click OK to close the dialog box.

The icon for the *FP7_Loader* symbol in the Library panel changes to a component icon. We're almost done. To wrap up, we just need to export the component so it can be stored in the Flash install directory and accessed via the Components panel:

1. Right-click (Windows) or Cmd-click (Mac) on *FP7_Loader* in the Library and choose Export SWC File from the pop-up menu. The Export File dialog box opens.

2. Name the file *FP7_Loader.swc* and save it in the *10* folder. The file extension for components created in Flash MX 2004 or Flash Pro must be *.swc*.

Now we have a compiled component file we can use in any project. All that's left to do is add it to the Flash install directory and test it:

1. Locate *FP7_Loader.swc* in the *10* folder and copy it to the clipboard.

2. Paste a copy of *FP7_Loader.swc* into:

   a) This folder on Windows:
   ```
   C:\Documents and Settings\UserName\Local
   Settings\Application Data\Macromedia\Flash MX
   2004\LANGUAGE_CODE\Configuration\Components
   ```

   b) On some Windows systems, the folder may be located at a path similar to:
   ```
   C:\Program Files\Macromedia\Flash MX 2004\
   LANGUAGE_CODE\First Run\Components
   ```

   c) Or this folder on Mac:
   ```
   Macintosh HD/Users/UserName/Library/Application
   Support/Macromedia/Flash MX 2004/LANGUAGE_CODE/
   Configuration/Components
   ```

3. I recommend creating a subfolder in the *Components* folder named *Custom* (or whatever you want) and putting the new loader component there to keep things organized.

4. Back in Flash, open the Component panel's Options menu and choose Reload. The new FP7_Loader component should appear in the list.

5. Save and close *FP7_Loader.fla*.

If your new *FP7_Loader* component doesn't appear in the list in the Components panel, you may need to restart Flash.

Now, we'll test the new component and make sure it does what it's supposed to:

1. Create a new Flash document and save it as *component_test.fla* in the *10* folder.

2. Drag the *FP7_Loader* component onto the Stage.

3. In the Properties panel's Parameters tab, enter **http://www.flashoutofthebox.com/water_2.jpg** in the File to Load field and **_level1** in the Where to Load It field, as shown in Figure 10-7. This loads the image into level 1.

4. Save and test the movie.

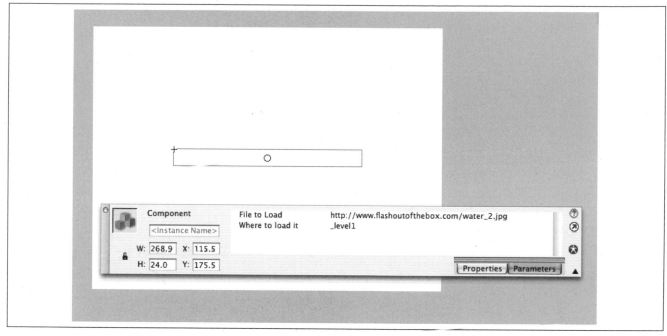

Figure 10-7. Configure and test the FP7_Loader component.

The preceding code won't work if you specify **1** (instead of **_level1**) for Where to Load It, because the component is expecting a string that represents a clip or level, not a number (and no clip named "1" exists). Of course, you could specify a clip such as **_parent.container_mc** as the destination, provided that a clip named container_mc exists on the parent timeline (the same timeline as the one containing the component).

Ideally, the user of the component could specify a level number instead of a string without worrying about the component's implementation. You can modify the code to convert the whereToLoadIt parameter to a number, if necessary, by replacing this code:

```
my_mcl.loadClip (fileToLoad, whereToLoadIt);
```

with this:

```
if (isNaN(parseInt(whereToLoadIt))) {
  // Treat the destination it as a string
  my_mcl.loadClip(fileToLoad, whereToLoadIt);
} else {
  // Otherwise, treat it as a level number
  my_mcl.loadClip(fileToLoad,
     parseInt(whereToLoadIt));
}
```

The preceding code will work even if the user specifies **1** instead of **_level1** in the Where to Load It field of the Parameters tab in the Properties panel. An ambitious developer might also warn the component user if the specified target clip or level doesn't exist. However, a full discussion of robust error handling when writing custom components is beyond the scope of this book. This exercise's goal is to help you understand universal issues, such as how to define parameters to generalize your components (i.e., make them flexible) and avoid possible errors when specifying clips and levels.

If you've followed along correctly, you now have a functioning preloader component. The percentage counter works and the image loads. Congratulations!

The best thing about this component is that it's less than 1 KB, which is 29 KB less than what it takes to do the same thing using the Macromedia components included with Flash. And now for some really good news. Now that you have a working preloader component, you never have to create one again (unless you want to).

There is one small catch to using the *FP7_Loader* component: it works only for Flash Player 7 or later. In fact, that's why I told you name it *FP7_Loader*. The *MovieClipLoader* class is new to Flash MX 2004, so ActionScript that uses it won't work in earlier versions of the Player. Although ActionScript 2.0 can be used when exporting to Flash Player 6 format, that version of the Player doesn't support new classes such as *MovieClipLoader*.

When creating Flash content, it's best to decide which version of the Flash Player you'll be publishing to prior to starting your project. Many of the most powerful features of ActionScript are supported only in Flash Player 6 or 7, but you can still do quite a lot with Flash Player 5. Decide which version to use before scripting your project so you

don't trap yourself into hours of revisions. If you're unsure about the ability to use a command or method in a particular Player version, double-click on the term in the Actions panel to select it, then click the Reference button in the panel to read the version compatibility information for that term in the ActionScript Dictionary included with Flash. (You can also access Help documentation by choosing Help → Help or Help → How Do I.)

To learn about creating preloaders for older versions of the Flash Player, check out the FlashKit site at *http://www.flashkit.com/movies/Scripting/Preloaders*.

We've solved the problem we set out to solve (finding the best way to load external assets into a movie) and learned quite a bit about ActionScript along the way. Problem-solving is an essential skill when working in Flash. There are usually multiple ways to do something in Flash, and knowing which method to use will make you a better developer, as your movies will be more efficient for people to download and use.

In this chapter, we've seen how to:

- Load external JPEG images into a Flash movie while it's running, shortening startup time for users

- Use ActionScript to create a preloader, which indicates to the user that something is loading

- Use Fireworks to decrease the file size of bitmaps before importing them into a Flash project

- Use Flash components for drag-and-drop functionality

- Create our own component, so we can spend less time writing code and more time having fun

Components can be as simple as the one we built in this chapter or as complex as the ones built by Macromedia. To stretch the powers of our *FP7_Loader* component, do some research in the Flash Help documentation to see what you can do with the text field in the component. Can you figure out how to make the font color and point size for the percentage counter customizable? Okay, that may still be a little difficult at this point, but if you're feeling adventurous, it would be nice addition.

For more information about building and using components, check out *Using_Components.pdf* on the enclosed CD-ROM, the URL *http://www.macromedia.com/devnet/mx/flash/articles/buildtest_comp.html*, and the resources cited in Chapter 13.

In the next chapter, we'll put our new ActionScript skills to work by creating a presentation that loads other assets such as external text files and CSS files. Again, modularizing projects like this makes each element of the project easier to create, update, and maintain.

11

BUILDING A REUSABLE AD TEMPLATE

In this chapter, we'll use some crafty Flash techniques to create a project template for a movie that contains formatted text, images, animation, and a form, all of which are updatable by altering external files. These techniques keep you productive and your clients happy even if a project's contents need to be updated repeatedly.

As stated in Chapter 10, one of the most significant benefits of modularizing Flash content is that you can easily update and maintain elements of a project.

To help you see why the modular architecture is important, here's a hypothetical situation for you (and yes, things like this do happen in real life):

Your client comes to you and says he needs a series of information pieces designed for the company's web site. Each piece should maintain a consistent look and feel, tell a story about what the company can do for its customers, and end with a screen where users fill out a small form to request a catalog and choose whether to join the mailing list. Each piece will appear in a priority section on the home page for one week.

Since the new campaign is meant to become the focus of the home page for the next several weeks, we've got some extra space to work with—we don't have to stick to the typical ad banner size (468 × 60). The maximum width we can use for the ads is 580 pixels. Height matters less, but we should try to make sure the piece can be seen completely by the user without scrolling down the page (borrowing from newspaper lingo, this is called "above the fold").

The best part? It's got to be ready to launch tomorrow, and you'll be on vacation next week when the images and text for the second piece in the series will be ready. What's a boy (or girl) to do?

The graphic designer for the company has designed the layout and animation for the pieces, but it's up to us to figure out how to turn this lone *.fla* file into a template for multiple home page ads that can be updated without interrupting your vacation.

USING EXTERNAL TEXT AND CSS

To start, let's take a look at what the graphic designer in our hypothetical situation has put together. The graphic designer doesn't know ActionScript very well, but she has been nice enough to add *stop( )* commands and button actions to the document so we can see a test movie.

Reviewing the .fla file

To see what the final movie is supposed to look like and how the *.fla* file is set up:

1. Open *ad_template.fla*, located in the *11* folder.

2. Expand the *learn more* and *animations* layer folders by clicking the small black arrow next to the layer folder names (on Windows, the arrow is white). Notice the animations.

3. Inside the *animations* layer folder, expand the *images* layer.

4. Test the movie. Click the button each time it appears to see how the movie looks.

After the initial fade-in animation, the button instances on the Stage send you through successive screens of the movie. The last screen features several small rectangles, each of which will be replaced with components to create the catalog-request form.

To turn this single piece of Flash content into a template for a series of ads, we'll take the text out of the Flash document and instead load it from an external text file. Then we'll create a way to dynamically format the text in case we need to change the typeface for one of the pieces in the series. We also need to pull the images out of the template and instead load them on the fly. Finally, we'll use components to create the form and write a script that pulls the data from the client-side form (in the *.swf* file) and sends it to a server-side script for processing.

Server-side scripting is beyond the scope of this book, but the necessary server-side script is on flashoutofthe-box.com, so we can complete the project without learning another programming language (nice, huh?).

> **NOTE**
>
> Data sent out of Flash must be processed by a server-side script, which is written in a language such as Perl, PHP, Python, ASP (Active Server Pages), JSP (Java Server Pages), or CFML (ColdFusion Markup Language). French works as well. (I'm kidding.)

Loading text dynamically

If we leave the text inside this *.fla* file, we'll need to re-open it and edit several symbols every time we update the ad. The same is true for the images. If we load everything dynamically, however, we can keep the maintenance requirements to a minimum.

The first thing we'll do is remove the text from the Flash document:

1. Drag the playhead to frame 15 and select the "Meet Joe" text.

2. In the Properties panel, choose Dynamic Text from the Text Type drop-down list. We can set the contents of a dynamic text field via ActionScript, something that is not possible with static text.

3. Double-click on the text field and delete the text. Then, drag the handle for the text field to resize it to match Figure 11-1.

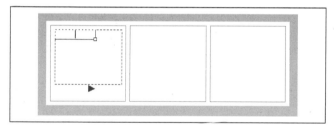

Figure 11-1. Resize the text field by dragging the handle.

4. Click outside of the text field to deselect it.

5. Repeat this process for the text fields at frames 45, 75, and 105, moving them to the upper-lefthand section of the box containing each item.

Next, we need to create a text file that defines each line of text as the value of a variable:

1. Open your favorite text editor. Flash Pro includes a text editor to edit external files, but the standard edition of Flash MX 2004 does not. You can use Notepad on Windows (under Start → Program → Accessories → Notepad), TextEdit on Mac (located in the *Applications* folder on your hard drive), or Macromedia Dreamweaver (included on the CD-ROM that comes with this book) just to name a few.

2. Create a new file and save it as *the_vars.txt* in the *11* folder. Be sure to use the *.txt* extension and save the file in plain-text format, as the Flash Player cannot read binary formats such as Microsoft Word documents (*.doc* files) or Rich Text Format (*.rtf*) files.

3. Enter the following text, starting from the first line of the document:

```
&leftText=Meet Joe.&
&middleText=He reads O'Reilly books&
&rightText=So does Serena.&
&learnMoreText=If you think they look happy,
just wait until you read them yourself.&
```

4. Save your text file and close your text editor.

The file we've just created sets up a series of variables. The first variable is `leftText`, and it holds the text "Meet Joe." Each line includes two ampersand symbols (&) so that Flash knows where each variable begins and ends once the file is loaded into a movie. Ampersands are the standard variable delimiter, which you might recognize from URLs that pass variables to server-side scripts. An ampersand is not necessary at the very beginning or very end of the variable list, but I think it makes the list easier to read. (Actually, it's mostly because I'm a designer, and I think text files should look as symmetrical as a nice design.) Two ampersands are required between the end of one variable and the start of another. In this case, we separated each line with a carriage return for readability.

To get this text into the Flash movie dynamically, we first need a script in the Flash document that will load it:

1. Select frame 1 of the *actions* layer in *ad_template.fla* and open the Actions panel.

2. Add a *stop( )* command: **stop();**.

3. Enter the following code to create a *LoadVars* object, which is used to load variables from an outside source:

```
var my_lv:LoadVars = new LoadVars();
```

4. Next, we need a function that tests the success of the load operation and, if it is successful, sends the playhead to a specific frame:

```
my_lv.onLoad = function (success) {
    if (success) {
        gotoAndPlay("start");
    }
};
```

The preceding script runs the *onLoad( )* method of the *LoadVars* object (my_lv). We're saying to Flash, "If the load is successful, go to the frame labeled start and play the movie."

Next, we just need to tell Flash which file to load:

1. To tell Flash which file to load, use the *LoadVars. load( )* method. The final code looks like this (addition shown in color):

```
stop();
var my_lv:LoadVars = new LoadVars();
my_lv.onLoad = function (success) {
    if (success) {
        gotoAndPlay("start");
    }
};
my_lv.load("the_vars.txt");
```

2. Create a new layer named *labels* underneath the *actions* layer, insert a keyframe at frame 6, and assign start as its frame label using the Properties panel.

3. Save and test the movie.

4. In the Preview window, choose Debug → List Variables.

The Output panel opens and lists all the variables for the movie. The panel lists the my_lv instance and the four variables that are loaded by my_lv (leftText, middleText, rightText, and learnMoreText). It also lists several other items, but these are the only ones we're interested in right now.

Now that we know the variables are loading correctly, let's move on. Next, we need to display the variable values in the appropriate text fields:

1. Close the Output panel and Preview window.

2. Assign an instance name to the text field at each point in the ad. Name the text field at frame 15 **left_txt**, the field at frame 45 **middle_txt**, the field at frame 75

right_txt, and the field at frame 105 **learnMore_txt**. You can assign instance names only to text fields that are of type Dynamic Text or Input Text. Static text fields do not support the use of instance names because they can't be controlled via ActionScript.

3. At frame 15, select the dynamic text field on the Stage and enter **my_lv.leftText** into the Variable field in the Properties panel. This tells the text field to display the value of the leftText variable, which was loaded into the my_lv instance and stored as a property there.

4. Save and test the movie.

The script on frame 1 loads the text file and sends the playhead to the start frame. The movie stops at frame 15, and the text field displays "Meet Joe."

Next, let's modify the remaining text fields similarly to display the other variables:

1. At frame 45, select the dynamic text field and enter **my_lv.middleText** into the Variable field in the Properties panel.

2. At frame 75, specify **my_lv.rightText** as the variable for the text field.

3. At frame 105, specify **my_lv.learnMoreText** as the variable for the last text field.

4. Save and test the movie.

The text of each loaded variable now displays in its respective text field as the playhead reaches those parts of the movie.

If it seems as if we're testing the movie too often, keep in mind that when writing ActionScript, it's very easy to mess something up (I speak from experience, people).

> **NOTE**
>
> The key to avoiding time-consuming or hard-to-find mistakes is a mantra in the development world: "Test early and test often."

That is, test small portions of your code to make sure they are working. Then you can test the next piece knowing that what you've already written is probably not the source of any problems that arise. Of course, it is an iterative process. You may have to revisit earlier code to enhance the feature set or fix a latent bug. ActionScript 2.0's strict typing, in which you declare each item's datatype—as we did earlier by specifying :LoadVars as the datatype for my_lv—helps keep you on the straight and narrow. For example, if we attempted to use a method or property with my_lv that wasn't supported by the *LoadVars* class, the compiler would alert us to the problem by displaying an error message in the Output panel. See the "Datatypes" and "Methods" sidebars in Chapter 10 for related information.

Next, we'll create a style sheet for the text so we can dynamically set the font and font size for the movie.

Formatting text using CSS

The use of Cascading Style Sheets (CSS) is increasingly common these days, so we'll assume you're at least somewhat familiar with CSS. If not, consult a book such as *Cascading Style Sheets: The Definitive Guide* (O'Reilly) or the chapter about CSS in *Dreamweaver MX 2004 Magic* (New Riders), written by my dear friend, Dreamweaver guru Stephanie Sullivan. CSS can be used to format text for an entire web site with only one file and design tableless layouts for individual web pages. Flash MX 2004 and Flash Player 7 offer the ability to use CSS in Flash, which means we can now control the format of all the text in a project using one external *.css* file.

To modularize our ad series even further, we'll create a style sheet and load it dynamically in the published movie. By doing this, we eliminate the need to ever reopen the template file to change the font properties for the dynamic text fields. (This example assumes you use a single set of font properties for all the text fields. In a more complex example, you could define multiple styles in the CSS file and apply different styles to each text field. The principles demonstrated here still apply.)

First, we'll create the style sheet:

1. Open your favorite text editor again (or use Flash Pro's built-in editor). You can use Dreamweaver for this as well; it features color coding for the various parts of CSS scripts.

2. Write the following to create a typical CSS style:

    ```
    myStyle {
        font-family: Verdana;
        font-size: 16pt;
        color: #666666;
    }
    ```

3. Save your work as a plain-text file named *the_styles. css* and close the text editor.

The *.css* file defines a style named myStyle. The style's font is 16-point Verdana and the font color is a medium gray. We can also create styles for links within the text, but none of the text in our movie includes hyperlinks, so it's not necessary.

We'll load *the_styles.css* into the Flash movie and use it to format all the text. This way, if we ever need to change the typeface used in one of the movies, all we need to change is the name of the font and/or font size in this *.css* file and repost it to the web server.

Next, let's write the ActionScript needed to load the CSS file:

1. In *ad_template.fla*, add the following code to frame 1 of the *actions* layer (underneath the other code) to create a new *TextField.StyleSheet* object named my_ss:

    ```
    var my_ss:TextField.StyleSheet = new TextField.
    StyleSheet();
    ```

2. Next, we'll test the success of the load operation, much as we did for the *LoadVars* instance we created earlier. To do so, add the following code (leave off the closing curly brace for now):

    ```
    my_ss.onLoad = function (success) {
        if (success) {
            trace("the_styles.css loaded");
        } else {
            trace("the_styles.css did not load");
        }
    ```

The script in Step 2 does several things. Much like the earlier *LoadVars* script, we're telling Flash to notify us when the load operation completes and to make sure it was successful. If so, it *traces* "the_styles.css loaded", which means it displays the specified data in the Output panel when you test the movie. That is, we use the *trace()* command to tell us whether the CSS has been loaded successfully.

The *else* statement tells Flash what to do if the load doesn't work. In this case, instead of reporting to us that the load was successful, the Output panel will report "the_styles.css did not load". The *if-else* statement is extremely common in ActionScript (and in other programming languages). The *if* part of the script tests the specified expression to determine if something is true or false (a Boolean value). If true, we tell the movie to do one thing; if false, we tell it to do something *else*. In this case, we're testing whether success is true or false. (The value of success is set by Flash depending on whether the load succeeded. It is automatically passed to the *onLoad( )* handler when the load operation completes.)

Now try to test the movie.

There is an error in the code, so the Output panel reports that the *onLoad( )* function is missing a closing curly brace. The curly braces essentially serve as a wrapper for a block of code. The closing curly brace must be included at the end of every function and *if-else* statement to tell Flash where the code block ends.

The actions for the `my_ss.onLoad` function must be enclosed in curly braces. We began the function with an opening curly brace, wrote an *if-else* statement inside of it, and closed the *if-else* statement with an ending curly brace, but did not include the closing curly brace for the *onLoad( )* function.

Let's fix it:

1. Add a closing curly brace and semicolon to the end of the *onLoad( )* function, after the closing curly brace for the second *trace( )* command:

    ```
    };
    ```

2. Save and test the movie again.

Now the script runs correctly, and we get no error messages. Next, we need to load the CSS file:

1. Add the following code (also on frame 1 of the *actions* layer) to load the CSS file:

    ```
    my_ss.load ("the_styles.css");
    ```

2. Save and test the movie. The Output panel dutifully reports "the_styles.css loaded" so we know it is working.

DICK TRACE-Y

The ActionScript *trace( )* command has no relation to the Trace Bitmap feature used in Chapter 6. In this context, the term *trace* is used in the investigative sense, as one might "trace" a phone call to track a criminal. In this case, we're hot on the trail of potential bugs.

The *trace( )* command displays the specified text in the Output panel when testing your movie in the authoring tool. It is one of your most important debugging tools. You can use it to display text messages or the result of any ActionScript, such as the value of a variable or property.

Displaying some identifying text along with an ActionScript expression makes it much easier to understand the results in the Output panel. That is, it is easier to interpret the results if the Output panel displays "The clip's width is 500" instead of just "500" with no identifying information. The identifying text is especially helpful to distinguish among the results of multiple *trace( )* statements in a large project.

If your program isn't working as expected, you should verify that your variables contain what you think they do. For example, your `my_lv.load( )` command won't work if `my_lv` isn't an instance of the *LoadVars* class. Thankfully, the *typeof* operator provides some information about the datatype of an item, and the *instanceof* operator checks whether an item is of a particular datatype (i.e., an instance of the specified class). Here are two *trace( )* statements that tell us whether `my_lv` is an object and an instance of the *LoadVars* class. The + operator concatenates (combines) the text with the values returned by the *typeof* and *instanceof* operators:

```
trace ("The type of my_lv is " + (typeof my_lv));
trace ("Is my_lv a LoadVars instance?: "
    + (my_lv instanceof LoadVars));
```

The first *trace( )* command should display "The type of my_lv is object" if `my_lv` is a valid object (as all instances should be). The second *trace( )* command should display "Is my_lv a LoadVars instance?: true" if `my_lv` is an instance of the

Finally, we need to apply the loaded CSS style (myStyle, as defined in *the_styles.css*) to the text fields. A CSS file often defines several styles, and Flash does not automatically know which style to apply to which text field. We can tell it what to do as follows:

1. At frame 15, add the following code to the *actions* layer:

    ```
    left_txt.styleSheet = my_ss;
    left_txt.wordWrap = true;
    left_txt.html = true;
    left_txt.htmlText = "<myStyle>" +
    my_lv.leftText + "</myStyle>";
    ```

2. Save and test the movie.

Here, we're accessing the styleSheet property of the text field and telling Flash to use my_ss as the style sheet for the left_txt instance. (When referring to the property, styleSheet starts with a lowercase s. Don't confuse this with the uppercase TextField.StyleSheet syntax used earlier to create a *TextField.StyleSheet* instance.) Then we tell Flash that we want the wordWrap property turned on for the text field (word wrap is disabled by default) so the text inside of it wraps to the next line when it runs out of space (the text field is only 160 pixels wide). Finally, we use the htmlText property to display formatted text in the text field (setting the html property to true, which is the same as setting the Render Text as HTML option in the Properties panel, tells Flash to obey the HTML tags so it renders the text in the desired style). In this case, it displays the value of my_lv.leftText using the <myStyle> tag to format the text. Don't forget the mandatory closing tag (in this case, </myStyle>).

At frame 15 of the movie, the text appears formatted according to the style in the CSS file, with no regard to how the text field is styled at authoring time using the Properties panel. To prove this:

1. At frame 15, change the properties of the dynamic text field on the Stage using the Properties panel. Change the font, font size, and font color to anything you want.

2. Save and test the movie.

Flash disregards the properties of the text field itself and instead uses the loaded CSS style to define the look of the text in that field.

LoadVars class. If either of these displays unexpected results, you know you have to correct some earlier problem. Maybe you forgot the command to create my_lv as an instance of *LoadVars* in the first place:

```
var my_lv:LoadVars = new LoadVars();
```

Once you've solved that problem, you can go about debugging your *onLoad( )* handler. Hint: to make sure your event handler is reached, add a simple *trace( )* statement as follows:

```
my_lv.onLoad = function (success) {
  trace ("Flash reached the onLoad event handler.");
  if (success) {
    gotoAndPlay("start");
  }
};
```

That is, one common problem is that code you think is being executed is never even reached by Flash! If you don't see the message in the Output panel, you know your *onLoad( )* event handler was never executed. So *trace( )* commands can help you determine what part of your program is executing (or failing to execute).

Of course, the Output panel isn't available when playing back Flash content in a web browser. If you need to display debugging information at runtime, you can display the results in a text field as follows (assuming a dynamic text field named debugDisplay exists on stage):

```
debugDisplay.text = "Your message here.";
```

Unlike the Output panel, displaying text in a text field ordinarily replaces the existing text. The following example adds text to the existing field (note the use of the += operator instead of =), starting on the next line:

```
debugDisplay.text += newline + "Your message here.";
```

Don't forget to make the field large enough and set its type to Multiline.

You can erase all the text in the field by simply using:

```
debugDisplay.text = "";
```

Chapter 11, Building a Reusable Ad Template

To finish up, let's apply CSS styles to the remaining text fields:

1. Add this code to frame 45 of the *actions* layer to apply the CSS to the middle_txt instance:

```
middle_txt.styleSheet = my_ss;
middle_txt.wordWrap = true;
middle_txt.html = true;
middle_txt.htmlText = "<myStyle>" +
        my_lv.middleText + "</myStyle>";
```

2. Add similar code to frame 75:

```
right_txt.styleSheet = my_ss;
right_txt.wordWrap = true;
right_txt.html = true;
right_txt.htmlText = "<myStyle>" +
        my_lv.rightText + "</myStyle>";
```

3. And finally, add this code to frame 105 to format the last text field in the movie:

```
learnMore_txt.styleSheet = my_ss;
learnMore_txt.wordWrap = true;
learnMore_txt.html = true;
learnMore_txt.htmlText = "<myStyle>" +
        my_lv.learnMoreText + "</myStyle>";
```

4. And here is the final code as it should appear on frame 1:

```
stop();
var my_lv:LoadVars = new LoadVars();
my_lv.onLoad = function (success) {
  if (success) {
     gotoAndPlay("start");
  }
};
my_lv.load("the_vars.txt");

var my_ss:TextField.StyleSheet =
     new TextField.StyleSheet();
my_ss.onLoad = function (success) {
  if (success) {
     trace("the_styles.css loaded");
  } else {
     trace("the_styles.css did not load");
  }
};
my_ss.load ("the_styles.css");
```

5. Save and test the movie.

Now every text field in the movie uses the loaded CSS style. If we need to change the typeface for one of the movies in the series, we'll need to change only one or two lines of formatting attributes in the CSS file.

Now that we know the CSS and text files are loading properly, let's take a moment to make sure the code is well-written.

Once these files are posted to the web server, we'll have no way to know if the CSS is loading properly, aside from simply looking at the text to see if it uses gray, 16-point Verdana (or whatever font we use for a particular movie). The *trace( )* command displays text within the Output panel in Flash's Preview mode only. No end user, including us, will ever see an error message if the load fails. So how do we make sure it's all working?

The first half of the script ends with the my_lv.load() method, used to load the text file containing the variables for the movie. If the load is successful, the playhead is sent to the start frame label. If the load fails, the movie simply stops at frame 1 and never does anything. This is conditional logic. The remainder of the script, dealing with the style sheet, however, has no such condition. The variables might load perfectly, sending the playhead to the start frame, but if the CSS isn't loaded, the text in the movie will display incorrectly (though you can set the font and font size for the text fields themselves via the Properties panel so there is a default font in place should the CSS fail to load).

To remedy this, we need to intertwine the two portions of the script a bit so that the movie does not play unless both files are loaded. The strategy is to use the my_lv.load("the_vars.txt"); statement to replace the trace("the_styles.css loaded"); statement. In the following revised code example, the lines we want to disable are commented out (changes shown in color):

```
stop();
var my_lv:LoadVars = new LoadVars();
my_lv.onLoad = function (success) {
  if (success) {
     gotoAndPlay("start");
  }
};
// Move this to my_ss.onLoad
// my_lv.load("the_vars.txt");

var my_ss:TextField.StyleSheet = new TextField.
StyleSheet();
my_ss.onLoad = function (success) {
  if (success) {
```

```
        // Disable this
        // trace("the_styles.css loaded");
        // Move this operation here
        my_lv.load("the_vars.txt");
    } else {
        trace("the_styles.css did not load");
    }
};
my_ss.load ("the_styles.css");
```

Save and test the movie.

Now the Flash Player loads the CSS file, checks to make sure the load is successful, and then loads the text file containing the variables. The my_lv.load() call, which loads the text file, triggers the my_lv.onLoad() method, which tests the success of that load and sends the playhead to the start frame. In other words, the variables do not get loaded until the CSS is done loading, and the playhead does not go to the start frame unless the variables have loaded correctly. Thus, if one of the two files does not load, the movie will stop at frame 1 and do nothing. You could modify the script to, say, display an error page if either the CSS file or variables file fails to load. (This code is meant as a demonstration of how to check the success of an initial load operation before performing a second load operation, not as a robust, deployment-ready solution. You might decide that the CSS loading is not crucial and structure your project to load the variables even if the CSS load fails.)

If you have experience with HTML, it may seem strange that the my_lv.onLoad() method is run after the CSS is loaded, despite the order of the scripts in the Actions panel. But the Flash Player does not always run code in the order it appears, as HTML does. Standalone commands are executed as they are encountered, but event handlers such as onLoad() aren't executed until they are triggered by an event. So the order of execution of the preceding code is:

```
stop();
var my_lv:LoadVars = new LoadVars();
var my_ss:TextField.StyleSheet = new TextField.
StyleSheet();
my_ss.load ("the_styles.css");
```

The my_ss.load() command triggers (i.e., executes) the my_ss.onLoad() handler. Finally, the my_lv.onLoad() handler is executed if the first load succeeded.

In other words, don't confuse defining the *onLoad()* event handler with actually executing it. The my_ss.onLoad() event handler just sits there and does nothing until the my_ss.load() method is run. If the my_ss.load() method is never run, the my_ss.onLoad() handler is never invoked.

We're all done loading and formatting text now, so let's move on to the button scripts.

Making code more efficient

The designer who put together this template added ActionScript to each button instance so we could see how the final movie would look, but this isn't the best approach for this particular project, as she added the code after she created the motion tweens. As a result, code is attached to the button at each point where the movie is stopped (at frames 15, 45, 75, and 105), so the code is written in the movie a total of four times. Let's see how to make the code more efficient:

1. Move the playhead to frame 15 and open the Actions panel.

2. In the Script Navigator, shown in Figure 11-2, click on one of the lines that says next_btn, <next_btn>. This displays the code attached to an instance of *next_btn* in the Script pane.

3. Delete the ActionScript.

4. Select the two other instances of *next_btn* listed in the Script Navigator and delete the code attached to them.

5. Select the *learn_btn* instance and delete the code for that as well.

The Script Navigator is a handy new feature of the Actions panel in Flash MX 2004 and Flash Pro. It lists every frame or object in an entire Flash document that has code attached to it. You simply select the script you want to see and Flash displays it in the Script pane. Simple as that.

Now that we've removed all the superfluous code, let's write a function that handles it all at once.

Fortunately, when the designer constructed the file, she gave the button an instance name that stays with it

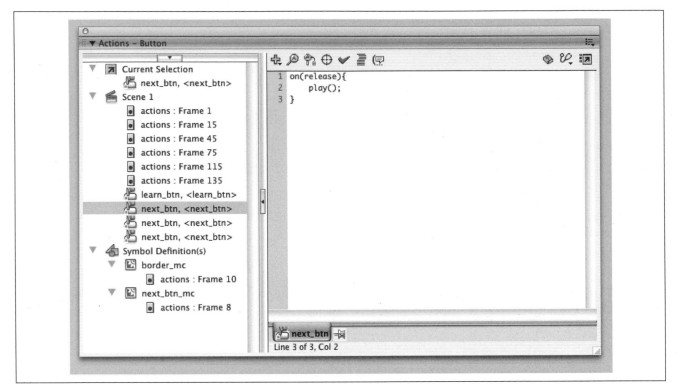

Figure 11-2. The Script Navigator section of the Actions panel.

through the entire movie, on every keyframe. (Multiple keyframes in a movie can contain separate instances of the same symbol, each using different instance names, but the designer used next_btn throughout.) All we have to do is write an *onRelease( )* handler for each button:

1. At frame 15, add the following to the Actions panel:

    ```
    next_btn.onRelease = function () {
        play();
    };
    ```

2. At frame 105, add similar code to make the learn_btn instance work:

    ```
    learn_btn.onRelease = function () {
        play();
    };
    ```

3. Save.

This example shows a situation in which it is beneficial to give multiple instances of a symbol the same instance name. Naturally, this would cause problems if you want different behaviors attached to each button, so use this only when the behavior is uniform for all buttons with the same instance name.

Since the code for the buttons is now in the *actions* layer instead of attached directly to the button instances, the Flash Player simply looks for existing button instances with the instance names next_btn and learn_btn and applies the appropriate code to them.

> **WARNING**
>
> Notice that we added button code to the *actions* layer only at the frames where the button instances actually reside. ActionScript cannot reference an object that does not yet exist in the movie, so adding the code to frame 1 would not work. Flash would look for the next_btn and learn_btn instances at frame 1, but since they don't appear until later in the movie, the code will not do anything.
>
> Code that references an object works only if the object has already been created and has an instance name. This caveat applies to symbol instances in a movie and objects created with ActionScript.

Now that we've simplified the button scripts, let's finish up by loading the images externally.

Pull images out, load images in

The last thing we need to make our project modular and easily updatable is to remove the images from the Flash document and load them as external *.jpg* files. When we need to create more movies in this series, we can just replace the images (using the same filenames), edit the variables in the text file, and call it a day.

To handle this process, we need to remove all instances of images from the Stage and replace them with instances of a container movie clip, into which we'll load external images.

1. Press Ctrl/Cmd-F8 to open the Create New Symbol dialog box and create a new movie clip symbol named *container_mc*.

2. In Edit mode for *container_mc*, draw a square and size it to 180 × 180.

3. Return to Scene 1 from Edit mode for *container_mc*.

4. Choose Edit → Find and Replace to open the Find and Replace dialog box, shown in Figure 11-3.

5. We want to find all instances of the symbol named *left* (the image that appears in the lefthand box in the movie) and replace it with instances of *container_mc*. So, in the dialog box, set the Search In option to Current Scene, set the For option to Symbol, and choose *left* from the Name drop-down list. Finally, choose *container_mc* from the Replace With drop-down list.

6. Click Replace All.

The statement "Found and replaced 5 items" appears at the bottom of the dialog box. Every keyframe that contained an instance of *left* now contains an instance of *container_mc*. Without this functionality in Flash, we would have had to delete each instance of the *left* symbol manually and drag *container_mc* from the Library to the Stage each time to replace it.

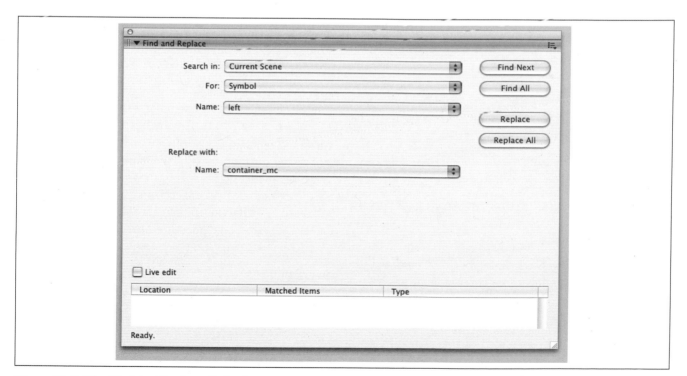

Figure 11-3. The Find and Replace dialog box.

Let's also replace the *middle* and *right* symbol instances, as images need to be loaded dynamically into each of those boxes:

1. Still in the Find and Replace dialog box, choose *middle* from the Name drop-down list and click Replace All.

2. Next, choose *right* from the Name drop-down list and click Replace All again.

3. Save your work.

All the instances of images in the Flash document (derived from the *left*, *middle*, and *right* symbols in the Library) have been removed and replaced with instances of *container_mc*. But each instance is still identified as a graphic symbol in the Properties panel, and we need instance names for each instance as well, so we need to change their types to Movie Clip (graphic instances cannot be assigned instance names):

1. At frame 15, select the *container_mc* instance on the Stage, choose Movie Clip from the Symbol Behavior drop-down list in the Properties panel, and give it an instance name of **left_mc**.

2. Repeat this process for every keyframe on the *left* layer (located inside the *images* layer folder).

Every instance on the *left* layer now contains a *container_mc* instance with left_mc as its instance name. Now we need to repeat the process for the *middle* and *right* layers.

1. Repeat the preceding Step 1 for the *middle* layer, naming each instance **middle_mc**.

2. Repeat this again for the *right* layer, naming each instance **right_mc**.

It's unfortunate there is no way to replace instance names with the Find and Replace dialog box, but Find and Replace is still a tremendous time-saver in many cases.

Next, we'll use the preloader component we built in Chapter 10 to load the images dynamically. We don't need to display the percentage of bytes loaded for each image being loaded into the movie because each one has a small enough file size to load almost instantly, but using the component we built means we don't have to write

ActionScript to load the images. (Aha! The benefit of using components suddenly hits you like a stiff shot of whiskey!)

1. Open the Components panel by pressing Ctrl-F7 (Windows and Mac).

2. At frame 15, drag an instance of our custom *FP7_Loader* component out from the Components panel and position it above the Stage. (We don't need to display it in the movie, but leaving an instance of *FP7_Loader* in the work area causes it to be exported as part of the *.swf* file so it can load and monitor the images.) Dragging an instance to the Stage or work area adds the component to the Library, so now we can create multiple instances without adding file size beyond that required for the component itself.

3. With the instance of the *FP7_Loader* component selected on the work area, in the Properties panel, enter **left.jpg** into the File to Load field and enter **_parent.left_mc** into the Where to Load It field.

4. Save and test the movie.

When you click the first button, the image loads and displays properly. See? Our component works in any situation because we built it that way. We're so smart (and good-looking too, I might add).

Also, notice that the file size of our test movie dropped from 20 KB to 3 KB. By removing the images from the movie, we saved 17 KB. The *.swf* file will load into a web page much more quickly (of course, the dynamic images will take some time to load). We've traded one initial load delay for smaller delays that occur when the user clicks a button to load the next image. This makes the Flash movie behave more like a traditional HTML web site in which content is loaded on demand rather than preloaded.

To finish up, let's do the analogous thing for the middle and right images:

1. At frame 45, create a new instance of the *FP7_Loader* component and use it to load *middle.jpg* into _parent. middle_mc.

2. Repeat this process at frame 75 and load *right.jpg* into _parent.right_mc.

3. Save and test the movie.

Each image loads and displays just as it should. And we didn't have to write separate ActionScript to do it for each image. Components rule.

Let's use more components to create the catalog-request form.

> Although the *FP7_Loader* component isn't visible on stage, it's still included in the published movie (this is true for any asset left in the work area). This fact is both a blessing and a curse.
>
> On the plus side, we can keep all kinds of graphics and movie clips offstage until they need to appear in the movie. On the downside, it means we have to make sure the work area of a *.fla* file is devoid of unused symbol instances and any raw artwork. Leaving that stuff lying around increases the file size of a published movie.

USING COMPONENTS

To complete the project, we need to create the catalog-request form for the end of the movie, which we'll build using Flash components. Part of Macromedia's intention for components is to standardize common Flash UI elements so they function like things the user is already accustomed to using, such as scrollbars and checkboxes typical to HTML pages and web browsers. Another intention is to add support for features like accessibility and keyboard-driven focus (tab) management.

As noted in Chapter 10, however, the so-called v2 components that come with Flash MX 2004 add substantial file size to a movie, as their architecture is optimized for cases in which you use five or six of them. If you don't need all the bells and whistles or if you are using only one or two components, the v2 components that come with Flash MX 2004 might be overkill.

The v1 components that came with Flash MX have a very small file size and work similarly to the Flash MX 2004 v2 components but with less overhead. However, the original Flash MX v1 components don't always work in Flash MX 2004, especially when exporting in Flash Player 7 format; therefore, Macromedia released a version

of the Flash MX v1 components updated for Flash MX 2004 and Flash Pro. In the next section, we'll download them from Macromedia's web site, install them, and create our form. (The updated v1 components are referred to as "Flash MX Components for Flash MX 2004"; don't confuse them with the v2 components shipped with Flash MX 2004.)

Using the Macromedia Exchange

An entire section of Macromedia's web site is devoted to components, behaviors, and other extensions built by Macromedia and third-party developers, like my geeky friend Ron Haberle, who supplied the Falling Text timeline effect used in Chapter 6. Many of the posted items are free.

To get the set of Flash MX v1 components updated for Flash MX 2004:

1. Go to the Flash Exchange (*http://www.macromedia. com/exchange/flash*).

2. On the Flash Exchange page, shown in Figure 11-4, click Search Exchanges.

3. The components we want are under the User Interface category, under the title "Flash MX Components for Flash MX 2004." You can either browse to them, or on the Exchange Search page, enter `Flash MX Components for Flash MX 2004` into the search box and click the Search button.

4. From the list of search results, locate "Flash MX Components for Flash MX 2004" and click the name of the extension. This takes you to another page with detailed information about the component set.

5. If you have not already registered on Macromedia's site, you'll need to do that to download the components. Don't worry—it's free, and you can opt out of email promotions.

6. Click the Download button. This downloads a file named *FlashMXUIComponents1.mxp*. Save it to your desktop.

An *.mxp* file is a packaged file that installs using the Macromedia Extension Manager, which is included with Studio MX and Studio MX 2004 (sorry, we couldn't

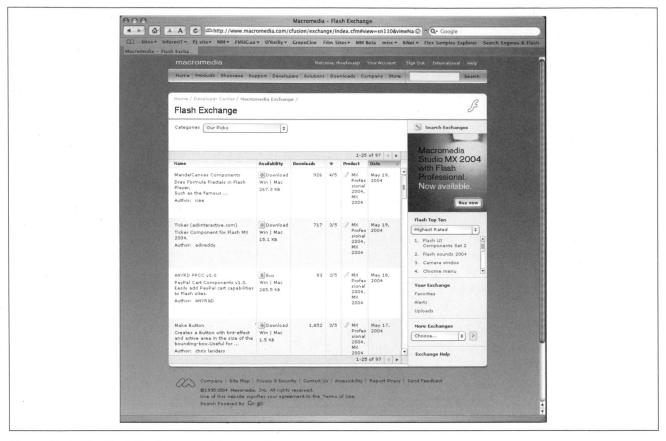

Figure 11-4. The Flash Exchange on Macromedia.com.

obtain a license to include it on the CD-ROM with the book). If you don't have the Extension Manager, you can download it from *http://www.macromedia.com/exchange/em_download* and install it.

When you have the Extension Manager installed and the component set downloaded, let's continue:

1. Double-click on the *.mxp* file on your desktop to open the Extension Manager, shown in Figure 11-5.

2. Follow the on-screen instructions to install the component set.

3. Quit the Extension Manager.

Before we can access the new components in Flash and build our form, we have to tell Flash to reload the newly installed components:

1. Open the Components panel.

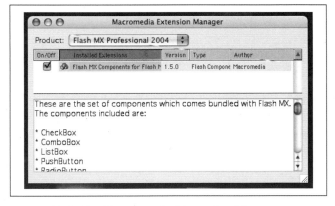

Figure 11-5. The Macromedia Extension Manager.

2. Open the Options menu in the upper-right corner of the Components panel and choose Reload. This reloads the list of components in the panel and displays the set of Flash MX UI Components, in

their own folder, as shown in Figure 11-6. (If the new components don't appear, make sure they are correctly installed and try restarting Flash.)

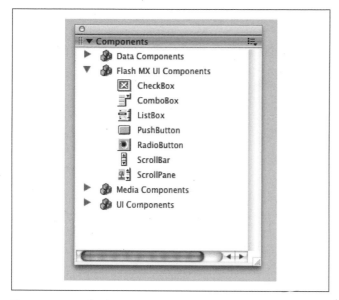

Figure 11-6. Flash MX UI Components.

3. Create a new Flash document and save it as *learn_ more.fla* in the *11* folder. Resize the Stage to 300 × 160.

We'll create the catalog-request form in this file and load it into the ad template later on. Creating this form as its own *.swf* file enables us to use it with other projects. After you've worked with Flash for a while, you may find yourself building up an arsenal of Flash widgets like this one, ready to load into any new project.

Creating a form

Let's create the form using our newly downloaded components. We'll set up some text fields and provide labels to identify them (here our "labels" are static text, not to be confused with frame labels in a timeline):

1. Instead of loading data into a text field with ActionScript, we'll use an input field so the user can type his own data into the field. Activate the Text tool and choose Input from the Text Type drop-down list in the Properties panel.

2. Click once on the Stage to create an input text field. Drag the handle in the corner of the field so the text field is about 225 pixels wide and 17–20 pixels high.

3. Activate the Selection tool and Alt-drag (Windows) or Option-drag (Mac) the text field twice to create two more instances of it.

4. For the third text field, double-click inside of it to make it editable and drag the handle to increase its height to about 60 pixels. We'll use this one as a Comments field. Use the Properties panel to set the line type to Multiline to allow comments to wrap across multiple lines.

5. Deselect the text field so the next step doesn't affect it.

6. Choose Static Text from the Text Type drop-down list in the Properties panel, and click on the Stage. This creates a static text field (static fields can be modified only at authoring time). The static text fields serve as labels for the user input fields. Enter the word **Name** in the text box.

7. Click twice on the Stage to create another static text field and enter the text **Email** in the text box.

8. Repeat Step 6 but enter the word **Comments**.

9. Organize the fields on the Stage to match Figure 11-7.

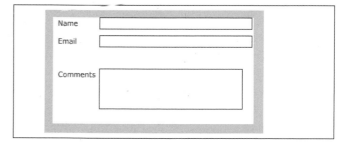

Figure 11-7. Organize the text fields on the Stage.

Now we'll add several components to the form to create the functionality for it. We need to write some ActionScript, but only to send the form data to a server-side script that will process the data:

1. Open the Components panel. Expand the *Flash MX UI Components* folder and drag an instance of

the CheckBox component to the Stage. Position it between the second and third text fields, as shown in Figure 11-8.

2. In the Properties panel, with the CheckBox component still selected, enter **promo_cb** as the instance name, and enter **Send email about promotions** in the Label field. The label field dictates what the text for the checkbox says.

3. The checkbox doesn't display the entire label, so use the Free Transform tool to widen it until the whole label appears. Then position it in a straight line with the text fields, as shown in Figure 11-8 (remember our old friend the Align panel?).

The checkbox now gives the user the option to receive information about promotions by email or to opt out by leaving the checkbox unchecked. Many people will simply leave the box unchecked to avoid getting more email, but conversely, many people might leave it checked if it were checked by default. We want to encourage the user to opt in to our company's mailing list (so we can hopefully increase business), so let's make sure the checkbox is checked by default:

1. With the checkbox still selected, choose True from the Initial Value field in the Properties panel. A checkmark appears in the checkbox.

2. Save your work.

Next, let's add a Scrollbar component instance to the Comments text field so users can scroll through the text if it's longer than the allotted space:

1. Select the bottom input text field—the largest one on the Stage. Assign it an instance name of **comments_ txt**. Make sure its type is set to Multiline.

2. Drag the Scrollbar component to the Stage and release it over the right edge of the comments_txt field, as shown in Figure 11-9.

The scrollbar should "snap" into place; it should automatically size itself to match the height of the text field, and the Target TextField option in the Properties panel should say comments_txt. This doesn't always work, however, so you may need to adjust it yourself. To manually associate the scrollbar with the text field:

1. Select the comments_txt field and note the H value of the field in the Properties panel.

2. Select the scrollbar instance and enter the height from Step 1 into the H field in the scrollbar's Properties panel. This resizes the scrollbar so it matches the height of the text field.

3. Enter **comments_txt** as the Target TextField option in the Parameters tab of the scrollbar's Properties panel.

4. Save and test the movie.

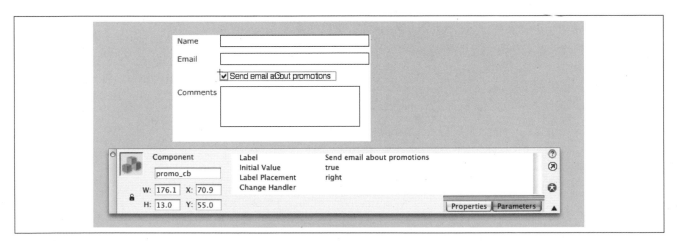

Figure 11-8. Add the checkbox to the Stage and align it.

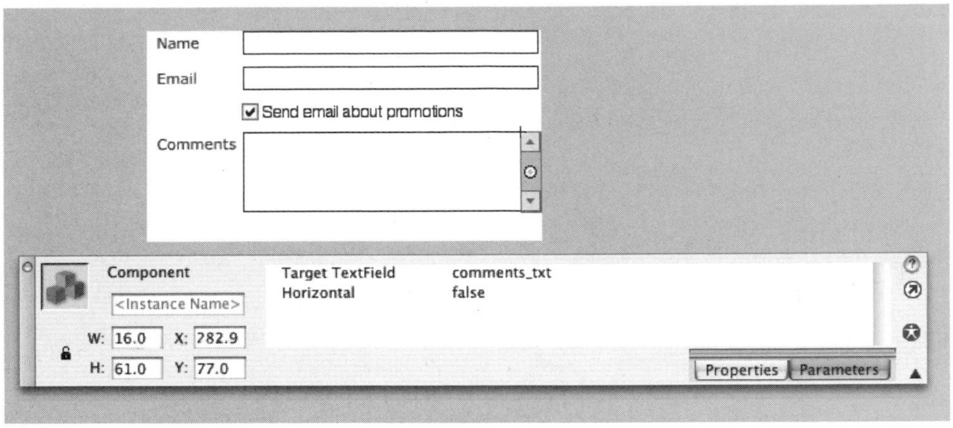

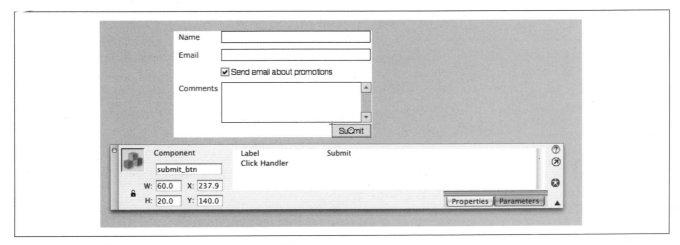

Figure 11-9. Add a scrollbar to the comments_txt instance.

Entering multiple lines of text into the Comments field triggers the scrollbar. A scroll handle appears and adjusts its own height as the input text gets longer, just like a scrollbar in a browser window.

The form needs just one more element: a Submit button. Let's add it now:

1. Close the Preview window.

2. Drag the PushButton component from the Components panel and position it at the bottom-right corner of the Stage, as shown in Figure 11-10.

3. In the Label field in the Properties panel, enter **Submit**. The word Submit appears in the button.

4. Assign the button an instance name of `submit_btn`.

5. Save and test the movie.

The Bandwidth Profiler in the Preview window indicates the file size is only 12 KB. (Recall from Chapter 2 that the Bandwidth Profiler gives us an indication of the relative download size of our movie. The Bandwidth Profiler included with Flash MX 2004 version 7.0.1 and later also accounts for some external assets in simple situations—a welcome enhancement although by no means a definitive measure of download times.) If we had used the v2 components that come with Flash MX 2004 (in which case we would use the Button, CheckBox, and TextArea components), the file size would be 40 KB. We saved 28 KB

Figure 11-10. Add a Submit button using the PushButton component.

of file size by using components from the set originally developed for Flash MX.

All we need to do now is add ActionScript that compiles the data from the form and sends it to the web server.

> **NOTE**
>
> If you think Macromedia messed up when they released such large components, you're not alone. Many Flash developers either build their own components or get third-party components from sites such as *http://www.flashcomponents.com* and *http://www.flashcomponents.net* (which are separate organizations offering different components, despite the similar domain names).

Compiling and sending form data

Once the user fills out the catalog-request form, the data needs to be sent to the web server for processing. The server-side script can email the data or add the information to a database. As stated earlier, server-side scripting is beyond the scope of this book, but I posted the server-side script necessary to complete this project on flashoutofthebox.com. In this section, we'll collect data from the form and send it to the server-side script, which will format an email and send it to you (thus making you an official Jedi Master).

Let's start by setting up the instance names for the text fields containing the form data of interest:

1. Assign instance names to the top two input text fields on the Stage. Assign name_txt to the top one and email_txt to the middle one. (The third one is already named comments_txt.) The fields must have instance names if we want to collect the data from them using ActionScript.

2. Create a new layer named *actions* and open the Actions panel.

Next, we need to create variables to collect the contents of each text field on the Stage and send them to the server. And we need all this to happen when the user clicks the Submit button. So we'll create a function that performs these tasks, then run it from the button:

1. On frame 1 of the *actions* layer, add this code to create variables that grab the data from each text field:

    ```
    var nameText:String = name_txt.text;
    var emailText:String = email_txt.text;
    var messageText:String = comments_txt.text;
    var promoOption:String;
    ```

The first three variables grab data from the three text fields on the Stage, all of which contain text strings (which is why we specified the variables' datatypes as *String*). The promoOption variable is empty at the moment. We're just declaring it here; we'll give it a value later. The promoOption variable simply holds the current value of the checkbox (either true or false) so we can send it to the server with the other variables. It's also a string, but instead of pulling data directly from a text field, we'll use a *change handler* to retrieve the value of the checkbox and assign that value to the promoOption variable.

A change handler is a function that notifies Flash if the state of the component changes. If the checkbox is checked, the value returned is true, and that value will be assigned to the promoOption variable (we'll do this in a minute). An unchecked box returns a value of false. You can set its default value to true by selecting the checkbox on stage and configuring it in the Parameters tab of the Properties panel.

Let's set up the necessary event handler:

1. First, we'll declare the handler that assigns the current value of the checkbox to the promoOption variable:

    ```
    the_handler = function (component) {
      promoOption = promo_cb.getValue();
    };
    ```

2. Next, we'll assign the_handler as the change handler for promo_cb:

    ```
    promo_cb.setChangeHandler("the_handler");
    ```

Now, if the value of the checkbox changes, *the_handler()* executes and the value of the promoOption variable changes as a result.

Next, we'll add an event handler that sends the variables to the server:

1. To send the variables to the server, we'll use the *loadVariablesNum( )* command from within the Submit button's click handler:

```
submit_btn.onRelease = function () {
  loadVariablesNum("http://www.
flashoutofthebox.com/FOTB_mail_form.cfm", 0,
  "POST");
}
```

2. In order to receive the email from the form, you'll need to send your own email address to the server as well. Add the following code to the script, replacing the email address with your own:

```
var myEmail:String = "me@mydomain.com";
```

3. Save and test the movie.

When a user fills out the form and clicks the Submit button, an email is sent to your own email address from whatever email address the user enters into the form.

The server-side script in this case determines the value of each variable and uses it to format and send an email. I already wrote the script in ColdFusion. The email you receive will look like Figure 11-11.

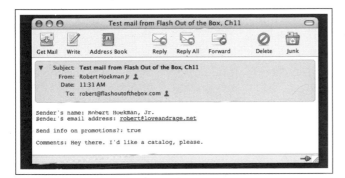

Figure 11-11. An example of the email you'll receive from this form.

Normally, the destination email address would go in the server-side script, but if that were the case here, all the email you sent would go directly to me, and that wouldn't help you at all (and it definitely wouldn't help me). This way, the server-side script receives a variable from Flash that contains your email address and sends the email there.

> **NOTE**
>
> You must enter a real email address into the Email field in the form, or the email cannot be sent.

If you want to see the server-side script, open *FOTB_mail_form.cfm*, located in the *11* folder, in an editor such as Macromedia Dreamweaver. It is a basic script that uses ColdFusion's <CFMAIL> tag to compose and send an email.

Our form is done and the *.swf* file is only 12 KB. Next, we'll load it into the main movie.

Loading the form into the main movie

We've already built a preloader component (in Chapter 10) that loads anything we need, so we can use an instance of it to load *learn_more.swf* at the end of the movie so the user can complete the form. Of course, we also need a container movie clip in which to load *learn_more. swf*. Otherwise, loading a new *.swf* would replace the current *.swf*.

To load the second *.swf*, we'll use our custom preloader component:

1. Close *learn_more.fla*.

2. In *ad_template.fla*, move the playhead to frame 125 and delete all the boxes on the *assets* layer. Don't delete the text.

3. Draw a box that's 300 × 160 and convert it to a movie clip symbol named *learn_more_mc*.

4. Assign the new clip the instance name learn_more_mc.

5. Insert a keyframe on the *loaders* layer at frame 125.

6. Drag an instance of the *FP7_Loader* component to the Stage and position it in the center of the learn_more_mc instance, as shown in Figure 11-12.

7. Enter **learn_more.swf** into the File to Load field in the Properties panel, and **_parent.learn_more_mc** into the Where to Load It field.

8. Save and test the movie.

Let's recap where we stand so far:

- The external text files, which contain variables and CSS, load into the movie to supply and format the text.

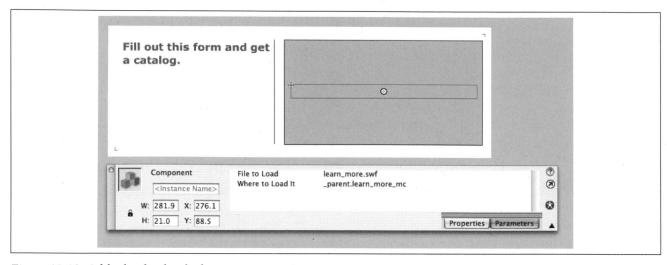

Figure 11-12. Add a loader for the learn_more_mc instance.

- Images load on demand.

- The *learn_more.swf* file (the fill-in form) loads at the end of the movie.

- If you fill out the form, it sends you an email.

And it all happens dynamically. There is just one more issue to resolve: when you click the Submit button, there is no visual feedback that the email has been sent.

Let's add a confirmation message so the user knows we've received his request:

1. Open *learn_more.fla*.

2. Add one frame to the *actions* layer so it's two frames long, and insert a keyframe on frame 2 of the *assets* layer.

3. On frame 2 of the *assets* layer, delete everything on the Stage and replace it with the text, "Thank you. A catalog will be sent to you by email." as shown in Figure 11-13.

4. On frame 1 of the *actions* layer, add the following code to the event handler for submit_btn:

   ```
   nextFrame();
   ```

5. On frame 2 of the *actions* layer, add a stop(); action.

6. Save and test the movie. When you're done, close *learn_more.fla*.

Now, when you click the button, the form disappears and you are thanked for requesting the catalog. Nice touch. (A more advanced version might display a custom message based on whether the user also opted into the mailing list.)

To see the real benefits of this modular architecture, we'll create a second movie from it in a few minutes. First, though, let's embed the movie into a web page.

Figure 11-13. Add a Thank You confirmation screen to the movie.

PUT THE MOVIE ONLINE

So far, we've talked a lot about things like decreasing the file size of Flash content, loading assets dynamically, and using buttons to navigate through a movie, but we have yet to put Flash content into a real web page, and this step in Flash development is an important one. After all, no one will ever see the results of our hard work unless we post it online. (You can also distribute Flash content by CD-ROM and on mobile devices, as we'll see in the next chapter, but most Flash content is published on the Web.)

Embedding Flash content into a web page

There are several ways to create an HTML page that will load our *.swf* (also known as "embedding a *.swf* file into a web page"). We can publish an HTML page directly from Flash, but that option leaves very little control over the published page. So instead, we'll put the *.swf* into the center of an existing HTML page (presumed to have been created in Dreamweaver or another HTML editor).

Let's start by publishing the final version of the movie:

1. In *ad_template.fla*, choose File → Save As and save the file as *ad_template_final.fla* in the *11* folder.

2. Click the Settings button in the Properties panel (or choose File → Publish Settings) to open the Publish Settings dialog box.

3. Choose the Formats tab and uncheck the HTML option. We don't need Flash to create an HTML page for us.

4. Choose the Flash tab and set the Version (the export format) to Flash Player 7. We're using a preloader built with the *MovieClipLoader* class, which requires Flash Player 7 or higher.

5. Set the Load Order to Top Down (so the *actions* layer loads first).

6. Set the ActionScript Version to ActionScript 2.0, because we're using strict datatyping.

7. Check the Protect from Import option to prevent users from opening the published *.swf* file in the Flash authoring tool. This isn't very secure because many third-party SWF decompilers are available, but it's a simple way to discourage casual pirates. For many more details on Flash *.swf* security, see Chapter 12 of *Flash Hacks* (O'Reilly).

8. Click Publish to generate the final *.swf* file. It is created in the same folder as the *.fla* file.

9. Click OK to close the Publish Settings dialog box.

10. Save and close *ad_template_final.fla*.

Next, we'll use Macromedia Dreamweaver to embed the *.swf* file into an HTML web page (a 30-day trial version of Dreamweaver MX 2004 is included on this book's CD-ROM). Although Dreamweaver makes it easy to publish Flash content, you can perform similar tasks using the HTML editor of your choice.

1. In the *11* folder, move the files we need for the site—*ad_template_final.swf*, *learn_more.swf*, *left.jpg*, *middle.jpg*, *right.jpg*, *the_styles.css*, and *the_vars.txt*—into the *SITE* folder (which is a subfolder of the *11* folder).

2. Launch Macromedia Dreamweaver (or your preferred editor) and choose File → Open. Open *index.html*, also located in the *11/SITE* folder.

3. Click once inside the table in the center of the page (we've already done some of the HTML work for you, but if you're not using a visual editor, you'll have to edit the HTML by hand).

4. Choose Insert → Media → Flash, locate *ad_template_final.swf*, and insert it. The Flash content appears in the page as a large gray box with a Flash icon in the center of it, as shown in Figure 11-14.

5. Select the *.swf* file in the page. In the File field in the Properties panel (common to all Studio MX 2004 applications), change the URL to `ad_template_final.swf` to make the path to the content relative to the site rather than your local drive.

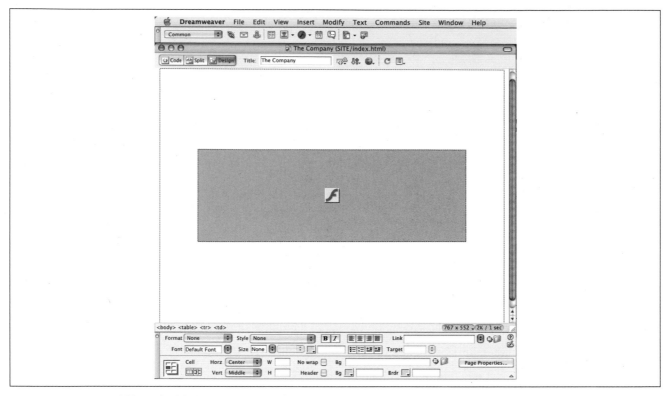

Figure 11-14. A .swf file embedded in a page created with Dreamweaver.

6. Save your work.

7. Press F12 to preview the page in a web browser.

We'll just pretend this page has other stuff in it, like a company logo and more content.

If you want to see the HTML code used to embed Flash content into the page, click the Code button in the top-left corner of Dreamweaver's Document window. This reveals all the HTML used for the page. The HTML related to embedding the .swf file begins with the <object> tag.

As mentioned at the beginning of this section, the world can't see your work unless you upload it to a web site. We've created all the files you need to deploy your site (including the .html page) and placed them in a SITE folder. Upload this folder's contents to a folder on your web site and it should work the same as it does when we tested it in a local browser. Dreamweaver includes site management features that make it easy to upload your site files (consult the Dreamweaver help files), but you can use any FTP program to transfer files to your web server (in some cases, your web server may be a local machine on your network, so ask your webmaster). When testing in a web browser, don't forget you may need to refresh the page or clear the cache to prevent it from displaying a previous version of the files.

Reusing our template

Now that we've finished the movie and popped it into a web page, we can see how a modular architecture helps speed up revisions. The client loves the first ad, but it's week #2 and the new ad needs to go up. He tracked you down on vacation and wants you to make updates. No one in-house knows how to use the Flash authoring tool. Can he really create a new movie without revising the *.fla* or *.swf* file?

Since you were smart enough to build the Flash content in pieces, all you have to do now is tell the client to replace the pieces. This is easy because they are just plain-text files, HTML pages, and external JPEG images.

Without even opening the Flash document, someone can change the text for the entire ad:

1. Open *the_vars.txt* in a text editor.

2. Write new values for each of the variables. The client or his staff can write whatever they want.

3. Save and close the file. Upload it to the server.

4. Open *index.html* in a web browser.

Mission accomplished!

GET OUT OF THE BOX

Wow! What a long strange trip it's been since we made a Jimi Hendrix poster in Chapter 1. It is hard to believe how far we've come and how much we've learned until you see it all come together to create a flexible application as we've done here. We've built on the foundation of skills and concepts learned in previous chapters and added quite a few more here.

In this chapter, we saw how:

- A modular architecture for a project allows for easy updates.

- Text can be loaded from an external source and formatted with CSS.

- External image files can be loaded dynamically.

- External .swf files can be incorporated inside another .swf.

- Data can be pulled into and sent out of Flash. It is this fact that makes Flash a viable and flexible option as a front end to web applications.

- Communicating with a server-side script to send an email from Flash isn't as hard as it might sound.

- Components can be used to quickly design user interfaces or implement preloaders.

- Embedding Flash content into web pages takes only a few steps with an editor like Dreamweaver.

The techniques you learned in this chapter can be applied to all kinds of projects. Flash sites are commonly built the same way as the ad template we created here. Images, text, other movies, and CSS are loaded into a main movie, and buttons are used to navigate through the site.

From here, try creating three new images for the ad, using the same filenames (*left.jpg*, *middle.jpg*, and *right.jpg*) and save them into the *SITE* folder. The new images will show up just like the originals. Also, try changing the font color specified in the CSS file (which may be necessary anyway if your new middle image has a darker background).

In this chapter, we only scratched the surface of Flash's ability to send and receive data from remote server-side scripts. There are many ways to do it. We used text variables, but you can also send XML or binary formats such as AMF (Action Messaging Format). For details on XML data transfers, see *ActionScript for Flash MX: The Definitive Guide* (O'Reilly). For many more details on AMF and how to use it with Flash Remoting to integrate server-side operations in Flash, see *Flash Remoting: The Definitive Guide* (O'Reilly).

Ready to move on? In Chapter 12, we'll explore the use of Flash content on CD-ROM and mobile devices.

12

FLASH FOR HANDHELDS AND CD-ROM

In addition to playback over the Web on PCs, Flash content can be delivered on handheld computers or CD-ROM. This chapter explores issues and opportunities for deployment via these alternative methods.

Believe it or not, not everyone has Internet access. I know, I know—it's crazy. And even when your audience does have access, desktop PCs aren't always the final answer with regard to the deployment of multimedia content.

In today's gadget-filled world, mobile devices have begun to see the dawn of the Flash age. Mobile devices can be used to keep employees in the know and deliver up-to-the-minute stock reports and news. That's right—mobile connectivity is the wave of the future. And Flash is already one of the most prevalent technologies connecting you and your valuable data.

The catch to publishing Flash content for mobile devices is that they tend to lag behind the Flash Player version for desktop PCs. While PC-based users can easily upgrade to Flash Player 7, PDA and handheld users have only Flash Player 5 or Flash Player 6. Even some cell phones can run Flash (albeit usually a scaled-down version). Nokia sells about a million Flash-enabled phones each month in Japan, and other markets can't be far behind. Your Pocket PC can get you the latest sports scores while the CD-ROM in your laptop bag can help get you certified and ready for your next career move.

CD-ROMs are still a serious contender for multimedia distribution. Companies use CD-ROMs for everything from product demonstrations to e-learning content used to update working stiffs like us on things such as changes in corporate policy and product promotions. For running a Flash application outside the browser, Macromedia provides the *Standalone Player*, which like any other desktop application can be launched from the Windows File Explorer or Mac OS Finder. If a user double-clicks a *.swf* file, his OS should open and play the Flash movie in the Standalone Player, much as double-clicking a PDF file typically launches Adobe Acrobat Reader. A *Projector* is also a self-sufficient executable that contains both the Standalone Player and a *.swf* file (allowing you to distribute your content and the application needed to run it in one bundle for users who don't have the Standalone Player installed).

CD-ROMs can run whatever version of the Standalone Flash Player you use to create the Projector (using the File → Publish command). That is, when you create a Projector from Flash MX 2004, the Flash Player required to run

the content is built into the published executable (*.exe* files for Windows and Projector files for Mac). This automatically adds about 1 MB of file size, but since you're distributing the content via CD-ROM, there is no need to worry about download time.

Flash does an excellent job of insulating developers from cross-platform differences (and differences among various OS flavors). To an overwhelming degree, Flash content behaves the same on different devices, provided the correct version of the Flash Player is installed.

As with all projects, however, there are a few things to consider when publishing content for CD-ROM or a mobile device. And that's what this chapter is all about.

WARNING

Be sure to test early and often on all target devices to avoid surprises, as platform differences are inevitable. Testing from the outset allows time for product redesign, if necessary. Ignore this advice at your own peril.

FLASH ON THE RUN: FLASHING YOUR DEVICES

Flash Players are appearing on more and more mobile devices, and if you're using Flash Pro, Macromedia has even included templates to help you develop Flash content for each device. If you're not using the Pro edition, you can still develop for devices—it just takes a little research to know which devices support which version of the Flash Player and the screen dimensions for each device. Information about each platform is available at Macromedia's DevNet center for mobile devices (*http://www.macromedia.com/devnet/devices*). For this chapter, we'll use a template that is built into Flash Pro. If you don't have Flash Pro, I'll tell you which publish settings to use before publishing the movie.

So, here's the situation: you're a photographer who's always on the go. And at almost every shoot you meet another potential client. You need a quick and easy way to show off your work. Sure, you have business cards to hand out, but your photography is what grabs the clients. So let's show them your work by putting a simple photo gallery onto your new Hewlett-Packard iPAQ (one of numerous so-called Pocket PCs, devices that run the Windows Mobile 2003 operating system, as described at *http://www.pdabuyersguide.com/ppc.htm*).

Flash Pro templates for mobile devices

The first thing to do is find a template for the iPAQ so we know what the photo gallery will look like on the device as we build it. If you're not using Flash Pro, skip to the next section, "Creating your own template." If you're using Flash Pro:

1. Choose File → New and choose the Templates tab to access the New from Template dialog box.

2. Choose Mobile Devices from the Category list in the dialog box, then choose iPAQ 1910 Full Screen from the Templates list. (If you're using Flash MX 2004 Professional update 7.2, choose the template named iPAQ 19x0 Full Screen). The template should be similar to the one shown in Figure 12-1.

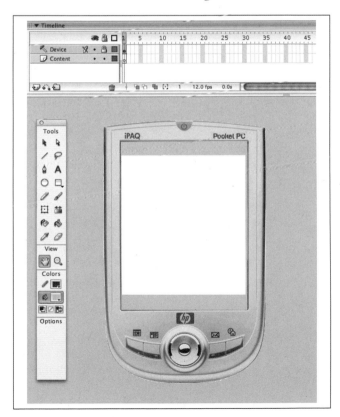

Figure 12-1. The iPAQ 1910 template built into Flash Pro.

The template opens and you see an image of the iPAQ 1910 with a white screen. The white screen represents the Stage for the Flash document. The iPAQ image surrounds the Stage, making it a whole lot easier to visualize how our finished project will look on the handheld device.

The image of the iPAQ itself is on a guide layer (remember guide layers from our animation in Chapter 7?), which does not export with the final movie. Guide layers are perfect for including notes in a *.fla* file or temporarily excluding layers from a test movie for debugging Action-Script or making design revisions.

In the Flash Pro 7.2 update, Macromedia changed the template naming to reflect differences in how iPAQ models are marketed in North America and Asia. The 1910 model in the U.S. is the same as the 1920 model in Japan; the iPAQ 19x0 template pertains to both. In addition, the mobile device templates in Flash Pro 7.2 include a *preview* layer (used to create a preview in the New from Template dialog box) that you should delete prior to using the template.

Creating your own template

Whether you're using Flash Pro or not, the ability to create your own template in Flash can be handy when you're working on a large project or using identical publish settings for multiple projects. Flash Pro includes built-in templates for all kinds of mobile devices, but more devices hit the market all the time. Fortunately, you can create your own template. (A template includes the publish settings, such as the Stage's default height and width. Don't confuse a Flash template with the generalized *.fla* file we created in the previous chapter, which was a template in the colloquial sense but not in the sense that Macromedia uses the term.)

If you're using Flash Pro, you should continue using your iPAQ template for this project, but you may want to read this section anyway.

To create a new template for the iPAQ 1910:

1. Create a new Flash document and save it as *iPAQ_ 1910.fla* in the 12 folder.

2. Change the Stage dimensions to 240 × 268.

3. Open the Publish Settings dialog box (by clicking the Settings button in the Properties panel) and under the Formats tab, uncheck everything but the Flash checkbox.

4. In the Flash tab, choose Flash Player 6 as the Version, Bottom Up as the Load Order, and ActionScript 1.0 as the ActionScript Version. Also, check the Compress Movie option.

5. Click OK to close the dialog box.

6. Choose File → Save as Template.

7. In the Save as Template dialog box, shown in Figure 12-2, enter **iPAQ 1910** in the Name field and choose Mobile Devices from the Category drop-down list. (If you're using Flash Pro 7.0, use a different name in the Name field—a template named iPAQ 1910 already exists in the Mobile Devices category.) Also, enter a description if you like.

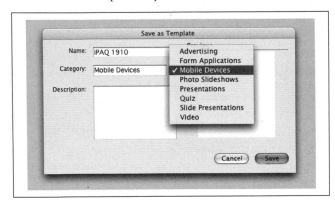

Figure 12-2. The Save as Template dialog box.

8. Click Save to save the template and close the dialog box.

9. Close *iPAQ_1910.fla*.

The file is now saved as a template into the *Templates* folder in your Flash install directory. The template is set to publish content for Flash Player 6, which is the current version available on the iPAQ, so the next time you create a file from this template you don't need to configure the publish settings. Let's see it in action:

1. Choose File → New and choose the Templates tab in the dialog box.

2. Choose Mobile Devices and then choose iPAQ 1910. This creates a new, unsaved document from the template file you created a moment ago.

With all this template stuff out of the way, let's build our photo gallery.

Building the photo gallery

The photo gallery we'll build here will use a very simple design based on our old friend, the box. The point is not to force you to design something elaborate; it's to show you how to make something for a handheld device. When we're done, you can add any design elements you want.

To get started with our photo gallery based on the template, let's create some arrow-shaped forward and back buttons:

1. Save the file you created from the iPAQ 1910 template as *photo_gallery.fla* in the *12* folder.

2. Create two new layers named *buttons* and *photos*, and delete any empty layers left in the timeline.

3. Draw a small box on the Stage using a light gray fill and dark gray stroke.

4. Activate the Selection tool and drag the top-right corner of the box toward the center of the box, as shown in Figure 12-3. This converts the top and right-side strokes into a single straight line, forming a triangle. Who says you can't teach an old box new tricks?

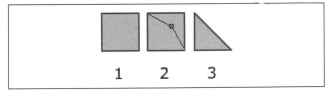

Figure 12-3. Drag the corner of the box to turn it into a triangle.

5. Select the fill and stroke for the triangle and use the Free Transform tool to rotate it until the triangle points to the right. (Holding down the Shift key constrains the rotation to 45-degree increments, making it easy to rotate the shape precisely.)

6. Convert the triangle to a Button symbol named *btn*.

7. Copy and paste the button to create a second instance, then select the second instance and choose Modify → Transform → Flip Horizontal to make it point left.

8. Assign the button pointing left the instance name back_btn and the one pointing right the instance name forward_btn.

9. Save.

Because this photo gallery is intended for a handheld device (which doesn't have a mouse), it's important to make sure the buttons are large enough to click with the stylus, so be sure to scale them appropriately.

I centered the buttons in the figures shown in this section, but you can position them anywhere you like.

Let's set up the button scripts:

1. Create a new layer named *actions* and drag it to the top of the layer stack. Select frame 1 of the *actions* layer and open the Actions panel.

2. Add a *stop( )* command: **stop();**.

3. The buttons need to send the user to the next and previous frames, so add event handlers that use the *nextFrame( )* and *prevFrame( )* commands to move the playhead forward or backward one frame:

```
forward_btn.onRelease = function () {
  nextFrame();
};
back_btn.onRelease = function () {
  prevFrame();
};
```

Next, we'll create a function that determines the current frame number. If the playhead is on the last frame of the movie, the forward_btn instance will appear dimmed (at 50% opacity). If we're on the first frame of the movie, the back_btn instance will be dimmed. This way, the user will have a visual indication that she is viewing the first or last photo in the series. Of course, we could get fancy and have the images wrap around if the user attempts to flip past the first or last image, but that is left as an exercise for you to figure out on your own. (Hint: use the *gotoAndStop( )* command.)

To dim the appropriate button when at the first or last photo:

1. Add the following code to frame 1 of the *actions* layer:

```
updateFrame = function () {
  if (this._currentframe == this._totalframes) {
    forward_btn._alpha = 50;
  } else {
    forward_btn._alpha = 100;
  }
  if (this._currentframe == 1) {
    back_btn._alpha = 50;
  } else {
    back_btn._alpha = 100;
  }
};
back_btn._alpha = 50;  // The back button
// begins dimmed on the first frame
```

2. To run the *updateFrame( )* function every time the user clicks a button, modify the button click handlers as follows (changes shown in color):

```
forward_btn.onRelease = function () {
  nextFrame();
  updateFrame();
};
back_btn.onRelease = function () {
  prevFrame();
  updateFrame();
};
```

3. Save your work.

The code in Step 1 creates conditional logic that sets the opacity of the button instances on the fly. It says, in plain English, "If we're viewing the first photo, dim the back button. If we're viewing the last photo, dim the forward button. Thank you." Okay—we're not really saying thank you, but you get the point, right?

Of course, Flash doesn't understand English and we have to tell it how to accomplish the preceding request. So at a more technical level, the code says, "If the current frame is equal to the total number of frames (the last frame in the movie), decrease the opacity (alpha value) of the forward_btn instance to 50%. Conversely, if the current frame is the first frame in the movie, decrease the opacity of the back_btn instance to 50%. Otherwise, leave them both at 100% opacity. Because we're starting at frame 1, start the movie with the back_btn instance at 50% opacity."

The code in Step 2 simply tells each button to run the *updateFrame( )* function whenever the button is clicked, which ensures that the buttons are always refreshed to the correct state (dimmed or active).

Yes, we could have simply written different scripts on the first and last frames of the movie that change the alpha value at those frames. But this way, we get to keep all the code for the movie in one place. Furthermore, we don't have to know how many images (and hence how many frames) the movie will contain, and we can change the number of images (and hence frames) used in the movie without updating the ActionScript. The Flash Player will automatically detect which frame the movie is on and adjust the alpha values accordingly.

Got it? Let's move on.

Now we need to import some images that show off your photography skills. But since I don't have your images, we'll use mine. (It's entirely possible that you're a better photographer than I am, but I win because I'm writing the book and you're not. So there.)

Why not load external images dynamically, as we learned in Chapter 10? This movie will be saved to your iPAQ, which means you won't have to wait for it to load from a web server. Since this is true, it's not necessary to keep the files external. We'll make the content in this movie self-contained so that it is easy to transfer between devices or email to potential customers (just transfer the one *.swf* file and you're in business).

To import the images for the photo album:

1. Select frame 1 of the *photos* layer, choose File → Import → Import to Stage (Ctrl/Cmd-R), and locate *1.jpg* in the *12* folder.

2. A message appears, as shown in Figure 12-4, asking if you want to import all the images. Click OK. This message appears because the images are named using a specific naming convention (each one has a number as its name).

3. Each image is imported and placed on its own keyframe on the *photos* layer, one image per frame for five frames.

4. At frame 1, make sure *1.jpg* is positioned in the center of the Stage (you can use the Align panel for aid if you need it).

5. At frame 2, drag *2.jpg* to the center of the Stage. Repeat this process with all five images on successive frames. (A faster way is to depress the Edit Multiple Frames toggle button at the bottom of the timeline, select frames 1 to 5, and then use the Align panel to center them to the Stage all at once. In the Align panel, depress the To Stage toggle button, then click the Align Horizontal Center and Align Vertical Center buttons.)

6. Add frames to the *actions* and *buttons* layers so they have five frames as well.

7. Save and test the movie.

FRAMES AND SCENES

The observant among you may say, "Wait a minute! The photo album code presented here dims the arrow buttons but the buttons aren't disabled (the scripts are still active)! What happens if the user clicks a dimmed button?" In this case, since we're using the *nextFrame( )* and *prevFrame( )*, although the script executes even when the button is dimmed, the playhead doesn't move. If the playhead is already at the last frame of a movie, *nextFrame( )* has no effect. Likewise, *prevFrame( )* has no effect if the playhead is already at the first frame of the movie. If your movie has frames that precede or follow the photo album, you'd need to add code to disable the buttons based on frame numbers other than the first and last frames.

Can you use a separate *scene* (Insert → Scene) without introducing a problem with *nextFrame()* and *getFrame()*?

Figure 12-4. Import all the images in the sequence? Um... sure. Why not?

When you click the Forward button, the movie advances one frame at a time, and the Back button sends the playhead back to the previous frame. On the first and last frames, the Back and Forward buttons are set to 50% opacity.

Running a test movie generates a *.swf* file based on the publish settings for the document, so we don't need to do it manually.

Your new photo gallery is ready to go. Just pop it onto your iPAQ or similar handheld and go grab a sandwich. The content is playable in a Pocket PC browser, a scaled-down version of a full PC browser. See also the "Content Development" sidebar on the next page.

FLASH ON CD-ROM

Many developers use Macromedia Director, another multimedia authoring program, for CD-ROM development, but Flash is a feasible option if you're not a Director guru. In all honesty, it's entirely possible that more people use Flash for CD-ROM development than Director because there are more Flash developers in the world. And they tend to use Flash even when it isn't sensible if they aren't familiar with Director. Suffice it to say, this is not the place to get into the Flash versus Director debate. But if you are considering a CD-ROM-based project, consult a knowledgeable Director developer. Director is designed to handle large amounts of data, offers better performance, is fully extensible, and can incorporate Flash assets (along with a boatload of other media types). Director even supports real-time 3D, but that is another story.

But for our purposes, let's assume you are creating a Flash-based CD-ROM. Everything from animations to ActionScript can be compiled into a self-contained file and run from a CD-ROM, so if Flash does what you need, there's no reason not to use it. In a modest project like this one, Flash is certainly up to the task.

No. You may have noticed we don't use Flash's scenes feature in this book. We avoid scenes because they don't work flexibly with ActionScript navigation. In general, you should avoid scenes and the associated commands, such as *nextScene( )* and *prevScene( )*. You can use frame labels as we've done throughout the book to create pseudo-scenes and then jump between them using *gotoAndPlay( )* or *gotoAndStop( )*.

When a movie with scenes is exported, the scenes get flattened into one continuous timeline. So if Scene 1 is 50 frames long, Scene 2 will start on frame 51. Using *nextFrame( )* at the last frame of Scene 1 would jump to the first frame of Scene 2. Conversely, using *prevFrame( )* at the first frame of Scene 2 would jump to the last frame of Scene 1.

There are, however, some extra steps to take when preparing Flash content for CD-ROM deployment, as well as several things to consider.

First, since the content runs from a CD-ROM, you don't have to worry so much about file size. It is always good to optimize your movies, but since the user will not be tapping his fingers to the tune of a phone line making a dial-up connection (the horror, the horror), bandwidth efficiency is not nearly as important. No downloading is required, and content tends to load quickly from a local drive. That said, runtime performance is still an issue, so although you don't have to optimize for size, you should still optimize for speed (and sometimes the two go hand in hand).

On a CD-ROM, you can do some pretty cool things to enhance the user experience. For example, you can automatically play the Flash content when the CD-ROM is inserted into the user's CD-ROM drive. You can also run the movie in full-screen mode and include a Quit button that closes the file (see the later "Projectors" sidebar). While the movie is running, you can grab user data, such as username and password, and save it to the user's computer (this is also true for Flash content on the Web).

> **WARNING**
>
> Make absolutely sure your movie functions correctly before you burn a thousand CD-ROMs. You can't update Flash content on a CD-ROM as you can when it's on the Web.

You can't guarantee that the computer being used to access the CD-ROM also has Internet access, so it's generally best to avoid making elements in the movie dependent on an online connection. If, for example, we created an online Flash application that requires the user to register and/or log in, the data might be saved to a database on the web server. If the *.swf* is posted on the Web, we know that, by definition, any user running it has Internet access. If, however, the application is on CD-ROM, we should save the data to the user's hard drive—you can't save files to the CD-ROM!—instead of trying to upload it to a web server. This way, we can guarantee that the Flash application running from the CD-ROM can still keep track of who is currently using the application and track information—such as quiz results (which can also be saved to the hard drive)—for that user.

Saving and retrieving local data

In this section, we'll create login and registration functionality for a CD-ROM application and store the username and password on the user's hard drive.

Here's another hypothetical situation for you: You have created a Flash game and want to pass it on to your friends on CD-ROM. Since more than one person uses the same computer at each of your friends' houses, we need Flash to keep track of who is currently playing the game so that person's high score can be displayed. You know that your friend Greg Brady has an Internet connection, but Peter and Bobby (Greg's brothers) do not (hence the CD-ROM distribution), so we can't save everyone's scores to a serv-

CONTENT DEVELOPMENT

Flash content for Pocket PCs can be either embedded into HTML pages that run on the Pocket PC version of Internet Explorer or converted into standalone files that play full screen. To learn more about the specifics of either method and more about developing Flash content for mobile devices, check out Macromedia's DevNet section covering devices at *http://www.macromedia.com/devnet/devices*.

Macromedia also offers the Pocket PC Content Development Kit (CDK), which contains a set of UI components de-

signed specifically for the Pocket PC platform. Despite being developed for mobile devices, these components can be used in any Flash project and look quite a bit better than the Flash MX components we used in Chapter 10, so use them as much as you need to. Simply download them from Macromedia's site and copy them into the *Components* folder in your Flash install directory (create a new folder in that directory to keep things organized). Then choose Reload from the Components panel's Options menu to access them.

er-side database. Instead, we'll save the scores and user login information to the user's hard drive and recall it when the user logs in.

To do this, we'll use a local shared object (LSO), which is the Flash analogue of a JavaScript cookie. Shared objects are often used in Flash projects to save important user data to the user's computer.

Sorry—we're not going to build a game here—just the login screen.

To set up the login and registration screen:

1. Open *login_widget.fla*, located in the *12* folder.

2. Save the file as *cd_login.fla* in the *12* folder.

The timeline of the *.fla* file, shown in Figure 12-5, has two layers: *assets* and *bg*. At frame 1, there are several items on the *assets* layer. There are input text fields on the Stage for the username and password (with instance names of name_txt and pw_txt), a Register button named register_btn, a Log In button named login_btn, and a dynamic text field named status_txt.

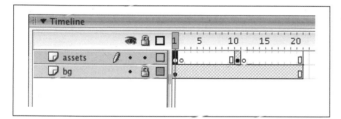

Figure 12-5. The timeline of the cd_login.fla file.

To make all this work, we need two new layers and some ActionScript:

1. Create two new layers and name them *actions* and *labels* (as usual, drag the *actions* layer to the top of the layer stack).

2. Select frame 1 of the *labels* layer and assign log_in as its frame label.

3. Convert frame 11 of the *labels* layer to a keyframe and assign logged_in as the frame label.

Now we have frame labels we can reference in the Action-Script, so let's start writing the code. First, though, let's figure out exactly what needs to happen.

First, we need the movie to stop at frame 1 so the user can log in or register. You should know by now that this means we need to add a *stop( )* command to the *actions* layer at frame 1.

Next, we need to create an instance of the *SharedObject* class so we can access the variables contained in the saved shared object file (assuming we've saved it previously, that is). Then we need two event handlers: one for each button. The Log In button will tell Flash to search the user's computer for a shared object file that starts with the user's username and ends with the *.sol* extension. (I'm told the *.sol* extension stands for "shared object local," not "shit out of luck," no matter how much frustration you experience debugging problems.) If it is found, the user needs to be sent to the logged_in frame. If it is not found (because the user is new or has entered an incorrect username), we'll tell the user he needs to enter a valid username and password or register a new one. The Register button, on the other hand, will create a shared object on the user's hard drive, using the new username as the name for the *.sol* file. In other words, we'll append *.sol* to the end of the username to generate a name for the file. This way, multiple users can use the game and keep their scores separate from one another. Once the user registers, he will be sent to the logged_in frame. No provision is made for users who forget their password.

Now that we know what needs to happen, let's make it work:

1. Select frame 1 of the *actions* layer and add a *stop( )* command to the Actions panel: **stop();**.

2. Create the event handler for the register_btn instance, which will take the data from the name_txt field and use it to create a shared object file:

```
register_btn.onRelease = function () {
  var so:SharedObject = SharedObject.
getLocal(name_txt.text);
  if (so instanceof SharedObject) {
    so.data.username = name_txt.text;
    so.data.pw = pw_txt.text;
    so.flush();
    gotoAndStop("logged_in");
  } else {
    status_txt.text = "Couldn't create or find
.sol file based on username.";
  }
};
```

In the preceding script the *SharedObject.getLocal()* method creates an *.sol* file based on the username by creating a *SharedObject* instance and storing it in the variable so. Data to be saved in the *.sol* file must be stored as properties of a data object associated with the shared object, namely so.data. When the user clicks the Register button, the code stores the username and password from the text fields in the username and pw properties of so.data.

Next, the *SharedObject.flush()* method writes the data stored in so.data to the *.sol* file on the hard drive. The so.data object contains the username and pw properties, so those two values are saved into the shared object file. Finally, the playhead is sent to the logged_in frame.

Now, let's set up the Log In button to search for a shared object file matching the user's name:

1. At frame 1 of the *actions* layer, add the following event handler to the end of the existing script on that frame:

    ```
    login_btn.onRelease = function () {
       var so:SharedObject = SharedObject.
    getLocal(name_txt.text);
    };
    ```

2. Save your work.

The preceding script tells Flash to search the hard drive for a shared object (*.sol*) file that uses the same name as the text in the name_txt field. To do this, we used the *SharedObject.getLocal()* method.

> **NOTE**
>
> The *getLocal()* invocation is literally prefixed by the keyword SharedObject rather than an instance of the *SharedObject* class because *getLocal()* is a so-called *class method*, not an *instance method*. That is, it is invoked on the class itself and not on an instance of the class. In fact, it creates a *SharedObject* instance, which is why it must be invoked in this way (we can't very well invoke it on an instance if the instance hasn't been created yet!). See the "Methods" sidebar in Chapter 10 for related information.

Flash determines the current contents of the name_txt instance (using the text field's text property) and appends .sol to the end of it, thereby arriving at the full name of the file it needs to locate.

This script, as it is, will locate the file (if one exists), but we also need to tell Flash what to do if it does not find the file. So we'll add a condition to the script. We'll say, "Check the file and tell me if the username and pw properties have values. If they do not have values (because the file didn't exist) or the values don't match, display an error message in the status_txt field."

1. To do this, add the following *if-else* statement, shown in color, to the event handler:

    ```
    login_btn.onRelease = function () {
       var so:SharedObject = SharedObject.
    getLocal(name_txt.text);
    ```

DETECTING KEYSTROKES

When running the photo gallery application from a CD-ROM, the user will have a full keyboard available. You might want to let the user scroll through the images using the keyboard instead of clicking on the Forward and Back buttons constructed earlier.

The following example detects the right and left arrow keys, allowing the user to use the keyboard to go forward and back in the photo gallery:

```
// Create a generic object to act as a listener
keyListener = new Object();

// Assign a function to the object's onKeyDown property
keyListener.onKeyDown = function () {
   // Check whether the right or left arrow was pressed,
   // as represented by the Key.RIGHT and Key.LEFT
   // properties.
   if (Key.getCode() == Key.RIGHT) {
      nextFrame();
      updateFrame();
```

```
        if (so instanceof SharedObject) {
            if (name_txt.text == so.data.username &&
pw_txt.text == so.data.pw) {
                gotoAndStop ("logged_in");
            } else {
                status_txt.text = "Please register or
enter a valid username and password.";
            }
        } else {
            status_txt.text = "Couldn't create or find
.sol file based on username.";
        }
    };
```

2. Save.

The second *if* clause in the script uses some strange syntax. Here's what it means: "If the value entered in the name_txt field is equal to (==) the stored username property, and (&&) the value entered in the pw_txt field is equal to the stored pw property, the username and password match, so go to the logged_in frame. Otherwise, display an error message." Technically, it is redundant to store the username in the *.sol* file, because no data is found unless the supplied username matches an existing *.sol* file. We could reduce the code to store only the password, but storing the username makes the code easier to read and demonstrates how to store multiple data items in a local file. Regardless, it is a bad idea to store or transmit unencrypted usernames or passwords that are used to protect any sensitive data, such as financial or health data. So this should not be interpreted as a robust, deployment-ready solution.

We're all done with the actions for the log_in frame. Let's move on to the actions for the logged_in frame.

The *assets* layer, at the logged_in frame, contains a dynamic text field named welcome_txt. We'll use this text field to display the user's name upon successful login:

1. Add the following code to stop the movie at the logged_in frame and display the username (from the shared object file) in the welcome_txt field:

```
stop();
welcome_txt.text = "Welcome " +
so.data.username + "!";
```

2. Save and test the movie.

3. In the test movie, enter a username and password.

4. Click the Log In button. If you've followed along, an error message appears in the status_txt field telling you to either register or enter a valid username and password. This occurs because there is not yet a shared object on the hard drive that reflects your name.

5. Click the Register button. This creates a shared object (named according to your username) and sends you to the logged_in frame, where a welcome message appears with your username in it.

6. Close the Preview window.

7. Test the movie again.

8. Enter the same username and password as in Step 3 and click the Log In button. This time, instead of getting an error message, you are logged in.

When you clicked the Register button, Flash created a shared object for you that contains your username and

```
    } else if (Key.getCode() == Key.LEFT) {
        prevFrame();
        updateFrame();
    }
};
// Register listener with Key class to detect key events
Key.addListener(keyListener);
```

When running in a web browser, the browser itself might intercept keystrokes. Keyboard events are triggered only if the Flash Player has mouse focus. Users must click the Stage of a movie before the movie's keystroke handlers will become active. Consider forcing users to click a button before entering any keyboard-controlled section of a movie. This ensures that the Flash Player has keyboard focus.

When keystroke detection is no longer needed, you can remove the listener as follows:

```
Key.removeListener(keyListener);
```

password. The shared object is saved on your hard drive. The next time you opened the movie, it looked for a shared object file that matched the username you entered. Because the shared object now exists, you are logged in without an error message.

Although the path can be specified explicitly when invoking *getLocal( )*, by default shared object (*.sol*) files are automatically placed in a folder based on the name of the *.swf* file from which they were created (in this case *cd_login.swf*). To prove that the login feature works for multiple users, run another test movie and register with a different username and password. Then locate a folder named *cd_login* (not the *cd_login.fla* or *cd_login.swf* file) on your hard drive. That folder is typically found in a directory similar to one of the following (substitute your user account name for *USER*):

Windows 2000, Windows XP
```
C:\Documents and Settings\USER\Local Settings\
Application Data\Macromedia\Flash Player\
#SharedObjects\cd_login
```

Macintosh OS X
```
Macintosh HD/Users/USER/Library/Preferences/
Macromedia/Flash Player/#SharedObjects/cd_login
```

Each *.sol* file generated by the *cd_login.swf* movie is saved into the *cd_login* folder, which in turn is located somewhere in the Flash Player folder on your hard drive.

> **NOTE**
>
> The exact location of *.sol* files varies by operating system and configuration. It's easiest to search your system for files with the *.sol* extension.

You may also find numerous other *.sol* files on your hard drive, but don't panic. It doesn't mean Big Brother is watching you. Much like JavaScript cookies, shared objects are often used by developers to save user data on your hard drive. Therefore, Flash-based web sites you've visited may have deposited one or more *.sol* files on your hard drive. Generally, the *.sol* files are for simple things like your username or the results of a quiz. If a movie needs to save more than 100 KB of data to your hard drive, a message appears in your Flash Player asking you for permission to do so. If you're worried, you can always

refuse permission. You can also disable this globally via the same message window.

The user can access her privacy settings from the Flash Player Settings pop-up window. It is accessible at runtime by right-clicking (Windows) or Cmd-clicking (Mac) and choosing Settings from the contextual menu that appears. A user can control additional privacy and security settings via the online Settings Manager on Macromedia's web site. The English language version is located at *http://www.macromedia.com/support/documentation/ en/flashplayer/help/settings_manager.html*.

For many more details on security and privacy (including ways to protect your Flash content), see Chapter 12 of *Flash Hacks* (O'Reilly). Also see the Macromedia Flash Developer Center security page at *http://www. macromedia.com/devnet/mx/flash/security.html*.

Running Flash content from CD-ROM

The *.swf* file format is designed to run in web browsers or the Standalone version of the Flash Player, but it's safe to bet that most users don't know that. After all, they're not Flash geeks—they're potential customers, friends, or employers. Yes, we could simply print some instructions on the CD-ROM label that tell the user to load the CD-ROM, open a web browser, and choose File → Open to open a specific file on the CD, but that's asking way too much. Remember, users don't like instructions. They like things to just work (as Steve Krug says, "Don't make me think!").

To solve this problem, we'll make the CD-ROM content run automatically. We'll publish the movie as a self-contained file that includes its own Flash Player and create an *autorun* file that tells the computer to open it as soon as the CD-ROM is inserted into the user's CD-ROM drive.

First, let's publish the file we need:

1. Choose File → Publish Settings to open the Publish Settings dialog box.

2. Under the Formats tab, uncheck Flash and instead check Windows Projector (*.exe*) and Macintosh Projector. Notice that tabs do not appear in the dialog box. There are no configurable options for either of these file types.

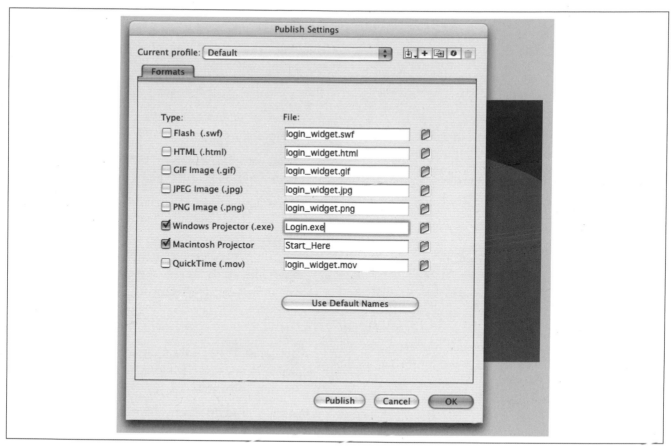

Figure 12-6. The publish settings for cd_login.fla.

3. In the File field for Windows Projector, enter **Login.exe**. In the File field for Macintosh Projector, enter **Start_Here**, as shown in Figure 12-6. If creating the Macintosh projector from Windows, name the file **Start_Here.hqx**, as Flash creates a BinHex archive that can be restored on a Mac. This is necessary to preserve the resource fork that is part of a Macintosh application.

4. Click the Publish button to generate a Windows *.exe* file and a Mac Projector. (If you click OK instead, you can still publish the executables at a later time using File → Publish.)

5. Click OK to close the dialog box.

Yes, you can create both Windows and Macintosh executables from either platform. If distributing CD-ROMs for both platforms, be sure to test on both operating systems. (For what it's worth, Macromedia Director MX 2004 has the ability to create executables for both platforms as well. This eliminates a long-standing objection of Director developers—namely that they had to buy Director for both platforms to distribute for both platforms, even if they developed primarily on only one platform.)

You are probably already familiar with *.exe* files. In the Windows operating system, *.exe* files (or *executable* files) are the files that constitute your programs. Microsoft Word's executable, for example, is named *Word.exe*.

To make our project run from a CD-ROM, we published an *.exe* file for Windows users, and a Projector file for Mac users. (Projector files are the Mac equivalent of *.exe* files and are usually known as *applications* in Mac terminology.)

Entire books have been written on PDA, handheld, and CD-ROM development, and the coverage here is not intended to be exhaustive. The *.exe* and Projector files we just created are enough to get started. Refer to the resources cited in Chapter 13 and throughout the book for additional help on CD-ROM development.

Next, we need to create the autorun file. Don't worry—this takes only a couple of lines of code and a text editor:

1. Open a text editor, such as Notepad, Macromedia Dreamweaver, or Flash Pro's built-in editor.

2. Enter the following into a new document, exactly as it appears here (no extra spaces, please):

```
[autorun]
open=Login.exe
```

3. Save this file as *autorun.inf* (note the extension is *.inf*, not *.ini*) in the *12* folder.

See? I told you it would take only a couple of lines of code. You may have noticed that the Mac Projector file isn't referenced in this code. This is because Macintosh operating systems don't use an autorun file to start CD-ROM content automatically. Instead, an icon for the CD-ROM appears on the user's desktop. The user simply double-clicks on the icon to view the content of the CD-ROM and then double-clicks the appropriate file, which, in this case, is named *Start_Here* (to make it obvious which file needs to be opened). That said, most Macintosh CD-ROM burning software can create an open window on the desktop showing the file to be double-clicked (this eliminates the step of having to double-click the CD-ROM icon itself).

Now we can put the files onto a CD-ROM:

1. Insert a blank CD-ROM into your CD writer (assuming you have a CD-RW drive).

2. Name the CD and copy the following files to it: *autorun.inf*, *Start_Here*, and *Login.exe*.

3. You want to burn a *hybrid* CD so that it is recognized on both Mac and Windows (which use different filesystems). If you want to get fancy, you can burn only the *Start_Here* file on the Mac partition and the other files on the Windows partition. This prevents Windows files from showing up on the Macintosh and vice versa. The details of this are specific to your CD-ROM burning software.

4. Burn the CD-ROM (again, the method for doing this depends on your operating system and CD-ROM burning software).

When the CD-ROM finishes burning, remove and reinsert it. If you're using a Windows operating system configured to autorun CD-ROMs (as most Windows machines

PROJECTORS

When running the Standalone Player, you may want it to behave more like a typical desktop application. Several third-party tools—such as SWF Studio (*http://www.northcode.com*) and SWF Kit (*http://www.swfkit.com*)—optimize or add features to Flash executables.

The versatile *fscommand( )* function supports some features not available when running Flash content in a web browser (where stricter security limitations are in place).

To run a Standalone Player full screen while maintaining the original movie's size, use:

```
fscommand("fullscreen", "true");
fscommand("allowscale", "false");
```

To quit a Standalone Player (Projector), use:

```
fscommand("quit");
```

For information on launching a movie full screen in a web browser window, see:

> *http://moock.org/webdesign/flash/launchwindow/fullscreen*

You can research *fscommand( )* in the Help documentation included with Flash. To do this, type **fscommand** into the Actions panel, select it, and click the Reference button in the Actions panel. The explanation of the term and its usage from the ActionScript Dictionary display in the Help panel.

are), the *Login.exe* file runs automatically. If you're on a Mac, an icon appears on your desktop, and you double-click *Start_Here* from the CD to run the Flash content.

Alternatively, it is possible to automatically start a Projector when the CD-ROM is inserted into a Macintosh computer. In Mac terminology, this feature is called AutoPlay, but it isn't controlled by a text file as is done on Windows. Instead, some CD-ROM burning utilities, such as Toast Titanium Pro, allow the developer to specify the file to be played when the CD-ROM is inserted. In our example,

you should configure it to play your Macintosh Projector, *Start_Here* (see your CD-ROM burning software documentation for details on how to specify the file to be automatically played). However, even in such cases, the Projector won't start automatically unless the user has AutoPlay enabled in his QuickTime control panel (and most Mac users have it disabled).

By now, you should have a solid idea of what can be done with Flash. Just in time, too, as we've just completed the last exercise in the book!

GET OUT OF THE BOX

In this chapter, we've seen how:

- Flash content can be modified to run on a handheld, PDA, or other mobile device, or can be specifically designed for it

- CD-ROM development requires some special considerations, such as the file types used for the published content

- You can in fact build something in this book without drawing a box (just thought I'd point that out)

One thing to keep in mind when constructing Flash content for CD-ROM: the Flash Player is built into *.exe* and Projector files, so your final project automatically has roughly 1 MB of file weight added to it. This does not mean you messed up—the additional file size generally does not affect the playback of the movie when it's saved to the user's computer or run from CD-ROM.

That said, you should still try to optimize your movies as much as possible when creating content for CD-ROM. It's not a free ride. The user may be using an older computer with less RAM and processing power than yours, and the power of the user's machine always plays a role in the performance of Flash content. Vector art, used exclusively in Flash except when adding bitmap images to movies (and text), is rendered from mathematical equations, so complex graphics and long animations can affect playback on any computer. On old machines, it can be downright unwatchable. A jerky animation does not look good.

The best way to avoid this problem is to test your content on a computer similar to the user's computer. This is not always easy, as many of us don't have old systems lying around. But if you can find a friend or relative with an old computer, start knocking on her door once a week to test out your Flash work. You may want to bring a gift.

Flash has become a ubiquitous development and distribution platform, and potential avenues are not limited to what we've discussed here. Macromedia Central (*http://www.macromedia.com/software/central*) is a new type of application—a so-called occasionally connected power browser. Central plays back *.swf* files, so Central content is generally developed using the Flash authoring tool.

Macromedia has also announced a version of the Flash Player known as Flash Lite and a server-side component known as FlashCast to broadcast content to cell phones and other processor-limited devices. Again, see Macromedia's DevNet center for mobile devices (*http://www. macromedia.com/devnet/devices*) for more information.

For more details on Flash Player distribution, see the Macromedia Player Licensing FAQ:

http://www.macromedia.com/support/shockwave/ info/licensing/faq.html

In Chapter 13, we'll recap, wrap up, and talk about where you can go from here. Our journey is almost over.

13

GET OUT OF THE BOX

As you may have noticed, Flash has billions of possible uses, and we've only begun to tap into its power. Now that you've mastered the basics, you may want to see some more advanced ways to use Flash.

In this chapter, I'll recap what we've done so far and point you toward other resources that can send you further down the path to Flash greatness.

THE RECAP

Using a simple box as the foundation of almost every exercise in this book, we've designed layouts, created custom commands, animated a cartoon character, loaded images, imported assets from other programs, embedded a *.swf* file into a web page, created some cool effects, loaded text and CSS into a movie, created a reusable template, and even streamed video with ActionScript. Hopefully, you've gotten a clear view of what you can do with the tools that come in the box with every copy of Flash MX 2004 and Flash Pro.

Here is a quick recap of some of what you've learned to do since the beginning of this book:

- Use the Rectangle tool to draw simple rectangles and boxes

- Manipulate fill and stroke colors, including gradient fills

- Customize a stroke style to achieve a new look

- Convert shapes into graphic symbols

- Create your own preloader component

- Automate tasks by creating commands via the History panel

- Use movie clips to create animations that run independently of one another

- Use ActionScript to control movie clips

- Create buttons that move the playhead from one frame to another, open web pages, and run custom ActionScript functions

- Analyze and revise ActionScript to make it more efficient

- Use ActionScript to control timeline and user events

- Use various drawing tools to draw and manipulate graphics

- Import sound to enhance a television static effect

- Import bitmaps

- Load *.jpg* and *.swf* files on the fly

- Share assets among multiple Flash documents

- Create text effects using animation and Flash MX 2004's timeline effects

- Convert video clips into *.flv* files that can be streamed into Flash

- Stream the video clips into a Flash movie using components and ActionScript

- Create a template for a series of ads

- Communicate with server-side scripts

- Create and publish a photo gallery for the Pocket PC platform

- Prepare Flash content for use on CD-ROM

- Store user preferences on the hard drive

Along the way, of course, we employed tricks that help make everything easier, and we saw how small additions to your designs, like a button rollover, improve usability. We've also seen how taking a few extra steps during development can improve the playback of a movie and lower file size.

All this is just the beginning of what you can do with Flash. It's quite amazing, actually, that the same program you'd use to create an animated cartoon can be used as the front end of a Rich Internet Application. But that's what is so great about Flash—the possibilities are almost limitless. Just when you think your idea is too difficult to pull off, Flash provides a way to accomplish it.

Top ten things we didn't cover

When I undertook this book, it was with the express intention of maintaining a reader-centric viewpoint. I tried to focus on the features that were most important to beginners and the majority of intermediate users. Having completed this book, you have a solid foundation for further study, but inevitably some will judge the book not by what it covered but by what it omitted. Here is a quick list of topics, many of which warrant their own books, which you may want to explore in more depth using the resources cited in this chapter:

Advanced ActionScript programming

Although this book helped you get your feet wet with ActionScript, it wasn't intended as a full-fledged programming course. ActionScript is covered in depth in other O'Reilly books. For a gentle introduction to programming basics in Flash, plus a detailed reference dictionary, see *ActionScript for Flash MX: The Definitive Guide*. For problem/solution-based example code, see the *ActionScript Cookbook*. And for complete coverage of ActionScript 2.0, including objected-oriented programming (OOP), design patterns, best practices, external *.as* files, classes, variable scope, and much more, see *Essential ActionScript 2.0*.

Advanced Flash design

Although we covered some design tips, this book was intended to get you up to speed with the Flash authoring tool's features; it isn't intended as an advanced course in online design or Flash design. See the resources cited later in this chapter, among others.

Advanced tips and tricks

Now that you understand how to use Flash and achieve basic goals, you're equipped to explore an infinite number of tips and tricks on your own. A good place to start is *Flash Hacks* for tips on optimization, security, and many other topics.

Flash Pro–specific features

For the most part, we didn't attempt to cover features supported only in Flash MX Professional 2004. For example, the Screens features—Slides and Forms—are used to develop user interfaces visually (a la Microsoft Visual Basic) and to create slide show presentations (a là Microsoft PowerPoint). Likewise, we didn't cover the Project panel, which helps developers manage complex projects with multiple files.

Accessibility

Accessibility and compliance with Federal Section 508 are increasingly important. See "Accessibility and Macromedia Flash MX 2004" (*http://www.*macromedia.com/macromedia/accessibility/features/flash*) for more on Macromedia's work and Flash's capabilities in this area. If accessibility is a concern to you, consider using the v2 components, which support accessibility features such as keyboard tabbing. Refer also to the *Accessibility* class and the System. capabilities.hasAccessibility property.

XML

Flash has a built-in XML parser, and it can send and receive data in XML format. For many details, see the *XML*, *XMLnode*, and *XMLSocket* classes, as covered in *ActionScript for Flash MX: The Definitive Guide*.

Extensibility

Skilled developers can create commands and tools for use in the Flash authoring environment. The Flash JavaScript Dictionary (*http://www.macromedia.com/support/documentation/en/flash/#flashjsdict*) includes the necessary information to get started in customizing the authoring tool. More details on component development, a topic we only scratched, are available at *http://www.macromedia.com/support/documentation/en/flash/#usingcomps*. Information on extensibility is also available in PDF format under the Flash MX 2004 trial folder on the enclosed CD-ROM. For some free extensions, complete with source files, see my WidgetMaker blog at *http://www.widgetmaker.net*.

Printing

End users can click the web browser's Print button to print the contents of the browser window, but more advanced printing requires ActionScript. You can perform basic printing using the *print( )*, *printNum( )*, *printAsBitmap( )*, and *printAsBitmapNum( )* commands. For fancier features, such as spooling multiple pages to the printer at once, see the *PrintJob* class (new in Flash MX 2004).

Flash-related companion technologies

This book doesn't attempt to cover companion technologies, such as Flash Remoting, Flash Communication Server MX, or Macromedia Central. O'Reilly currently offers *Flash Remoting: The Definitive Guide*, and expects to publish books on other Flash-related technologies.

Rich Internet Application development

Although we touched on many of the principles and basics, this book didn't attempt to teach full-fledged Rich Internet Application (RIA) development. An RIA is a web-based application such as a mortgage calculator that you might find on the site of a financial services company. If you're an experienced programmer, you should now better understand how to create the Flash front end for such an application. If you are a graphic or UI designer, you should now better understand Flash's programming environment and some of its capabilities. The resources cited throughout this chapter should help you take it from here.

A rant about my "other" agenda

The purpose of this book wasn't just to teach you how to use Flash, but also to teach you why and when to use Flash and how to use it well. The Internet is not perfect—there are all kinds of limitations to web distribution that affect every decision you make when it comes to Flash development. As designers, we must get to know the medium and create within its constraints. Design is not a science, and using the medium to your advantage is a key factor when trying to master the art of good design.

It's important to see the limitations of the Internet as an opportunity. Instead of being frustrated that dial-up Internet connections are the majority, let that fact guide you toward a more minimalist design that communicates effectively while using smaller file sizes. Instead of being bothered by the fact that users likely won't read all the text you have written for a site, see if you can make your point more efficiently or communicate without text altogether. A guideline I use in my own designs is this: if you can't say it in 25 words or less using a bullet point, don't say it (unless it's an article or tutorial or something else that mandates a lot of text). Bullet points aren't usually my chosen method for the presentation of text on a site, but this mantra reminds me that each and every point I make must be as efficient as short bullets. The same is true for graphics and animations. If you can find a way to communicate more effectively, do it. Your users will appreciate it.

The point to all this is that thinking outside the box is invariably a required skill when trying to create something great inside the box. You have to understand how your proverbial box works, what it's capable of handling and doing, and what tools you have at your disposal. Once you understand how your delivery medium works, you can take advantage of its full potential. Whether you're designing content for the Web, a CD-ROM, the Pocket PC platform, a PDA, or even a cell phone, your box is defined for you. Each medium has its own limitations. To create your best work, you must identify the limitations, study them, and work within them. In doing this, you transcend the limitations and convert them into opportunities to make you better at what you do. In short, getting completely *inside* the box can only help you get *out* of it.

RESOURCES

As you may expect, this book is not the end of your journey. *Flash Out of the Box* is not a reference guide for all things Flash, nor is it an encyclopedia of tips, tricks, and ActionScripts (hey, that could be the title of my next book!). This book is here to show you the path and get you walking. What happens from there is up to you.

If you're not already using Flash MX 2004 or Flash MX Professional 2004 version 7.2, which is included on the book's CD-ROM, you can download the update, code name Ellipsis, from:

> *http://www.macromedia.com/software/flash/ special/7_2updater*

The article "What Is the Significance of Ellipsis?" talks about the changes in update 7.2:

> *http://www.macromedia.com/devnet/mx/flash/ articles/context.html*

The following subsections list resources to expand your Flash knowledge and arsenal of assets. I've used each of them myself on more than a few occasions and can personally attest to their greatness.

Online Flash help and assets

Tons of Flash tutorials are available online, and it can be awfully difficult to know which ones are worth reading.

Well, I've read just about all of them (it feels like it, anyway), so I thought I'd make it easier on you. Here's a list, along with some resources for assets you can use in your own projects:

FlashKit (http://www.flashkit.com)
> Get sound loops, sound effects, sample *.fla* files, fonts, reviews, and news all in one place. FlashKit rocks, and just about every Flash geek I know has it bookmarked.

Macromedia DevNet (http://www.macromedia.com/ devnet/mx/flash)
> Macromedia's site features Developer Centers for each of its major products, and the Flash Developer Center contains all kinds of articles, tutorials, product updaters, and sample files. Developer Centers are updated frequently, so check in often to take full advantage.

Macromedia Flash Exchange (http://www.macromedia. com/exchange/flash)
> As you saw in Chapter 11, the Flash Exchange is an excellent resource for components and extensions built by Macromedia and third-party developers. Categories include User Interface, Navigation, Design, Commerce, and more.

Miniml (http://www.miniml.com)
> Miniml is a site devoted entirely to fonts, and they all work very well with Flash.

Community MX (http://www.communitymx.com)
> Community MX (a.k.a. CMX) is a little different from most knowledge sites in that you have to pay a subscription fee to get to the best stuff, like components, extensions, and multipart tutorials on all of Macromedia's major applications. But for $25 per month (currently), you know you're learning from experts. The CMX team is made up of the same people who wrote the books you see on the shelf in your favorite bookstore. They are the masters; you can trust them.

InformIT.com's Flash Reference Guide (http://informit. com/guides/guide.asp?g=flash)
> Hosted by author Matthew David, this section of InformIT.com features articles, tutorials, and a blog

devoted exclusively to Flash. You'll find me there as well—I wrote an entire series for the Flash Reference Guide called *10 Minutes with Flash*.

Macromedia User Group Program (MMUG) (http://www. macromedia.com/usergroups)
> As a MMUG manager, I must tout the incredible power of being in a room full of other Flash geeks. Some know more than you, some know less, but everyone is there because they love Flash. Most groups have regular raffles and software giveaways. The presenters could be anyone from a group member to a Macromedia staff member, like Mike Downey (Flash Project Manager) or Greg Rewis (Product Evangelist). One thing's for sure: you'll learn a lot and have fun doing it.

Macromedia's events listing (http://www.macromedia. com/events)
> There are a ton of online seminars and international conferences to get in on, and Macromedia's web site lists all the ones they know about.

Flash-related blogs (http://www.markme.com/mxna/ index.cfm?category=Flash)
> Keep up with Macromedia Flash news and views with this blog aggregator. Of particular interest is the "mesh on mx" blog (*http://www.markme.com/mesh*) by Mike Chambers, Flash's Product Manager for Developer Relations.

moockmarks (http://www.moock.org/moockmarks)
> Links to all things Flash-related, vetted and organized into categories by Colin Moock.

Flash in books

Much like the online resources, quite a few Flash books are on the shelves these days. They can cost an average of $40 or more, likely preventing you from buying them all, so here are my official recommendations for more advanced Flash topics.

Essential ActionScript 2.0 (O'Reilly)
> The title says it all. This book covers the in and outs of ActionScript 2.0, including object-oriented design, object-oriented programming, and design patterns. Indispensable for serious scripters, but not

for beginners. That said, it is very approachable for people with intermediate ActionScript 1.0 skills or OOP experience in another language.

Flash Hacks (O'Reilly)

A fun and informative exploration of a wide variety of Flash-related topics from animation to ActionScript. You'll learn how to optimize content and code, protect your SWF files from prying eyes, simulate 3D, and more. An excellent resource to bring beginners up to speed with the larger Flash universe and to reinvigorate the creative spark in more experienced developers.

ActionScript for Flash MX: The Definitive Guide, Second Edition (O'Reilly)

Affectionately known as ASDG2, this book is exactly what it says—the definitive guide for Action-Script. The author, Colin Moock (*http://moock.org*), is a very well respected ActionScript guru. Although this book covers ActionScript 1.0, it is still the best resource for learning ActionScript syntax and the API. It covers ActionScript programming in a comprehensive and intelligent way, including a detailed reference section. For details on OOP development in ActionScript 2.0, see Colin's latest book, *Essential ActionScript 2.0*.

Flash Remoting: The Definitive Guide (O'Reilly)

This book covers using Flash Remoting to communicate between the Flash Player (on the client) and various server-side scripting technologies. Copious server-side examples are provided for ColdFusion, Java, .NET, PHP, and Server-Side ActionScript. Open source implementations are available for various server scripting languages, including Perl, Java, and PHP.

Flash MX 2004 Magic (New Riders)

The Magic series by New Riders is meant for people who have mastered the basics and want to increase their knowledge and skill. This book comprises 12 projects, created and taught by 10 different authors. Each shows off the new features in Flash MX 2004 and shows you how to take your existing skill a little further. And hey, I wrote Chapters 1 and 2, so you know it can't be bad. (Hehehehe...)

MTIV: Process, Inspiration and Practice for the New Media Designer (New Riders)

This is not a how-to book, but it's worth every penny. In *MTIV* (Making the Invisible Visible), world-renowned Flash designer Hillman Curtis offers brilliant insight into the more cerebral and emotional aspects of design. The book is broken into three major sections—process, inspiration, and practice—and almost functions like an oracle for designers. Whenever I'm stuck on a design, I grab this book, pick a random page, and read it. And I always walk away with a clearer view than I had when I started.

Stock photography

Need some images for your Flash or web project? Check out the following stock photography web sites. Stock photos generally cost money, but if you find the one you desperately need, it's usually worth it.

Comstock (http://www.comstock.com)

This site is the home of thousands of beautiful, multifunctional images from great photographers and illustrators.

Punchstock (http://www.punchstock.com)

Inventive, playful, useful, and generally brilliant images abound on this site.

Library of Congress (http://www.loc.gov/rr/print/catalog.html)

Many, but not all, of the images found in the LOC's Prints and Photographs Reading Room are in the public domain, which means many are royalty- and cost-free. Note that some are not. You'll have to weed through them yourself to determine which you can use legally.

The author himself

Should you come across anything in this book you desperately need help with, or just feel like telling someone how much you loved reading *Flash Out of the Box*, feel free to go straight to the source: me. I can be reached by email at *robert@flashoutofthebox.com*.

Whew! I'm about ready for a sandwich. How about you?

You've come a long way since the beginning of this book, and I commend your efforts. By jumping headlong into Flash design and development, you've proven that you're no ordinary cat. You've got ideas and you want to start putting them together. You started this book with nothing more than a simple box and have since learned about ActionScript, streaming video, animation, and many other things that can help bring your ideas to life. I hope that this book has been as rewarding for you to read as it was for me to write. I've taken you as far as I can go within the scope of this book, but you should be well prepared for what lies ahead.

This book has tried to offer you practice with the tools, techniques, and terminology of Flash. You should be able to communicate effectively (even if it is only to ask questions) within the larger Flash community. You should definitely take advantage of the camaraderie, inspiration, and assistance available from this interesting and diverse group of people.

Alas, a final note:

I got into web design almost by accident. When my small-time rock band was in need of a web site, my wife (a librarian formerly employed as a web designer) spent an afternoon teaching me HTML. Roughly two and a half months later, I was employed as a code geek for a local startup, banging out one five-page web site after another, each for a different product sold by my employer. Since then, I've played the roles of webmaster, print ad designer, marketing guy, UI designer, and even writer (it's been a strange ride). Along the way, I learned Flash and ended up using it in almost every project. Sometimes I need to create a simple banner ad, and sometimes I need an entire web application. Sometimes I sit at my desk and design just for fun. Whatever the case, Flash is an integral part of my work, and it's usually the best part of my job. Simply put: I love using Flash.

Hopefully, now that you've seen some of what Flash can do and begun your experience with my favorite program, your (stunning and brilliant) ideas will get to see the light of day. Hopefully, your journey will be just as rewarding.

Have fun, experiment, and learn! And, to quote Larry Mullen, Jr. (drummer for U2), "Stay vertical and don't get shredded."

Happy Flashing!

WORKFLOW AND WORKSPACE TIPS

Now that you've worked with Flash for a while, you may have noticed that it has a tendency to take over your desktop with panels and dialog boxes, and not everything functions quite the way you might prefer.

You're still here? Oh. Well then I guess I'll keep talking.

Here are some tips that can improve your workflow while using Flash. I hope this appendix answers some of the questions that may be lingering in your head.

PREFERENCES

Just like every program out there, Flash has a Preferences dialog box. Flash's Preferences dialog box has five tabs, and each tab has several sections. The following subsections suggest ways you can improve or enhance the performance and functionality of Flash by adjusting the preferences under each tab. I won't tell you about every tab and every option in Preferences, just the ones I think will help you (I've excluded the Clipboard and Warnings tabs because they're just not very exciting).

To follow along, open the Preferences dialog box by choosing Edit → Preferences on Windows, or Flash (Professional) → Preferences on Mac.

The General tab

The General tab, shown in Figure A-1, contains miscellaneous preferences that don't seem to belong anywhere else. Here, I highlight some preferences of particular interest.

Undo levels

When you first install Flash, the number of undo levels is set to 1000 (although it defaults to 100 in the 7.2 update). But the undo stack requires memory that your computer may not have to spare. Everything you do must be remembered by Flash so that it can be undone if requested. With this number set so high, your computer is doing more work than you probably realize just to track every step you take. Lowering this number decreases the amount of memory required to run Flash. I leave mine set to 200, but you can choose whatever number you are comfortable with. Don't set it too low—you still want to be able to undo.

Highlight color

Selecting an object on the Stage highlights it with a blue bounding box by default. You can change the highlight color using the nearby color swatch if you set the Highlight Color option to Use This Color. Alternatively, each layer in the timeline has its own colored square next to the layer name. To highlight all the objects on a particular layer using the layer color, change the Highlight Color option to Use Layer Color. This makes it easier to tell the objects on one layer apart from another. This color is also used when viewing content in outline mode (View → Preview Mode → Outlines). You can set the color for the selected layer in the Layer Properties dialog box (Modify → Timeline → Layer Properties).

On launch

This section of the General tab enables you to choose what to show upon launching Flash. By default, the Start screen is shown, but you can choose to have Flash open either a new document, the last document you had open, or no document at all. Personally, I find the Start

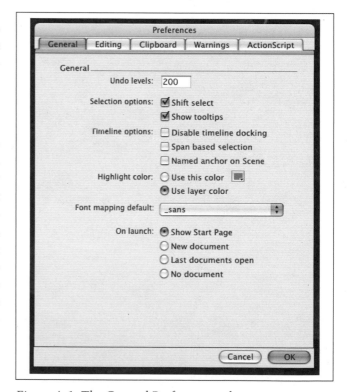

Figure A-1. The General Preferences tab.

screen pretty handy, as you can use it to quickly open various types of new templates or reopen any of the last 10 opened documents. There are also options in the Start screen to search Macromedia's web site and launch the Flash Exchange. Nonetheless, you may find it more desirable to open the last document you worked on.

The Editing tab

The Editing tab, shown in Figure A-2, contains preferences for the Pen tool, drawing settings, and project settings. Following are some highlights.

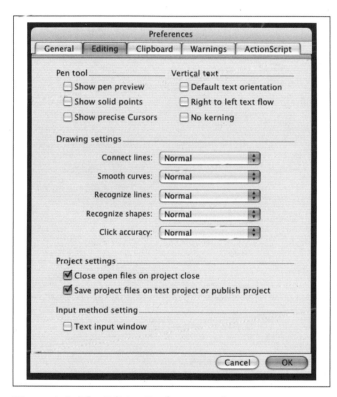

Figure A-2. The Editing Preferences tab.

Drawing settings

Change the drop-down list choices in this section to accommodate your particular drawing needs. Need smoother curves? Choose Smooth from the Smooth Curves menu. Bad at drawing shapes freehand but still want Flash to recognize them? Choose Tolerant from the Recognize Shapes menu.

Project settings

For those of you using Flash Pro, this section enables you to close project files when you close a project in the Project panel (Window → Project) and save project files when you test or publish an opened project. If you don't tell Flash to close all the project files at once, you'll have to do it yourself. And that's just no fun.

The ActionScript tab

The ActionScript tab, shown in Figure A-3, lets you configure all sorts of things related to writing code in Flash, such as the font used in the Actions panel, how reserved keywords are color coded, and whether you want to use code hints.

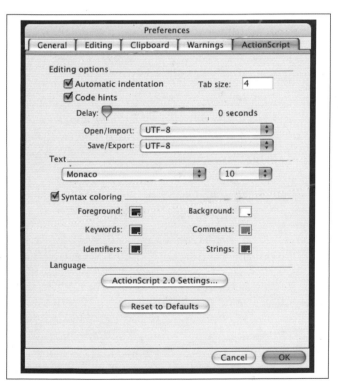

Figure A-3. The ActionScript Preferences tab.

Editing options

Here, you can set the amount of time delay for code hints when typing in the Actions panel, from 0 to 4 seconds. If you like code hints, four seconds can be a long time to wait, so leave it set to 0. If you want to disable code hints entirely, simply uncheck the Code Hints checkbox.

Text

Some developers swear that they absolutely must use certain types of fonts when writing code, but you can use whatever you want. In this section of the ActionScript tab, you can change the font and font size of ActionScript in the Actions panel to something you might find easier to read. The default is 10-point Monaco (on Mac) or 10-point Courier New (on Windows).

KEYBOARD SHORTCUTS

Many commands and features in Flash already have corresponding keyboard shortcuts, such as pressing V to activate the Selection tool. But you may want a speedier way to run a command or open a custom panel set (which I'll show you how to create in a minute). Here's how to customize the keyboard shortcuts:

1. Choose Keyboard Shortcuts from the Edit menu on Windows (or the Flash (Professional) menu on Mac) to open the Keyboard Shortcuts dialog box, shown in Figure A-4.

2. Click the Duplicate Set button in the dialog box, name the new keyboard shortcut set (name it after your dog, perhaps), and click OK.

3. In the Commands section of the dialog box, expand the File menu and select Close All (which closes all open documents and libraries).

4. In the Shortcut section, click Add Shortcut, and press the keys you want to use as the new shortcut. For example, you might press Ctrl+Shift+W on Windows or Cmd+Shift+W on Mac. The keys you press appear in the Press Key field.

5. Click the Change button. This opens a message warning you that the shortcut is already assigned to the Work Area command, which is, in my opinion, completely useless (all it does is shove the Stage up against the timeline, eliminating the work area space between them).

6. Click Reassign.

7. Click OK to close the dialog box.

Now, when you have more than one document or more than one library open, simply use this keyboard shortcut to close all your Flash files at once.

You can set up whatever custom shortcuts you like using the preceding procedure.

You want another tip? When you need to see the Stage a little better and get some of those panels out of the way, press F4 to hide all the panels at once. Press it again to show the panels.

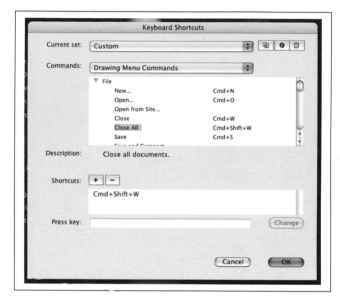

Figure A-4. The Keyboard Shortcuts dialog box.

PANEL LAYOUT

Customizing the panel layout in Flash enables you to organize your workspace exactly the way you want, but first you need to know how to dock and undock panels:

1. To undock a panel, locate two panels that are docked together. Click on the titlebar (more specifically, click on the little dots on the left side of the titlebar) of one of them and drag the panel away from the other panel, then release the mouse button.

2. To redock the panel, drag it over the top of the titlebar of another panel until a heavy black line appears between them. Then release the mouse button.

When you've got that mastered, here's how to customize your panel layout:

1. From the Window menu, open any panel you believe you'll use often.

2. Next, choose Window → Design Panels, Window → Development Panels, and Window → Other Panels to locate any panels that are currently not open. Open the ones you think you'll use often.

3. Arrange the panels in any way you like. Leave a nice view of the Stage, Tools panel, Properties panel, and Timeline panel (you use those a lot in Flash).

4. When everything is arranged how you like it, choose Window → Save Panel Layout to open the Save Panel Layout dialog box.

5. Give your panel set a name and click OK to close the dialog box.

My preferred setup is shown in Figure A-5 (note that my preferred setup is on a Macintosh, with iTunes running—it's what keeps me sane). In fact, I've saved this custom panel set as *Flash Out of the Box Panel Set* and included it on the enclosed CD-ROM (in the *Appendix* folder). You can install it by placing it in the *Panel Sets* directory in your Flash MX 2004 installation folder.

Flash remembers your current layout the next time you launch it, but you might move things around while working. Any time you want to restore your workspace to your saved panel layout, simply choose Window → Panel Sets → *your panel set*. Choose the Default Layout or Training Layout panel set from this menu if your windows become hopelessly misarranged or if you can't locate a panel you need.

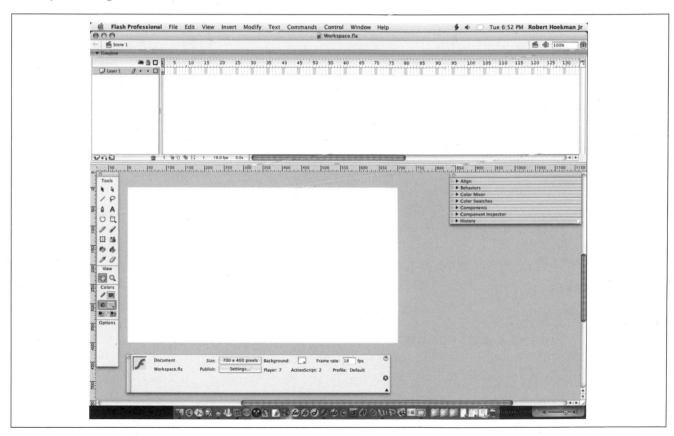

Figure A-5. My preferred workspace setup.

MISCELLANEOUS TIPS

And here are a few tips that don't seem to fit into the previous categories.

Save and compact

Adding assets to a Flash document, whether they're bitmaps, symbols, or scripts, can substantially increase the size of the *.fla* file. In the event you need to FTP the document or email it to someone, a large file can be a huge problem. To remedy this, choose File → Save and Compact. This menu option can cut the file size of a large file in half. Generally, it decreases file size by even more than half, especially if you have deleted unused assets from the Library. Using File → Save, which performs an incremental save, doesn't ordinarily lower the file size of the *.fla*, but Save and Compact squashes your file nicely.

Quick edits

To quickly enter Edit mode for a Library symbol, click the Edit Symbols button in the Edit bar attached to the timeline, as shown in Figure A-6.

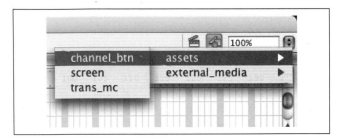

Figure A-6. The Edit Symbols menu in the Edit bar.

Simply locate the symbol name and click. Voilà! You're in Edit mode.

Tabbed documents

Windows users get a little bonus when working with multiple *.fla* files. If the document windows are maximized within the Flash authoring window, each open document adds one tab to the top of the Flash document window. Click through the tabs to access each open document quickly. Otherwise, you can access open documents from the bottom of the Window menu.

Transfer software license

This is one of my favorite new features. Suppose you have one licensed copy of Flash MX 2004 installed on two computers (allowed by the End User License Agreement or EULA) and suddenly find yourself needing to take Flash with you on your laptop for a business trip. Well, go right ahead and do it, mister; I'm not stopping you.

To do this, choose Help → Transfer Your Software License to open the Macromedia Product Activation screen. Click Transfer License and wait. The license is transferred to a Macromedia server, which tracks your registration information with the serial number for your copy of Flash. Next, install Flash on your laptop and register it with the same serial number.

The key here is that you can legally register one copy of Flash on two computers and install Flash on as many computers as you want. You can't, however, use Flash on both computers at the same time (according to the EULA). So before you head for the airport, transfer the license from one computer and then register the copy on your laptop. Instantly, you have a portable copy of Flash. When you get back from your trip, transfer the license from your laptop and register the copy on your main computer. Everything is legal and everyone's happy.

Enable simple buttons

Need to see how a button looks but don't want to go to the trouble of running yet another test movie? Choose Control → Enable Simple Buttons. You can now roll over and click those buttons on stage just as you would in a test movie. They do not, however, run any ActionScript associated with them. Enabling simple buttons allows you to see the button in context.

Check spelling

Now, I'm an excelent speler. I don't mean to boste, but realy, I am very guud. I wun speling beez in skool and everything. But you mite not bee az good az me.

Once again—Flash to the rescue. To check your entire *.fla* file for spelling mistakes, choose Text → Check Spelling. A dialog box opens through which you can verify every word Flash does not understand. And if your typing skills are as bad as mine, it might take a while.

CONCLUSION

In conclusion, ladies and germs, not all features are documented. Sometimes you just have to hunt them down and find your own ways to make working with Flash easier and faster. I've done what I can for you. Now go away. I'm all done with you. Check the resources in Chapter 13 if you need more than I can offer.

Happy Flashing!

About the Author

Robert Hoekman, Jr., is a Certified Macromedia Professional who has worked with Flash since version 3. He is the founder and manager of the Flash and Multimedia Users Group of Arizona (FMUG.az), an official Macromedia User Group (MMUG) with more than 150 members. In the past several years, Robert has worked in corporate environments as a multimedia designer, web designer, and webmaster and has designed for audiences ranging from music-memorabilia collectors to executives at Fortune 1000 companies. He currently works in the engineering department of Thomson NETg, the e-learning industry leader located in Scottsdale, Arizona, as a Flash developer.

Robert's publishing credits include two chapters for *Flash MX 2004 Magic* (New Riders) and an extensive series of articles for InformIT's Flash Reference Guide called *10 Minutes with Flash*, about how to do fun and useful things with Flash in roughly 10 minutes. Robert also served as the consultant for *Flash MX 2004 Beyond the Basics* (Peachpit Press), and technical reviewer and editor for *Flash MX 2004 Hands On Training* (Peachpit Press), *Photoshop CS/ImageReady CS for the Web Hands On Training* (Peachpit Press), and *Flash MX 2004 Magic* (New Riders).

To learn more about Robert, visit WidgetMaker (*http://www.widgetmaker.net)*, his Flash blog and widget-resource site (complete with free source files), or love+rage (*http://www.loveandrage.net*), his online portfolio.

Colophon

Our look is the result of reader comments, our own experimentation, and feedback from distribution channels. Distinctive covers complement our distinctive approach to technical topics, breathing personality and life into potentially dry subjects.

Emily Quill was the production editor and proofreader for *Flash Out of the Box*. Norma Emory was the copyeditor. Rick Schlott and Emily Quill did the typesetting and page makeup. Sanders Kleinfeld and Claire Cloutier provided quality control. Julie Hawks wrote the index.

Ellie Volckhausen designed the cover of this book using Adobe Photoshop CS and Adobe InDesign CS, and produced the cover layout with InDesign CS using Adobe Rotis Sans and Adobe Helvetica Condensed fonts. The cover illustration was drawn by Dan Masi and is copyright © Mayzee Illustration. David Futato designed the CD label using Adobe InDesign CS.

David Futato designed and implemented the interior layout using Adobe InDesign CS. This book was converted from Microsoft Word to InDesign by Julie Hawks. The fonts are Linotype Birka, Adobe Helvetica, and Helvetica Condensed; the code font is TheSans Mono Condensed from LucasFont. The illustrations and screenshots that appear in the book were produced by Robert Romano and Jessamyn Read using Macromedia FreeHand MX and Adobe Photoshop CS.

Related Titles Available from O'Reilly

Web Programming

ActionScript Cookbook

ActionScript for Flash MX:
The Definitive Guide, *2nd Edition*

Dynamic HTML: The Definitive
Reference, *2nd Edition*

Flash Hacks

Google Hacks

Google Pocket Guide

HTTP: The Definitive Guide

JavaScript & DHTML Cookbook

JavaScript Pocket Reference,
2nd Edition

JavaScript: The Definitive Guide,
4th Edition

Learning PHP 5

PHP Cookbook

PHP Pocket Reference, *2nd Edition*

Programming ColdFusion MX,
2nd Edition

Programming PHP

Web Database Applications with PHP
and MySQL, *2nd Edition*

Webmaster in a Nutshell, *3rd Edition*

Web Authoring and Design

Cascading Style Sheets: The Definitive
Guide, *2nd Edition*

CSS Cookbook

CSS Pocket Reference, *2nd Edition*

Dreamweaver MX 2004:
The Missing Manual

Essential ActionScript 2.0

Flash Out of the Box

HTML & XHTML: The Definitive
Guide, *5th Edition*

HTML Pocket Reference, *2nd Edition*

Information Architecture for the
World Wide Web, *2nd Edition*

Learning Web Design, *2nd Edition*

Web Design in a Nutshell, *2nd Edition*

Web Administration

Apache Cookbook

Apache Pocket Reference

Apache: The Definitive Guide,
3rd Edition

Perl for Web Site Management

Squid: The Definitive Guide

Web Performance Tuning, *2nd Edition*

O'REILLY®

Our books are available at most retail and online bookstores.
To order direct: 1-800-998-9938 • *order@oreilly.com* • *www.oreilly.com*
Online editions of most O'Reilly titles are available by subscription at *safari.oreilly.com*

Keep in touch with O'Reilly

1. Download examples from our books

To find example files for a book, go to:

www.oreilly.com/catalog

select the book, and follow the "Examples" link.

2. Register your O'Reilly books

Register your book at *register.oreilly.com*

Why register your books?
Once you've registered your O'Reilly books you can:

*   Win O'Reilly books, T-shirts or discount coupons in our monthly drawing.
*   Get special offers available only to registered O'Reilly customers.
*   Get catalogs announcing new books (US and UK only).
*   Get email notification of new editions of the O'Reilly books you own.

3. Join our email lists

Sign up to get topic-specific email announcements of new books and conferences, special offers, and O'Reilly Network technology newsletters at:

elists.oreilly.com

It's easy to customize your free elists subscription so you'll get exactly the O'Reilly news you want.

4. Get the latest news, tips, and tools

www.oreilly.com

*   "Top 100 Sites on the Web"—PC Magazine
*   CIO Magazine's Web Business 50 Awards

Our web site contains a library of comprehensive product information (including book excerpts and tables of contents), downloadable software, background articles, interviews with technology leaders, links to relevant sites, book cover art, and more.

5. Work for O'Reilly

Check out our web site for current employment opportunities:

jobs.oreilly.com

6. Contact us

O'Reilly & Associates
1005 Gravenstein Hwy North
Sebastopol, CA 95472 USA
TEL: 707-827-7000 or 800-998-9938
          (6am to 5pm PST)
FAX: 707-829-0104

order@oreilly.com
For answers to problems regarding your order or our products. To place a book order online, visit:

www.oreilly.com/order_new

catalog@oreilly.com
To request a copy of our latest catalog.

booktech@oreilly.com
For book content technical questions or corrections.

corporate@oreilly.com
For educational, library, government, and corporate sales.

proposals@oreilly.com
To submit new book proposals to our editors and product managers.

international@oreilly.com
For information about our international distributors or translation queries. For a list of our distributors outside of North America check out:

international.oreilly.com/distributors.html

adoption@oreilly.com
For information about academic use of O'Reilly books, visit:

academic.oreilly.com